AF352487

In Deference to the Other

In Deference to the Other

Lonergan and Contemporary Continental Thought

Edited by
Jim Kanaris
and
Mark J. Doorley

Foreword by John D. Caputo

State University of New York Press

Published by
State University of New York Press, Albany

For information, address State University of New York Press,
90 State Street, Suite 700, Albany, NY 12207

Production by Judith Block
Marketing by Susan Petrie

Library of Congress Cataloging-in-Publication Data

In deference to the other : Lonergan and contemporary continental thought /
edited by Jim Kanaris and Mark J. Doorley ; foreword by John D. Caputo.
    p. cm.
  Includes bibliographical references and index.
  ISBN 0-7914-6243-9 (alk. paper)
  1. Lonergan, Bernard J. F. I. Kanaris, Jim 1964– II. Doorley, Mark J.

BX4705.L7133I5 2004
191—dc22

                                                          2003070440

10 9 8 7 6 5 4 3 2 1

Contents

Foreword

John D. Caputo

In the current revival of interest in religion among recent Continental philosophers, the name of Bernard Lonergan is an unlikely partner. But if the studies that are collected in the present volume succeed, that is likely to change and Lonergan will assume a growing importance in this discussion, if not as an "integral postmodern," as Fred Lawrence puts it (since, if I may say so, a certain measure of disintegration is integral to the postmodern scene), at least as integral to the discussion. That assessment is also based upon a sea change that has taken place among Continental philosophers in the last two decades. A constructive confrontation of Lonergan and postmodernism thus involves a twofold movement: first, a movement beyond entrenched doctrinaire polemics against postmodernism by Lonerganians of the strict observance, and second, a movement on the part of postmodernists beyond their cultured—and modernist to the core—disdain of religion. As the present volume speaks to the first movement, allow me to say something about the second and the possibilities that these two movements create.

What Mark Taylor once said in his landmark work *Erring*,[1] nearly twenty years ago now—that deconstruction is the hermeneutics of the death of God—has suffered the fate of all such pronouncements about God's death: it has been stood on its head. Instead of Taylor's reductionist atheology, nowadays one is more likely to hear arguments that postmodern thought is the hermeneutics of the desire for God, where desire has the deeply Augustinian tone of the *cor inquietum*, the restless heart that cannot rest until it rests in God. A seemingly secular philosopher like Jacques Derrida finds himself asking, along with Augustine, "Quid ergo amo cum deum meum amo?" (What do I love when I love my God?), where it is not a question of whether one loves God but of what that love means and where it is directed.[2] Without simply repudiating pyschoanalysis, the theme of desire has twisted free of its psychoanalytic imprisonment and become the basis of an affirmative relationship to what we have been calling the *tout autre*, the "wholly other," ever since Levinas installed this word from negative theology at the heart of contemporary Continental thought. Far from representing a form of skepticism, or relativism, or a reductionist rejection of religion and theology, the various postmodern critiques of the "metaphysics of presence" or "ontotheology" are now seen to have an affirmative and even positively religious quality in clearing away the idols of presence or of the ontotheological manipulation of the idea of God in order to make room for a more religious God, what Meister Eckhart called the truly godly God, *der göttliche Gott*. For desire cannot be satisfied with the idols of metaphysics, desire being a kind of self-transcending desire beyond desire, a desire beyond anything that eye has seen or ear heard. In Derrida—to me the most interesting example in the present scene—a critique that seemed like a merciless exposure of the "undecidability" in things at the cost of being able to hold or think anything decisive, that seemed to issue in nothing but nihilism, is now widely regarded as the affirmation of the gift or of a justice to come that exceeds every thing that presently calls itself justice or the gift, an affirmation that has a deeply religious, prophetic, and even messianic tonality.

This is a philosophical scene with which Lonergan's conception of intelligence as dynamism toward God, of the mind's relentless work of questioning, and of God as the totality of answers to the totality of questions, the complete intelligibility of being, while hardly congruent, can undertake a serious dialogue.[3] That this is not a wild conjecture is confirmed by the work of the late Charles Winquist, for whom Lonergan was an explicit formative influence and a powerful provocation, along with Tillich and Whitehead.[4] One of the luminaries in postmodern theology, Winquist's work, once associated primarily with Mark Taylor and the death of God movement, evolved in the direction of what he called a "desiring theology." In my view, that evolution followed a firm rule. The death of God in any simple and straightforward sense would be the death of desire, for the name of God is the name of what we desire. The death of God in any straightforward sense would be the death of questioning, for the name of God is the name of what we are always already inquiring into.

In Winquist the momentum of Lonergan's conception of the dynamism of questioning desiring intelligence was brought together with Tillich's notion of "ultimate concern," which exerts a certain pressure on the everyday things of common concern, forcing them to give way to the theological force of radical questioning and thus open up the radical and religious depth in things. Without the force of this desiring questioning and questioning desire, our desire would be abandoned to wander the shopping malls in search of what we desire (a result that perhaps would be important for James L. Marsh's study in this volume). To be sure, the theological glow given by things under the pressure of radical questioning is confined entirely to what Winquist calls, following Deleuze, the "plane of immanence." Incidentally, Winquist would fault Lonergan for attaching an ontological reference to the word "God," inasmuch as for Winquist this word gives expression to a subjective concern and transcendental desire; but it does so in the manner of what Jaspers would call a "cipher" for something I know not what. Winquist would in effect fault Lonergan for his theism. At this point his desiring theology and Lonergan part ways; but the idea is not to stress obvious differences but to see the range of views in postmodern theory with which Lonergan's views intersect and can be articulated or "integrated," to use Nicholas Plants's vocabulary.

The point is that while postmodern thinkers do not share the critical realism that underlies Lonergan's theory of judgment and insight, or his metaphysics of the intelligibility of being, with its Aristotelian and Thomistic roots, that is not because they advocate a sceptical antirealism but because the notion of the *tout autre*, the wholly other, commits them to a radical theory of alterity which I would describe not as antirealism but as hyperrealism, that is, as advocating a reality beyond reality corresponding to a desire beyond desire.[5] Postmodern thought, or at least the brand of it that is proving congenial to a renewal of religious discourse, is driven not by a logic of the "anti" or the oppositional, but by a logic of the beyond, of the "hyper" or "*au-delà*", let us say a hyperbolic logic not of "anything goes" but of what goes beyond, not incidentally or by accident, but in principle. For example, postmodernists emphasize interpretation over pure facts not out of scepticism, but out of a respect for the irreducible complexity of the real, and a recognition that—and Lonergan would agree—the world is not blocked off from us by mediating interpretations but delivered over to us, mediated, through them, but this mediation also delivers us over to a play of interpretations with which we must learn to cope.

To see the sense that what I am calling here hyperreality has for post-modernists, consider two things. First, consider how much they owe to Husserl's famous analysis of the alter ego in the fifth of the *Cartesian Meditations*. Here one encounters a paradigm, a paradoxical paradigm, of an appearance constituted by its nonappearance, an appearance whose essential and irreducible distance constitutes in a positive and affirmative way its very proximity. To be in the living presence of the other person is an experience not of total presence but of having set out for a shore that one never reaches.[6] The proximity is constituted by the distance, which is not simple or total distance, for that would be death. The relation to the other is a relation of endless exploration and passage to the limit, an exposure to a realm of irreducible surprise and novelty. The other is not the unreal or absent, but the excess beyond the reality that presents itself, in a way that reminds us of the God of negative theology. Second, consider that the postmodernist emphasis on the "singularity" arises not from a perverse insistence that everything is different so that no one can say anything sensible, but because they have taken to heart, and radicalized, the classical idea of the *individuum ineffabile*: the singular being of the individual flies below the radar of language's universals; the singular one is not a specimen of a species or a token of a type, but uniquely and singularly itself. That preoccupation with the primacy of the individual over the universal is the reason why Aristotle thought that you could only get so far in ethics and that if you wanted more precision, you should take up mathematics. As Mark J. Doorley's chapter on Lonergan and Levinasian ethics shows, there is clearly room here for a substantive dialogue between postmodern insights and Lonergan's critical realism—in ethics, and not only in ethics, but in the metaphysics of individuality as well.

Inasmuch as the question of the self and subjectivity is a central and deep concern in the studies that follow, allow me also to say a word about this which can accommodate both a postmodern and Lonerganian gloss. Following the hypothesis I pursued above about the death of God, I am prepared to say that the death of God in any straightforward sense would be the death of the self. But what is a self? The self for the quasi-Augustinian, unmistakably Jewish "circumfessions" of Derrida, to again take up my favorite example, is a divided, questioning and self-questioning being, one whose being is disturbed by questions that in disturbing it also constitute it as a self. Far from being a principle of simple self-identity, the self is a self not when it rests in simple, substantial identity with itself, but only when its selfhood is contested, when who it is is at issue for itself. The idea of the self arises from the question of who I am, for that self-questioning is indeed what I am, namely, a question unto myself. Just as there would not be a hermeneutical issue if there were but one received view and not a play of contesting and contested views, in the same way there would be no self if the self languished in self-identical contentment with itself. When Paul said that the things that I wish to do I do not do, and the things that I do I do not wish to do (Rom. 7:15, 19), he was describing not a temporary distress under which we labor but the quasi-transcendental condition of the self. In questioning the idea of the self or of the human, one affirms the self as a question. That is all profoundly and economically stated by Augustine when he said, "Quaestio mihi factus sum."

Once one has gotten over the idea that what we variously call postmodernist, poststructuralist, or recent Continental thought is nothing more than a quagmire of relativism and nihilism, the possibility arises for a constructive engagement between these thinkers and Lonergan on the ideas of God and subjectivity, of knowledge and desire. To their credit, the studies that Mark J. Doorley and Jim Kanaris have collected here are organized around just such a hypothesis. While their several contributors are all more or less squarely in or sympathetic to Lonergan's camp, they are also rightly convinced that Lonergan studies would be enriched by this exposure and that there is nothing to gain from playing an insider's game, in doctrinaire denunciations of competing theories, and engaging in discourse only with one another. To be sure, it would also be instructive to postmodern readers to discover the resonances of thinkers like Foucault and Derrida in a religious and metaphysical thinker like Lonergan, even as they have something to learn from the seriousness with which Lonergan treats mathematical and scientific rationality, which is something they neglect. The business of putting one's own assumptions at risk and in play is never a unilateral affair, a point Kanaris stresses in his essay. Translating the other into one's own categories, grinding the other up in one's own writing machine, compromising the other by capturing the other in advance in one's own terms—that is what always menaces dialogue, on every side. It menaces not only Lonerganians but Heideggerians, not only Whiteheadians but just as much postmodernists who make a profitable living out of writing about openness to the other while writing unreadable essays for a small group of insiders. That is what the contributors to the present volume have tried to resist, and for that we are all in their debt.

Notes

1. Mark C. Taylor, *Erring: A Postmodern A/theology* (Chicago: University of Chicago Press, 1984).

2. For an account of the religious, biblical, and even Augustinian dimension of Derrida's work, see John D. Caputo, *The Prayers and Tears of Jacques Derrida: Religion without Religion* (Bloomington: Indiana University Press, 1997).

3. "Complete intelligibility" is a notorious term in Lonergan. The adjective is what usually sparks controversy. Lonergan insists, however, on its importance. This is brought out in a public discussion between Lonergan and David B. Burrell published over thirty five years ago: Burrell, "How Complete Can Intelligibility Be? A Commentary on *Insight:* Chapter XIX," *Proceedings of the American Catholic Philosophic Association* 41 (1967): 250–3; Lonergan, "Response to Father Burrell," *Proceedings of the American Catholic Philosophic Association* 41 (1967): 258–9. While Burrell does not take issue with the phrase as postmoderns might, disturbed by its totalistic overtones, Lonergan's response may quell knee-jerk reactions. Lonergan notes that besides knowing, there is intending. By "the real is completely intelligible," he does not mean that complete intelligibility is knowable, which would be to enjoy an unrestricted infinite act of understanding. Lonergan and Burrell think from within a tradition that reserves such understanding to God. For Lonergan, intending drives an unrestricted question-and-answer process, there being no prospect of this coming to an end. In other words, intending is not knowing, but the sine qua non of proportionate knowledge, proportionate, that is, to our limited acts of understanding: "It follows that our intending intends, not incomplete, but complete intelligibility. If it intended no more than an incomplete intelligibility, there would be a point where further questions could arise but did not, where the half-answer appeared not a half-answer but as much an answer as human intelligence could dream of seeking. If the dynamism of human intellect intended no more than incomplete intelligibility, the horizon not merely of human knowledge but also of possibly human inquiry would be bounded. Whether or not there were anything beyond that horizon, would be a question that could not even arise" (259). Thus Lonergan concludes that complete intelligibility is not an empty phrase. In fact, if we understand intending as a cognate for meaning, complete intelligibility, he argues, can be seen to lie "at the root of all our attempts to mean anything at all." Thus it's important to understand Lonergan's phrase in terms of its constitutive intentional value. [Eds.]

4. See Charles E. Winquist, *Desiring Theology* (Chicago: University of Chicago Press, 1995); for Winquist's treatment of Lonergan, see his *The Surface of the Deep* (Aurora, CO: The Davies Group, 2003), ch. 2.

5. For more on hyperrealism, see John D. Caputo, "For Love of the Things Themselves: Derrida's Hyper-Realism," *Journal for Cultural and Religious Theory* 1, no. 3 (August, 2000). <http://www.jcrt.org/archives/01.3/index.html?page=caputo.shtml>.

6. One may parallel this Levinasian sentiment concerning proximity/distance with that of Lonergan concerning the interminable course of self-

transcendence incited by the question of God: "The question of God, then, lies within man's horizon. Man's transcendental subjectivity is mutilated or abolished, unless he is stretching forth toward the intelligible, the unconditioned, the good of value. The reach, not of his attainment, but of his intending is unrestricted" (*Method in Theology* [New York: Herder and Herder, 1972], 103). The resemblance is not surprising since Lonergan, too, borrows, finally, from a Jewish theology of the transcendence of Yahweh.

Introduction

JIM KANARIS AND MARK J. DOORLEY

[T]he Greek mediation of meaning resulted in classical culture and, by and large, classical culture has passed away. By and large, its canons of art, its literary forms, its rules of correct speech, its norms of interpretation, its ways of thought, its manner in philosophy, its notion of science, its concept of law, its moral standards, its methods of education, are no longer accepted. What breathed life and form into the civilization of Greece and Rome, what was born again in a European Renaissance, what provided the chrysalis whence issued modern languages and literatures, modern mathematics and science, modern philosophy and history, held its own right into the twentieth century; but today, nearly everywhere, it is dead and almost forgotten. Classical culture has given way to a modern culture, and, I would submit, the crisis of our age is in no small measure the fact that modern culture has not yet reached its maturity. The classical mediation of meaning has broken down; the breakdown has been effected by a whole array of new and more effective techniques; but their very multiplicity and complexity leave us bewildered, disorientated, confused, preyed upon by anxiety, dreading lest we fall victims to the up-to-date myth of ideology and the hypnotic, highly effective magic of thought control.
—Lonergan, Dimensions of Meaning

Contributors to this volume wrestle with elements of the philosophy of theologian-methodologist Bernard Lonergan (1904–84) vis-à-vis contemporary concerns in Continental philosophy and theology. "Continental" is a precarious term. It is usually invoked to earmark a particular mode of thought, largely of German and French origin. We use it in this typical fashion. Foundational are the works of Kant and Hegel. As with Analytic philosophy, to which we will turn shortly, Continental philosophy has many shades. In 1987 Kenneth Baynes, James Bohman, and Thomas McCarthy serviceably, and somewhat courageously, divided the field into radical, systematic, and hermeneutic trends.[1] Grappled with in this volume are by and large the challenges of the radical stream. Its key instigators are the so-called masters of suspicion: Nietzsche, Marx, and Freud. The dialogue tends to focus on the aftermath of their progeny, whose work has in many ways come to characterize contemporary forms, "postmodern" as they are often called. "Postphenomenological" and "poststructuralist" are probably better terms, especially if we are thinking of the philosophies of the masters' sons: Martin Heidegger, Michel Foucault, and Jacques Derrida (to name only a few).

Astute readers will immediately recognize that Lonergan's discourse resembles the concerns of systematic and hermeneutic proposals. Incidentally, the systematic and hermeneutic seek to transform, not to overthrow or to bring an end to, Enlightenment thought. And so a more likely fit would be comparisons with, say, Karl-Otto Apel and Jurgen Habermas on the systematic side and Hans-Georg Gadamer, Paul Ricoeur, and Charles Taylor on the hermeneutic side. No doubt. A number of our contributors make such connections. However, there is much in Lonergan that resonates with the concerns of poststructuralists like Derrida and Foucault, Levinas and Kristeva. It is here that more work is required. Our hope is that this volume will facilitate this development as it seeks to address the radical wing of Continental thought in the light of Lonergan's systematic- and hermeneutic-like proposals.

Before developing this further, some things should be said about what is often assumed to be the nemesis of Continental thought: Analytic philosophy.[2]

Analytic means of reflection are carried out largely by English-speaking academics indebted historically to the empiricist philosophies of John Locke and David Hume, "Continentals" of a different stripe. Now classic expressions of Analytic philosophy proper, in its nascent state, are identified with the works of Bertrand Russell, G. E. Moore, and the early Ludwig Wittgenstein. They honed classical empiricist concerns through discourse on the precise nature of concepts and propositions. The concern there was to arrive at a language that lays bare, as much as humanly possible, the logical structure of reality; the school known as logical positivism developed as a result. The history and fate of logical positivism is well known. Suffice it to say that analytic philosophy is not synonymous with positivism. In fact, it was philosophers identified as Analytic who contributed to the demise of logical positivism as an all-embracing theory of empiricism. The mere mention of Karl Popper and W. V. O. Quine suffices as examples.

A wide variety of Analytic philosophers exists today; their concerns tend to be as various. John Heil makes the significant observation that despite differences among them, Analytic philosophers have "an implicit respect for argument and clarity, an evolving though informal agreement as to what problems are and are not tractable, and a conviction that philosophy is in some sense continuous with science."[3] Logic as fundamental, its principles and formal explicitation (symbolic and otherwise), is deeply ingrained. It gives us a handle on things, it is presumed, without which, were Nietzsche right, we would be on a rudderless vessel, facing an expanse too frightening to contemplate.[4] Of course, for many an Analytic philosopher Nietzsche's logic, and that of those who appreciate it, is flawed because self-contradictory. One cannot impose a logic to destabilize logic and then pretend that the destabilizing logic is not simply an alternative, somehow more basic than the destabilized logic; both are logics, presupposing the principles of logic. It is difficult to speak about such matters in the abstract. To appreciate Nietzsche's critique of logic, religion, and other issues requires an understanding of the proper object of his diagnosis. This object is as multifarious and dynamic as the history of thought itself. However, if we may be permitted to speak in the abstract, it is important to recognize a basic insight characteristic of this wing of Continental thought, of which Nietzsche is something of a patron saint. It is this: clarity and logic are important. But they are not fundamental, that is, if we appreciate our historicity and the all-pervasive nature of language. Fundamentality itself is a historical concern and the function of language. The thought often is that Continentals have no appreciation of logic and her principles. As a result, their thought degenerates into relativism due to sparse insights about existence, the art of living, interpreting, and so on. Not to dismiss this, but Continental thought is not a monolithic achievement. Each thinker pinpoints the relativity of thought in a way closely tied to the thinker's presuppositions and alternatives. Those are as complex as they are idiosyncratic; they lead in different directions and even oppose each other. But the insight here, on a sympathetic reading, concerns not the eradication of logic or epistemology, but its destabilization. Nothing can serve as our ticket out of the flux.

Because Lonergan was not schooled in either approach, one finds flexibility in his philosophy to accommodate Analytic and Continental concerns. He shares with Continentals the concern that epistemology be given a central place in questioning; he does not share with many of them the belief that epistemology is corrupt through and through. Rather, he understands epistemology as secondary, cognitional theory, which grounds it, being the more basic task.[5] Cognitional theory is Lonergan's entry ticket into the discussion, however we might feel about it as in step with contemporary Continental concerns. That said, cognitional theory does give him the needed flexibility to accommodate insights that so many reduce to either way of thinking. By distinguishing cognitional theory from epistemology and the concerns of logic, Lonergan can situate Analytic and Continental concerns relative to differing patterns of experience (that is, artistic and intellectual) outlined in his theory of cognition. The short of it is that Continental thinking resembles what Lonergan describes as purely experiential. In its thinking, which experientially is artistic, this mode of thought attempts to think past, by destabilizing, instrumentalized meanings of society. Lonergan pinpoints Heidegger as an exemplar. What people like Heidegger try to effect are worlds of meaning that are "other, different, novel, strange, remote, intimate."[6] The objective is to get us past our accepted modes of thought into a place where we are totally and constantly surprised by the totally other.

The pattern that represents the analytic is easily identifiable with Lonergan's intellectual pattern of experience. Someone who thinks according to this pattern is, in Lonergan's terms, after a scientific-like explanation of observed data. We might think of it more generally in terms of any potentially theoretical disposition preoccupied with the nature or state of things. And so the attempt to lay bare the logical structure of reality easily lines up with this kind of pattern of experience. Structurally the operations of consciousness function identically in both patterns, artistic and intellectual. The mode by which things are thought, however, will determine how the concerns of each pattern function and how their respective insights are brought to expression. Often these insights are placed in critical tension, as evidenced by the impasse reached in both types of philosophizing, artistic (Continental) and intellectual (Analytic). Hints of a rapprochement in Lonergan can be traced to his concept of a differentiated consciousness. Briefly, a differentiated consciousness is one that is able to distinguish between patterns of experience and their specialized differentiations, to integrate them at levels in which one can spot the difference between them, and to adjust one's aspirations accordingly. The concept is key to understanding why Lonergan scholars bother negotiating the differences, often irreconcilable.

The dynamic, brusquely stated here, is detailed elsewhere.[7] It is offered as a means of understanding the orientation of Lonergan scholars in tackling a "crisis of our age." We have come a long way since Lonergan penned the words in the epigraph, but we are of the opinion that a serviceable balance has yet to be reached. We agree with Lonergan that our "modern culture has not yet reached its maturity." Offered in this volume are ways of thinking the differences briefly outlined above en route to some sort of rapproachment. The authors entertain different visions but they are united in the assumption that Lonergan has something important to contribute.

Nicholas Plants's chapter, "Decentering Inwardness," continues a project that seeks a critical integration of the thought of Lonergan and Charles Taylor. As Plants points out, both Lonergan and Taylor are committed to a notion of authenticity that avoids the slide into subjectivism. In his chapter Plants explores Taylor's insight into the hermeneutic dimension of engaged subjectivity that rests on the self-transcending movement of the subject. Authentic subjectivity is a subjectivity engaged by sources other than the self. Hence the charge of an immanentist subjectivity is escaped. However, Taylor, in Plants's opinion, does not offer a sufficient account of consciousness to justify his normative claims about authentic subjectivity. It is here that Plants turns to Lonergan.

Lonergan also wants to make use of the authenticity trope. However, his approach to authenticity is to identify the subject and its operations made available to us by consciousness. Plants's analysis of Lonergan's thought on this subject depends on a crucial distinction that Lonergan makes between understanding oneself as an object of perception and understanding oneself as a subject of experience. For Lonergan the goal of philosophy is to appropriate oneself as conscious and as a knower, engaged in the intentional and conscious operations of experiencing, understanding, judging, and choosing. Plants identifies a subtle trap that Lonergan's analysis of consciousness is vulnerable to, namely, identifying the subject as the self that is appropriated rather than as the self that one is conscious of. He details the consequences of this trap being sprung. The prime consequence is that the self as conscious, as appropriated, is a centered self, thus incapable of the radical decentering that Taylor identifies as the mark of self-transcendence.

Both Lonergan and Taylor have valuable insights to offer to the contemporary Continental debate about the human subject. Both want to situate authentic subjectivity as the point of departure for philosophical reflection without either succumbing to the flaws of modernity or despairing of a way forward from the deconstructive moment. Plants's chapter provides a way of reading both thinkers as complementary to each other and as providing necessary astringents to each other's work.

In his chapter "To Whom Do We Return in the Turn to the Subject? Lonergan, Derrida, and Foucault Revisited" Jim Kanaris analyzes a fundamental problem shared by thinkers generally identified as contemporary Continental thinkers. This group runs from Nietzsche thru Heidegger to Derrida and Foucault. The fundamental problem remains Kant. Although Nietzsche and Heiddeger are prodigious in their destruction of the pretensions of Kant and Hegel, they are still beholden to the same metaphysical claims that Kant and Hegel espoused. Kanaris argues that for Lonergan the principle of immanence continues to haunt Nietzsche and Heidegger, thus necessitating a return to Kant, the modern thinker who brought the subject to its greatest prominence. Lonergan's criticism is radical, in that he wants to get at the root of the problem, a problem that is clearly evident in Kant

Kanaris turns to Derrida and Foucault as contemporary Continental thinkers who want to disengage themselves from modern narratives about the subject. For Derrida everything is text, so that a re-turn of the subject will negotiate the presence/absence dichotomy that characterizes any text.[8] Derrida's subject is nothing more than a trace that can be uncovered in the play of presence and absence. Foucault, on the other hand, finds Derrida's analysis lacking. He prefers to speak of the subject via the institutional "technologies" that have formed the subject and that condition the kinds of questions that are raised. In both thinkers, in the end, one finds still the workings of the principle of immanence, such that the re-turning of the overturned Nietzschean/Heideggerian subject is essentially a return to Kant's subject.

Kanaris argues that Lonergan does concern himself with the same problems that Derrida and Foucault have identified in the modern as well as the Nietzschean/Heideggerian subject. Kanaris shows that Lonergan's attempt to articulate the structure of the human subject as knower and chooser offers an unique account of subjectivity that overcomes the limitations of the Kantian account. However, in his self-avowed spirit of critical reciprocity, Kanaris also wants to recognize the vulnerability of Lonergan's account of subjectivity to the very criticisms that both Derrida and Foucault have leveled at modern thinkers. There is a tendency in Lonergan scholarship, as well as in Lonergan himself, to put the structure of intentionality beyond question. This is dangerous. The structure must always be submitted to regular criticism. The return to the subject is always an ambiguous one and so a fertile field for ongoing challenges, criticisms, and questions.

In his autobiographical chapter entitled "Self-Appropriation: Lonergan's Pearl of Great Price" James L. Marsh takes the reader on a quick march through his own self-appropriation. An examination of Lonergan's invitation to self-appropriation is followed by a discussion of that invitation in the context of contemporary Continental philosophy. Marsh then looks at his own journey and intellectual achievements in tracing the path to his own self-appropriation. Ironically, his appropriating himself as a knower, a chooser, and a lover frees him from his tutelage to Lonergan. Having decisively chosen to be his own person, yet connected to universal humanity, Marsh finds that self-appropriation must lead to radical conversion and political action. For Marsh a radical conversion manifests itself in political action. Today the radically converted political actor must confront the excesses of both late capitalism and state socialism.

Most significant in Marsh's essay is the insight that self-appropriation is the gateway to the philosophic life. Commentators on the thought of Lonergan can be successful without decisively choosing themselves in the way that Marsh indicates. The "pearl of great price" is precisely the insight that I am responsible for who I am and who I will become. People who identify themselves as intelligent, reasonable, and responsible step out from the shadow of their mentors. That is the final end, as it were, of Lonergan's invitation to self-appropriation.

In her chapter "Subject for the Other: Lonergan and Levinas on Being Human in Postmodernity" Michele Saracino offers a reflection on the dialectical tension between these two thinkers. Her reflection begins with the recognition of the inattention that the Other has received from the Western Subject as it has pursued its own notion of the good life. The concern for the marginalized, the voiceless, the hidden and powerless peoples motivates much of contemporary Continental thought, particularly that of Emmanuel Levinas. Saracino's essay argues that Lonergan has a commitment to openness to the Other that provides an entry point for a dialogue between these two seemingly disparate thinkers.

Such a dialogue is necessary at this point in time because contemporary Continental thought has demonstrated its ability to pinpoint the problems of the contemporary world, but, to date, has had little that is constructive for moving beyond the problems. Christian theology, on the other hand, does offer a point of departure for decision and action in response to contemporary crises. By placing Lonergan and Levinas in dialogue in relation to their approaches to the Other, Saracino hopes to identify ways in which the thinking of these two people can be advanced.

Saracino begins with a discussion of Lonergan's notion of the patterns of experience, his notion of the transcultural, and his notion of the subject as radically open to the Other. These three notions underpin an anthropology that can meet Levinas's identification of the Other as the one to whom we are hostage. Rather than a subject that is self-sufficient, Lonergan's subject is clearly not self-sufficient in any way that would exclude or devalue the Other.

Tracing his roots to Talmudic and Cartesian sources, Saracino discusses the metaphor of facing and the feminine as ways in which Levinas locates the obligation to the Other that is the starting point for any adequate anthropology. Both the metaphor of facing and the feminine make it clear that any relation to the Other must always make evident the asymmetrical character of that relation. The Other can never be just a subset of the Subject, a horror perpetrated through much of human history.

By placing these two thinkers in relation to each other, Saracino suggests a variety of ways in which both Lonergan and Levinas scholars can proceed to enrich their work and directions in which Christian theologians need to move in the new millennium. Two very different thinkers, in their openness to the alterity of each, provide a space for fruitful dialogue leading to important and necessary insights into possible solutions to the problems of contemporary society.

Christine E. Jamieson finds in Lonergan a way to make sense of Julia Kristeva's analysis of the "split subject." In "Kristeva's Horror and Lonergan's Insight: The Psychic Structure of the Human Person and the Move to a Higher Viewpoint" Jamieson presents Kristeva's analysis of the person. Kristeva begins her reflection by noting the disturbing relation between the increasing presence of women in the public realm and the increase in violence against women. Kristeva's focus on the speaking subject leads her to identify a lacuna that exists in attempts to explain this tension "between humanity's progress and decline in relation to women."[9] Kristeva is often criticized for presenting women as forever trapped in oppressive and deterministic situations. Jamieson argues that Lonergan provides a conceptual analysis that can account for what she argues is a liberating movement in Kristeva's argument. That analysis depends on Lonergan's notion of a higher viewpoint emerging from the limits of more restricted horizons.

Kristeva's analysis of the split subject, the speaking subject constituted by the semiotic and symbolic realms, leads to a recognition of the threat that the semiotic represents to the symbolic. The semiotic is the maternal materiality of the subject that threatens the meaningful and ordered symbolic realm. Women become a threat, the object of violence. This threat is experienced as preconscious. The unforgiving analysis reveals a permanent split in our identities that is preconscious and fuels antagonism toward women. Birth is the originary and fundamental experience of separation between the semiotic and the symbolic. Kristeva's analysis is both deterministic and liberating. How can that be? Jamieson argues that Kristeva raises questions that cannot be answered in the horizon of questions that generated her project to begin with. A higher viewpoint is required.

Jamieson argues that Kristeva actually moves the feminist critique to a higher viewpoint by providing a framework for a discussion of women's rights that can answer questions that arise but are beyond the horizons of either liberal or social constructivistic theories.

In his chapter "Lonergan's Postmodern Subject: Neither Neoscholastic Substance nor Cartesian Ego," Frederick Lawrence traces the emergence of naïve realist and idealist strategies from the medieval and modern worlds. The subject as object, as the "already out there now" substance and the subject as subject, as the "already in here now" consciousness, rests upon a subject/object split that gives rise to more common ground between idealist and naïve realist than is normally admitted. The criticisms of contemporary Continental thinkers are aimed at this subject that is hopelessly cut off from reality or naively holds onto sense perception as the really real.

Lawrence argues that Lonergan's subject as self-transcending avoids the mistakes of both naïve realism and idealism. The subject as other, as self-transcending, can be the centerpiece of a social and political discourse that is genuinely open to difference, yet able to distinguish between reality and illusion. This genuineness requires conversion on the part of human subjects: intellectual, moral, and religious. Lawrence indicates the necessity of religious conversion as the condition for the possibility of a self-transcending subject.

Mark J. Doorley's "In Response to the Other: Postmodernity and Critical Realism" presents a response to the idea that ethics must be abandoned. Ethics always has a victim. Doorley suggests that a dialectical reading of thinkers like Levinas and Derrida can reveal positional moments that underlie the judgment about ethics. The importance of the Singular, the notion of obligation, and the process of clôtural reading are moments in contemporary Continental thought where Doorley finds important claims about ethics and the conditions for its possibility.[10]

The chapter turns to Lonergan's thought and suggests two approaches to addressing the postmodern concern about ethics. The first approach is a positional account of metaphysics that answers the criticism about totalizing reason. Doorley examines the patterning of experience, the operation of judgment, and the notion of objectivity. This approach, however, does not quite answer all the questions raised by the contemporary Continental critique. In the second approach, then, he appeals to the role of conversion and the inbreaking of the Other in religious, moral, and intellectual conversion. This approach seems to meet the demands of the postmodern critique. Throughout, Doorley is quick to point out where Lonergan does not quite escape the postmodern critique.

In a very intriguing chapter "Lonergan and the Ambiguity of Postmodern Laughter," Ronald H. McKinney, S.J. takes up the topic of humor and satire in Lonergan's *Insight*. He argues that humor and satire may be the key to understanding the way in which Lonergan appreciates and attempts to address the concerns of contemporary Continental philosophy.

His argument begins with an examination of Umberto Eco's *The Name of the Rose*, in which the role of humor and laughter is examined. McKinney then turns to Aristotle's discussion of *eutrapelia* and Kierkegaard's three stages to begin to develop an understanding of humor that both admonishes us to develop virtue and reminds us of our finitude.

McKinney then examines Lonergan's short reflection on satire and humor in *Insight*. Lonergan's notion of development, and his "thick" understanding of the existential subject provide space for the use of satire and humor to serve the role that Aristotle most clearly articulates: to nudge a person toward greater genuineness and to keep the person in touch with the fragility of human achievement. The former encourages development toward greater and greater authenticity; the latter keeps in question all achievement. It is here that McKinney thinks Lonergan is most postmodern.

The objective of these chapters is not to decide whether Lonergan defines or defies the postmodern, a most precarious term anyway. To many he represents the epitome of that against which postmoderns rail. This contention is as precarious as the term "postmodern." Different visions exist regarding what it means to be post-Cartesian or post-Hegelian. All these visions do not hinge on some essence relative to which postmoderns ironically define themselves. What exists rather is a tapestry of varying concerns oftentimes negotiated contrarily by family responses. Continentals have taught us that this is okay, something to be expected given our finitude. But none of the representatives of the radical wing discussed here propose their views as a license for chaotic thinking, for a relativistic free-for-all. That chaos, which seems to mark what appears as postmodern, may be the result of pop culture or muddled thinking. However, it is not necessarily the intention of those who have helped forge its tools.

Lonergan's idiosyncratic thought, the depth of which has been plumbed seriously only recently with respect to this question, is dynamic and flexible. If we understand modernity and postmodernity in bipolar terms, the former involved in the art of argument, the latter in that of persuasion and narration, few will be swayed. But as Maurice Wiles has shrewdly argued, this kind of bipolarity is overstated. Proponents of narratival thinking, so to speak, are also involved in argument not totally unlike that employed by their nemesis.[11] Moreover, modernists are not bereft of the inclination that draws some into the agonistics of out-narrating each other.[12] Bipolar characterizations have their limits and should not dictate the rules of the game. In Lonergan an appreciation exists for both concerns, however different its intonation from the bipolarity mentioned.[13] Those open to it and not predisposed to rule it out of court based on tenuous characterizations (which turn out finally to be unhelpful caricatures anyway) may find it refreshing. Doubtless they will find familiar elements in it. But should the familiar bewitch, the issues, which are new and discussed here, should predominate. This should serve to rebuff delusional comfort zones and to buff the apparent lackluster of the familiar.

Notes

1. See Kenneth Baynes, James Bohman, and Thomas A. McCarthy, eds., *After Philosophy: End or Transformation?* (Cambridge, MA: MIT Press, 1987).

2. It is interesting that Derrida has gone on record recently claiming that he is after the same sort of truth coveted by Analytic philosophers. Of course, we must always understand such public statements in the larger context of Derrida's philosophy as a whole. See Derrida in *Arguing with Derrida*, ed. Simon Glendinning (Oxford, UK; Malden, MA: Blackwell, 2001), 83–4.

3. See *The Cambridge Dictionary of Philosophy*, s.v. "analytic philosophy."

4. See Friedrich Nietzsche, *The Gay Science*, trans. Walter Kaufmann (New York: Vintage Books, 1974), 180–1 (aphorism 124).

5. The main argument for the centrality of cognitional theory is developed most elaborately in Lonergan's *Insight: A Study of Human Understanding*, volume 3 in *Collected Works of Bernard Lonergan*, edited by Frederick E. Crowe and Robert M. Doran, (Toronto: University of Toronto Press, 1992). The editors take this opportunity to alert the reader to the fact that the authors of the chapters in this book cite different editions of *Insight*: the edition already noted here as well as an earlier edition [Bernard J. F. Lonergan, *Insight: A Study of Human Understanding* (London: Longmans, Green, and Co., 1958; reprint, San Francisco: Harper & Row, Publishers: 1978).] The notes will clearly indicate which edition is cited by each author.

6. Bernard Lonergan, *Topics in Education*, volume 10 in *Collected Works of Bernard Lonergan*, edited by Frederick E. Crowe and Robert M. Doran (Toronto: Univerity of Toronto Press, 1993), 216.

7. See Jim Kanaris, "Lonergan and Contemporary Philosophy of Religion," in *Explorations in Contemporary Continental Philosophy of Religion*, ed. Deane-Peter Baker and Patrick Maxwell (New York: Editions Rodopi, 2003), 65–79.

8. See chapter two of this book for a discussion of the term "re-turn."

9. See Jamieson's chapter 5 in this volume.

10. See chapter seven of this book for a discussion of the term clôtural.

11. Wiles makes this point in a recent review of Gavin Hyman's book, *The Predicament of Postmodern Theology: Radical Orthodoxy or Nihilist Textualism?* in *Theology Today* 60, no. 1 (2003): 116.

12. According to Wiles, Hyman, although on the same page with John Milbank's postmodernity, is displeased with the latter's narratival tactics. As a result, Hyman tries to "out-narrate" Milbank.

13. This dimension of argument in Lonergan is relatively well known. For the lesser known dimension of rhetoric, see John Angus Campbell, "Insight and Understanding: The 'Common Sense' Rhetoric of Bernard Lonergan," in *Communication and Lonergan: Common Ground for Forging the New Age*, ed. Thomas J. Farrell and Paul A. Soukup (Kansas City, MO: Sheed & Ward, 1993), p. 3–22. For Lonergan's appreciation of what approximates narratival-type thinking, see Kanaris, "Lonergan and Contemporary Philosophy of Religion," 65–79.

Chapter 1

Decentering Inwardness

Nicholas Plants

Rather than recoiling from the devastating wisdom made available by the deconstruction of the modernist project, Lonergan scholars are confronting the contemporary Continental critique of the metaphysics of presence on their way to a much-needed critical integration of postmodernism and transcendental method.[1] The fact that several obstacles continue to block the path to such an integration, including the difficulties inherent in circumscribing postmodernism and the unfortunate proclivity of some Lonergan scholars to "treat rival philosophies in too polemical a manner,"[2] only underscores the significance of the contributions that have already been made. These contributions all highlight a postmodern theme which is pivotal in that it is both directly relevant to Lonergan studies and has generated a significant level of current philosophical interest: the decentering of the modern subject. My aim in this chapter is to further advance the ongoing critical integration of contemporary Continental thought and Lonergan studies by exploring the specific impact the decentering of the modern subject has upon the self-appropriating subject as subject.

Despite its being contentious, this exploration is partly motivated by my genuine conviction that Lonergan studies has as much to learn from postmodernism as it has to offer in return. The strength of Lonergan's philosophical enterprise lies not in its departure from, but rather in its complementarity with the ongoing deconstruction of the modernist project. Such is particularly the case with regard to the spirit of genuine openness and moral concern that ultimately animates and sustains them both. Another motivation is to further address the concern I share with Jim

Kanaris: that his emphasis on the centrality of the knowing human subject leaves Lonergan vulnerable to charges of subjectivism.[3] Although I believe there are good reasons to mitigate this charge, it is a charge that arises more from an internal awareness of a problematic tendency within Lonergan's thinking than from an external critique, and therefore merits further consideration rather than a defensive response alone. More specifically, I would like to address Kanaris's concern by reconsidering Fred Lawrence's claim that Lonergan's postmodern conception of the human subject entails "a radical decentering of the conscious subject correctly conceived."[4] For just what the correct conception of the conscious subject is and exactly what a radical decentering consists in are two questions that even from the Lonerganian perspective are open to further discussion. After engaging in such a discussion, I will be able to resolve the concern I share with Kanaris by providing a response to the definitive question it prompts: can the plausibility of transcendental method as the cognitional theory that overcomes the epistemological distortions of modernism be maintained if the subject as subject which lies at its heart is decentered, as it must be in order to avoid charges of subjectivism?

An affirmative answer to this crucial question emerges when we critically integrate Lonergan's transcendental method with Charles Taylor's philosophical anthropology.[5] For not only do Taylor's insights into subjective engagement enable us to detail what a "radical decentering of the conscious subject correctly conceived" consists in, they thereby put us in the position to offer a Lonerganian account of authentic subjectivity that is not vulnerable to the charge of subjectivism. Unlike many contemporary philosophers, Taylor aims to provide an account of authenticity that retains normative force at the same time that it overcomes subjectivism. Lonergan has as much to contribute to this challenging endeavor as Taylor, but fails to do so in terms of subjective engagement, which he must if he is to fully escape the charge of subjectivism. Taylor's reflections on subjective engagement, meanwhile, do not include an adequate account of the structure of intentional consciousness, which they must if they are to retain the degree of normative force he intends. It is because Lonergan and Taylor each achieve what the other requires that their critical integration makes it possible for the aims which animate their philosophical projects to be realized.[6] Above and beyond the significant differences between the two, Lonergan and Taylor are allies in that they both labor to overcome the epistemological and anthropological distortions incurred by modernism without becoming nonrealists in the process. When they are critically integrated, transcendental method and philosophical anthropology not only enable Lonergan and Taylor to achieve their shared endeavor, therefore, but do so in such a way that critical realism remains relevant in the postmodern philosophical landscape. The ongoing critical integration of postmodernism and transcendental method is thereby furthered, as it must be if the study of Lonergan is to make its much-needed contribution to contemporary Continental thought.

Subjective Engagement and Authenticity

Taylor chronicles the modern ideal of disengagement and the distortions it leaves in its wake (subjectivism, reductionism, naturalism) with more subtlety than many contemporary thinkers.[7] It is no surprise, then, that he details its alternative—subjective engagement—with its associated moral ideal—authenticity—in a more nuanced manner as well.[8] His primary contribution has been to work against the contemporary grain by recovering, rather than divesting, the normative dimension of authenticity. Taylor sees authenticity as a crucial philosophical issue that must be understood if we are to ever overcome the distortions—especially subjectivism—incurred by the modern ideal of disengagement. Such understanding is extremely difficult, of course, because authenticity, no less than subjectivity itself, is continually susceptible to distortion. More specifically, Taylor believes authenticity is a contemporary ideal that is often stripped of its normative force.[9] Lacking all normativity, authenticity is reduced to a self-centered individualism that is driven more by self-fulfillment and narcissism than by a search for purpose and meaning. "This individualism involves a centering on the self and a concomitant shutting out, or even unawareness, of the greater issues or concerns that transcend the self, be they religious, political, or historical."[10] Taylor believes such individualism is ironically self-defeating, however, because by precluding demands emanating from anything more than, or even other than, human desires, it undermines the conditions for realizing authenticity: "Authenticity is not the enemy of demands that emanate from beyond the self; it supposes such demands."[11] Rather than making authenticity possible, human desires that preclude demands emanating from beyond themselves actually fly in the face of its requirements. And when authenticity is stripped of its normative force, Taylor concludes, the result is a pervasive "slide to subjectivism" that ironically precludes the very authenticity it seeks to achieve.[12]

In order to restore normative force to the contemporary ideal of authenticity, Taylor, like Lonergan, insists that authenticity is only achieved in self-transcendence.[13] If we are to overcome the contemporary slide to subjectivism, Taylor argues, we must reconnect the disengaged subject with, and thereby reengage it in, a reality larger than itself.[14] Human subjects must be engaged by subject-transcending sources if we are to participate in authenticity as a normatively conceived ideal. Although transcendent sources such as society, religion, history, nature, and politics are independent of us as human subjects, they engage us in a manner that calls us beyond ourselves, and thus operate as the conditions for the possibility of authenticity: "Otherwise put, I can define my identity only against the background of things that matter. But to bracket out history, nature, society, the demands of solidarity, everything but what I find in myself, would be to eliminate all candidates for what matters."[15] Authenticity is a matter of being true to ourselves, but defining who we are as selves first involves being engaged by transcendent realities so that our self-interpretations might be informed by these sources.[16] As Taylor conceives of it, then, authenticity requires rather than precludes the demands transcendent sources place upon us: "[W]e ought to be trying to persuade people that self-fulfillment, so far from excluding unconditional relationships and moral demands beyond the self, actually requires these in some form."[17] Determining the form these demands take is the primary challenge that the ideal of authenticity still poses to its advocates. Taylor therefore concludes that "the struggle ought not to be *over* authenticity, for or against, but *about* it, defining its proper meaning. We ought to be trying to lift the culture [of authenticity] back up, closer to its motivating ideal."[18]

Taylor's many contributions to this struggle over authenticity are informed by the hermeneutic emphasis on engagement in the background within which we constitute ourselves. His attempt to define the proper meaning of authenticity is inseparable from his attempt to promote the crucial role subjective engagement plays in self-understanding. Understanding authenticity, like understanding human subjectivity itself, is a matter of interpreting our lived experience from within the background of subjective engagement. Because they provide us with our understandings of ourselves, our self-interpretations partly constitute us in such a way that self-interpretation, and thus engagement in a hermeneutic background, is essential to human existence.[19] Subjective engagement is normative as well as hermeneutic because the self-interpretations that constitute us are themselves informed by subject-transcending sources. The self-interpretations these normative sources inform constitute the hermeneutic background from which we must first disengage in order to achieve the modern stance of disengagement. Taylor contextualizes the modern disengaged subject within this background of subjective engagement for this reason: "Disengaged description is a special possibility, realizable only intermittently, of a being who is always 'in' the world in another way, as an agent engaged in realizing a certain form of life."[20] Because we necessarily disengage from this background in order to adopt the disengaged perspective in the first place, he believes that subjective engagement is the primordial reality whose true nature must first be articulated if authenticity is to ever be properly understood. According to Taylor, then, subjective engagement and its associated ideal of authenticity operate within a dimension that is as distinctly hermeneutic as it is normative.

Although they both operate normatively, subjective engagement and authenticity only do so when they involve self-transcendence. Being engaged *in* the background within which we constitute ourselves necessarily requires being engaged *by* the subject-transcending sources whose norms make authenticity possible. Being engaged by transcendent sources such as history, religion, and nature enables us to transcend ourselves, as we must if we are to participate in the sources which, when they inform our self-interpretations, partly constitute us as subjects who constitute ourselves within the background of subjective engagement. We thereby participate in the subject-transcending sources that guard against the slide to subjectivism Taylor identifies within contemporary culture. It is by explicitly linking self-transcendence with subjective engagement in this way that Taylor restores normative force to the contemporary ideal of authenticity. Because we must be engaged by subject-transcending sources if we are to participate in authenticity as a normatively conceived ideal, the subjectivism that often precludes such engagement is definitively overcome. Coupled as it is with self-transcendence, therefore, subjective engagement is singularly crucial to Taylor's understanding of authenticity, and so to his entire philosophical anthropology.

The Structure and Appropriation of Subjectivity

Lonergan's many contributions to the struggle over authenticity are made possible by his crucial breakthrough to the subject as subject—the primordial reality in whose intentional consciousness he discerns the structure of human subjectivity. Lonergan's breakthrough is a breakthrough to the reality that is the subject as subject[21]: "The subject as subject is reality in the sense that we live and die, love and hate, rejoice and suffer, desire and fear, wonder and dread, inquire and doubt. . . . Reality in that ontic sense, prior to any ontology, prior to any conception of himself as *there*. Here we are, it is true of all of us."[22] The subject as subject is the human subject of experience whose lived experience is prior to any objectification of oneself. "It is Descartes' *cogito* transposed to concrete living. It is the subject present to himself, not as presented to himself in any theory or affirmation of consciousness, but as the prior non-absence prerequisite to any presentation, as *a priori* condition to any stream of consciousness."[23] As such, the subject as subject is the center as well as the source of all intentional and conscious operation—the "experienced center of experiencing, the intelligent center of inquiry, insight, and formulations, the rational center of critical reflection, scrutiny, hesitation, doubt, and frustration."[24]

Although discoverable in consciousness and capable of being understood, affirmed, and chosen via intentionality analysis, the subject as subject is a primordial reality that is opaque as well as luminous. "It is reality in a very prior and probably conceptually incomplete sense, but nonetheless in a very real sense."[25] Thus, "that prior opaque and luminous being is not static, fixed, determinate, once and for all; it is precarious; and its being precarious is the possibility not only of a fall, but also of fuller development."[26] The struggle over authenticity is the struggle Taylor claims it is, according to Lonergan, because the subject as subject is a precarious reality—a reality which is as vulnerable to falling short of authenticity as it is to achieving fuller development through this contemporary ideal. For human subjectivity like authenticity itself has already endured, and remains susceptible to, continuous distortion. More specifically, Lonergan believes that the common failure to advert to the presence we have to ourselves as subjects prevents us from recognizing the constitutive role this unique presence plays in human subjectivity. His main contribution to the struggle over authenticity has been to mitigate this shortcoming by exposing the intentional structure of human subjectivity that our presence to ourselves makes available to us, thereby enabling the fuller development of authentic subjectivity.

By engaging in intentionality analysis Lonergan distinguishes four levels of intentional operation that are intrinsically conscious as well as intrinsically intentional. Our intentional operations at the empirical, intellectual, rational, and responsible levels all share the added dimension of occurring consciously: "Just as operations by their intentionality make objects present to the subject, so also by consciousness they make the operating subject present to himself."[27] In addition to the presence of the object to the subject as made possible by intentionality, there is the presence of the subject to the subject as made possible by consciousness. Thus we are present to ourselves as subjects at the same time that objects are correlatively present to us. "The object is totally present to you, and you are present to yourself; but your presence to yourself is in another dimension. It is not on the side of the object. . . . As the object is present to the spectator, simultaneously and concomitantly the subject is present to himself."[28] Above and beyond the objects we regularly advert to, therefore, we can also advert to the unique presence we have to ourselves as human subjects.

Precisely because this presence to ourselves is in a further dimension, though, it often remains unarticulated within our self-interpretations, and we thereby prevent ourselves from recognizing the constitutive role it plays in our lived experience as subjects. Since we can experience ourselves not only as presented but as that to whom presentations are made, we are human subjects for whom consciousness is an experience, not simply the perception of an object.[29] The presence of the subject to herself is not the presence of an object to a subject. Our consciousness does more than reveal us to ourselves as objects; it constitutes us as subjects of experience, and thereby pertains to the very constitution of human subjectivity, just as our intentional operations do. Because consciousness renders us present to ourselves as subjects of experience, and not simply as objects of perception, it constitutes human subjectivity. Consciousness constitutes us as subjects, as subjects whose range of experience includes consciousness—our experience of our experiencing, understanding, reflecting, and choosing. When we understand ourselves as objects of perception rather than as subjects of experience we miss the constitutive dimension of consciousness. To fail to advert to this unique presence we have to ourselves as subjects is to diminish our lived experience by failing to recognize the intentional structure of human subjectivity that it makes available to us.

Lonergan therefore encourages us to advert to the presence we have to ourselves as subjects so that we might assume possession of our intentional consciousness through the decisive personal act of self-appropriation—the indirect process in which we objectify our intentional consciousness. He identifies this process, in which we apply our operations as intentional to our operations as conscious in order to thereby heighten our intentional consciousness, as the primary function of philosophy.[30] The primary function of philosophy is the self-appropriation of one's interiority: "one's subjectivity, one's operations, their structure, their norms, their potentialities."[31] As such, this indirect process necessarily requires an explicit advertence to the unique presence we have to ourselves as subjects. Self-appropriation requires a move into the subject as subject—a move which leads us out of the worlds of common sense and theory and into the world of interiority[32]: "Moving in there is self-appropriation; moving in there is what is pre-predicative, preconceptual, pre-judicial. In what may resemble Heidegger's terminology, it is moving from ontology, which is the *logos*, the word about being, the judgment about being, to the ontic, which is what one is."[33] Lonergan conceives of this move as involving a "withdrawal and return."[34] Moving into the subject as subject is a movement into interiority in which one withdraws "from the outer realms of common sense and theory to the appropriation of one's own interiority,"[35] but that culminates in a return to common sense and theory once self-appropriation has been achieved. Although not an end in itself, then, the withdrawal into interiority is therefore as challenging as self-appropriation is definitive: "It is only through the long and confused twilight of philosophic initiation that one can find one's way into interiority and achieve through self-appropriation a basis, a foundation, that is distinct from common sense and theory, that acknowledges their disparateness, that accounts for both and critically grounds them both."[36] This achievement is the primary function of philosophy for Lonergan, moreover, because when we fail to adequately appropriate the intentional operations that constitute the structure of human subjectivity, we hinder ourselves from being genuinely attentive, intelligent, reasonable, and responsible, as Lonergan claims we must if we are to incarnate authentic subjectivity.[37]

Like Taylor, Lonergan insists that authenticity is only achieved in self-transcendence, however, and so we must recognize that although the world of interiority is an inner realm, it is one that is always already ruptured by subject-transcending sources. When we move into ourselves as subjects we find ourselves performatively engaged in transcendental method: "The trick in self-appropriation is to move one step backwards, to move into the subject as intelligent—asking questions; as having insights—being able to form concepts; as weighing the evidence—being able to judge."[38] Thus engaged *in* transcendental method, however, we have already been engaged *by* a subject-transcending source to the degree that we are transcending ourselves so as to fully participate in it. And so the movement into ourselves as subjects is a movement into ourselves as self-transcending subjects, that is, as already swept up by the mystery of lived experience, as already caught in the arduous search for understanding, as already engrossed by the rigors of reflection, and as absorbed in the gravity of choosing. Moving into ourselves as subjects is a movement into ourselves as already engaged by the subject-transcending source whose call has ennobled us to transcend ourselves via engaging in transcendental method.

The spirit in which we engage in this process is definitive because transcendental method is a normative pattern of operations that is only authentically realized through the donative ecstasis of self-transcendence. When we move into ourselves as already engaged in transcendental method, we move into the norms of our conscious and intentional operations, and not simply their structure and potentialities. Before the transcendental precepts that express these norms are themselves formulated and expressed, they "have a prior existence and reality in the spontaneous, structured dynamism of human consciousness."[39] Self-appropriation aims to bring the normative force of these imperatives to life by heightening our consciousness, not only of their existence, but also of the truth that our unfailing fidelity to these norms is the condition for the possibility of authentic subjectivity. We are our true selves when we observe the transcendental precepts because these demands authenticate our subjectivity as human subjects.[40] In order to incarnate unfailing fidelity to the normative demands these precepts express, we must heighten our consciousness regarding the four levels of conscious and intentional operation they pertain to. Doing so is just what self-appropriation aims to achieve, beginning as it does with the move into ourselves as subjects. Engaging in transcendental method authentically is not simply a matter of experiencing, inquiring, judging, and choosing, however, because although this pattern is already operative and conscious, it must be appropriated before what is meant by genuine attentiveness, intelligence, rationality, and responsibility are incarnated in the human subject. We are called to such incarnation by the transcendent sources whose call is a call to authenticity. In order to fully participate in the subject-transcending sources whose calls ennoble us to engage in transcendental method in this manner, then, we must fully give ourselves over to these transcendent sources, as we do in and through self-transcendence. When we do so with an unfailing fidelity to the transcendental precepts, we engage in the donative ecstasis of self-transcendence and thereby incarnate authentic subjectivity.

The Adequacy of Self-Appropriation

Although Lonergan invites us to engage in the indirect process of self-appropriation so that we might be at home in transcendental method, doing so "is a matter of heightening one's consciousness by objectifying it, and that is something that each one, ultimately, has to do in himself and for himself."[41] Self-appropriation is as personal a process as it is definitive. In and for ourselves, each of us must heighten our consciousnesses if we are to adequately appropriate transcendental method. As definitive as this personal heightening of consciousness is, it is not without its traps. I believe one of these traps accounts for Lonergan's tendency to emphasize the centrality of the subject and thus explains his vulnerability to the charge of subjectivism: the trap of appropriating one's consciousness of oneself rather than the self of which one is conscious.[42]

Self-appropriation as Lonergan conceives of it necessarily involves what Taylor refers to as a "two-place relation": the relation between (1) the self as appropriator and (2) the self that is being appropriated.[43] As in any attempt at self-interpretation, the self is simultaneously the interpreter and that which is interpreted as one is engaged in self-appropriation.[44] Since the self is both experiencer and experienced, understander and understood, judger and judged, and chooser and chosen during this process, there is a two-place relation which has as its poles the self as appropriator and the self that is being appropriated. As Jerome Miller reminds us, a crucial distinction must therefore be drawn between the subject as *noesis* and the subject as *noema* throughout self-appropriation.[45] Doing so is necessary because what is meant by experience during this indirect process is not the data of sense but rather the data of consciousness. Self-appropriation is an indirect process because what it adverts to are not the objects that our intentional operations make present to us but rather these operations themselves, as made available to us through consciousness. It is only because they are conscious as well as intentional that we can apply our operations as intentional to our operations as conscious and thereby heighten our consciousness. As such, drawing a distinction between the self as experiencer and the self as experienced necessitates drawing the more specific distinction between the self as conscious and the self of which one is conscious. This latter distinction parallels the umbrella distinction between the self as appropriator and the self which is appropriated since the self as conscious is the appropriator of the self of which one is conscious—the self that is appropriated during self-appropriation.

The trap of appropriating one's consciousness rather than the self of which one is conscious is set by the fact that self-appropriation is a process whose primary aim is to heighten one's consciousness, and is sprung when the self-appropriating subject uses one's heightened consciousness to center oneself within this process. Self-appropriation is an exercise in consciousness-raising that aims to elevate the level of consciousness one has regarding oneself. Thus although he does not perhaps intend it, Lonergan's conception of this process as a heightening of consciousness itself encourages us to appropriate the first pole of the two-place relation—the consciousness one has of oneself—rather or more than the second pole—the self of which one is conscious. If we are to objectify our consciousness, as we clearly must in order to appropriate the whole of transcendental method and not simply the first level of experience, we need to heighten our consciousness of our operations at the four levels of experience, understanding, judgment, and decision. Since doing so necessarily involves the two-place relation between the consciousness one has of oneself and the self of which one is conscious, though, appropriating the first pole of this relation rather than the second cannot result in what Lonergan himself refers to as an "adequate" self-appropriation.[46] Such is the case because the self-appropriating subject as subject is both the self as appropriator and the self that is appropriated during this process. To appropriate the first pole of this relation rather than the second, whether at the crucial level of experience where experience translates into consciousness, or at any of the other three levels, is to therefore do nothing less than appropriate half of one's subjectivity, and so render authentic subjectivity an impossibility.

Surprisingly enough, doing so is as tempting as it is advantageous, however, precisely because the consciousness we have of ourselves leaves us at a remove from the self each of us is conscious of being: the self who, far from simply being conscious of itself, is already ensnared by mystery, already searching for the crucial insight, already weighing the evidence for definitive judgment, and already overwhelmed by the necessity of choosing—the self who is already subjectively engaged by some subject-transcending source to the degree that she is equally engaged in the donative ecstasis that is transcendental method. Though one's heightened consciousness of this process can be secured by appropriating one's consciousness of oneself alone, thereby seemingly centering the subject amid what is a radically decentering process, it does not and cannot exempt one from actually being the self of which its heightened consciousness is conscious. Being this self means being a subjectively engaged subject—a subject who is engaged *by* some subject-transcending source as she responds to its call by remaining engaged *in* transcendental method. Thus understood, subjective engagement is as inherently decentering a venture as can be imagined. Far from leaving a subject at one remove from this decentering engagement, adequately heightening one's consciousness of oneself as caught within it is itself as decentering as it is personally definitive. Such is never the case more than when this radical process culminates in the donative ecstasis of self-transcendence whereby authentic subjectivity is incarnated. Thus authentic subjectivity is no more centered than it is constituted by one's consciousness alone. As necessary and definitive as it is, heightening one's consciousness of oneself while engaged in transcendental method does not constitute an adequate self-appropriation unless it includes a concomitant appropriation of the self of which one is conscious—an appropriation that is as uninviting as it is perilous from the perspective of the self-appropriating subject who hopes to remain centered throughout one's appropriation of transcendental method.[47]

If the extent to which Lonergan's vulnerability to the charge of subjectivism ultimately remains ambiguous, as I believe it does, such is the case because his commitment to self-transcendence is in tension with his emphasis on the centrality of the knowing subject. The fact that Lonergan articulates the intentional structure of self-transcendence more fully than any philosopher before him would lead one to dismiss the charge of subjectivism as a misapprehension. And yet Lonergan simultaneously insists that the subject is the source and center of all cognitional operation—the "experienced center of experiencing, the intelligent center of inquiry, the rational center of reflection, and the responsible center of decision." Similarly, the fact that Lonergan, like Taylor, claims authenticity can be achieved only in and through self-transcendence might lead one to assume that Lonergan's conception of the human subject entails a "radical decentering of the conscious subject correctly conceived," just as Lawrence claims. And yet, according to Lonergan, the conscious subject correctly conceived is the subject as the "rock" upon which transcendental method is built: "The rock, then, is the subject in his conscious, unobjectified attentiveness, intelligence, reasonableness, responsibility."[48] Can the subject so conceived ever be radically decentered? Is not his conception of the subject as subject, despite its initial perspicuity with regard to the intentional structure of conscious subjectivity, only distorted by Lonergan as soon as he then conceives of it as a rock? Thus conceived, the subject is thoroughly centered precisely because it remains impervious to the radical decentering Lawrence associates with Lonerganian self-transcendence. And can self-transcendence be ultimately, not to mention radically, decentering if the subject engaged in this donative ecstasis remains centered throughout the process whereby it is personally appropriated? So goes the unresolved tension between Lonergan's emphasis on the centered subject as rock and his commitment to the decentered self-transcending subject— the tension which perpetuates the ambiguity regarding his vulnerability to the charge of subjectivism, and thereby threatens the plausibility of transcendental method within the contemporary Continental landscape.

The Sources of Authenticity

That this unresolved tension in Lonergan's thought is not an unresolvable one is revealed when Lonergan's articulation of the normative structure of conscious intentionality is critically integrated with Taylor's insights into subjective engagement. Taylor's hermeneutic claim that we must remain engaged in the interpretive background within which we constitute ourselves as subjects is coupled with his assertion that doing so itself involves being engaged by the subject-transcending sources that inform our self-interpretations. Whereas the former requires Lonerganian interiority, or what Taylor refers to as "inwardness," because it is only insofar as we advert to our presence to ourselves as subjects that we can properly form the self-interpretations which partly constitute us, the latter requires being engaged by transcendent realities to the degree that we fully participate in the process of self-transcendence within which we are radically decentered.[49] By going beyond ourselves so as to connect with subject-transcending sources, as we do when subjective engagement culminates in the donative ecstasis of self-transcendence, we participate in the transcendent sources that inform our self-interpretations, and which thereby serve as the conditions for the possibility of authentic subjectivity. It is not human subjects ourselves, but rather these subject-transcending sources, which, by issuing the normative demands they place upon us in the form of the transcendental precepts, call us to self-surrendering self-transcendence, and so to authentic subjectivity. If we are to ever incarnate the unfailing fidelity to these precepts that this ideal requires, however, each of us must heighten our personal consciousness of the intentional structure of human subjectivity—a structure that, once it has been appropriated, can be authenticated through our incarnation of the transcendental precepts as issued to us by the subject-transcending sources which call us to subjective engagement. As self-interpreters engaged in transcendental method, therefore, we are one source of ourselves, while the transcendent sources we are engaged by are another.[50]

This unique entwinement of the subjective with the subject-transcending is definitive in that it requires both an inward turn to and a radical decentering of the human subject. We are inwardly decentered when authentically engaged in transcendental method because we are participants in a process that requires us to both complete the indirect process whereby we inwardly appropriate the structure of conscious intentionality and surrender our very selves to the transcendent sources whose normative demands ennoble us to engage in the radically decentering process of self-transcendence. Although these sources thus lead us beyond ourselves, "the road to them passes inescapably through a heightened awareness of personal experience,"[51] a heightening of consciousness that is achieved, as Lonergan insists, by appropriating one's interiority. Authentic subjective engagement therefore requires inwardness as well as radical decentering. Such is the case, according to Taylor, because "decentering is not the alternative to inwardness; it is its complement."[52] The complementarity of inwardness and radical decentering is what animates Taylor's conception of subjective engagement, informed as it is by the closely related entwinement of the subject and the subject-transcending. The complement to the inwardness that reveals the normative structure of human subjectivity is the lived experience of being radically decentered while engaged in the process of self-transcendence through which we participate in transcendent sources. The subject-transcending sources that call us to such subjective engagement are calling us to *decentered inwardness,* or authentic subjectivity. Authentic subjectivity is the consequence of genuine attention, genuine intelligence, genuine reasonableness, and genuine responsibility, just as Lonergan claims it is, but we only incarnate these norms if, as Taylor claims, we are radically decentered during our subjective engagement in self-transcendence. Authentic subjective engagement is therefore the only adequate response to the transcendent sources that, together with the self-interpretations which also partly constitute us as human subjects, serve as the dual sources of our selves.

Concluding Implications

The implications of this critically integrated account of the sources of authenticity are numerous, but can be grouped into three general conclusions. First, human subjects cannot be the center of our cognitional operations because we are not the only source of these operations. Being subjectively engaged means being engaged in the background within which we constitute ourselves as human subjects. Because this background is partly constituted by the subject-transcending sources we are engaged by as well as by our self-interpretations, however, we are no more the only source of the cognitional operations whereby we formulate these interpretations than we are their center. Secondly, self-transcendence entails a radical decentering of the conscious human subject correctly conceived, just as Lawrence claims it does, but such a conception is one which successfully avoids the trap of appropriating one's consciousness of oneself rather or more than the self of which one is conscious. Subjects who appropriate their consciousness of themselves alone with the hope of remaining centered throughout self-appropriation are disengaged subjects—subjects who, precisely because they are not engaged by a subject-transcending source to the degree that they are radically decentered, are thus not authentically engaged in self-transcendence, as they must be if they are to adequately appropriate this process. When the conscious subject is correctly conceived, the consciousness it has of itself serves to bring it closer to, rather than leaving it at one remove from, the self of which it is conscious—the self whose subjective engagement in transcendental method is as radically decentering as its appropriation of this process is personally definitive. The withdrawal into interiority is not a withdrawal into one's

consciousness alone. If it were, self-appropriation would be an appropriation of a centered but disengaged subject, half of whose subjectivity was
amputated for the sake of centrality. When an adequate appropriation is
achieved, on the other hand, the self returns to the worlds of theory and
common sense as a unified self whose heightened consciousness of transcendental method is inseparable from its being the self who lovingly sur-
renders itself in the donative ecstasis of self-transcendence.

Finally, the presence we have to ourselves is a constitutive presence
because, not despite, the fact that it is a decentering presence. Our presence to ourselves as subjects is constitutive of human subjectivity, not
because it enables us to center ourselves within transcendental method,
and to thus become the center of the universe this process makes available
to us, but rather because it brings us closer to ourselves as engaged in a
process which can provide us with access to the intelligible universe, but
only when we willingly surrender all of ourselves to the radically decentering process whereby we participate in transcendent sources of meaning
and value. Thus our presence to ourselves is not, as many contemporary
Continental thinkers claim, yet another instance of the metaphysics of
presence, but such is the case because neither is this unique presence a
centering presence. Although it is abused when it leaves us at one remove
from the selves we are conscious of, the consciousness we have of ourselves
as subjects simultaneously brings us face to face with our selves as radically
decentered by the transcendent sources whose call to authentic subjective
engagement is as harrowing as it is mysterious. The contemporary Continental critique of self-presence need not render the notion of interiority
absurd, therefore, especially if it serves as the impetus to conceive of the
presence we have to ourselves as subjects, and therefore of authentic subjectivity, as decentered inwardness.[53] Modern, and with it postmodern,
inwardness will assume the form of self-exploration rather than that of
self-control, if and when the contemporary Continental critique of the
metaphysics of presence is critically integrated with self-transcendence as
Lonergan, together with Taylor, formulate it.[54]

Doing so involves overcoming modern assumptions, and thus
requires postmodern wisdom. The critical integration of contemporary
Continental thought and transcendental method is as necessary as it is
challenging, therefore. The result of such an integration is, likewise, as
definitive as it is hard won. At its end, transcendental method emerges as
the cognitional theory which, because the subject as subject that lies at its

heart has been decentered, can plausibly overcome the epistemological and anthropological distortions of modernism. Critical realism can thereby emerge intact and relevant in the contemporary Continental philosophical landscape that so desperately needs it.

Notes

1. See, for example, Jerome Miller, *In The Throe of Wonder: Intimations of the Sacred in a Post-Modern World* (Albany: State University of New York Press, 1992), and "All Love is Self-Surrender: Reflections on Lonergan After Post-Modernism," *Method: Journal of Lonergan Studies* 13 (1995): 53–81; Fred Lawrence, "Lonergan, The Integral Postmodern?," *Method: Journal of Lonergan Studies* 18 (2000): 95–122, and "The Fragility of Consciousness: Lonergan and the Postmodern Concern for the Other," *Theological Studies* 54 (1993): 55–94; Elizabeth Morelli, "Oversight of Insight and the Critique of the Metaphysics of Presence," *Method: Journal of Lonergan Studies* 18 (2000): 1–15; and Jim Kanaris, "Calculating Subjects: Lonergan, Derrida, and Foucault," *Method: Journal of Lonergan Studies* 15 (1997): 135–50. Miller's contributions have advanced this critical integration the furthest in my view, and are ones that substantially influence my upcoming reflections.

2. See Ronald McKinney, "Deconstructing Lonergan," *International Philosophical Quarterly* 31 (1991): 81.

3. See Jim Kanaris, "Engaged Agency and the Notion of the Subject," *Method: Journal of Lonergan Studies* 14 (1996): 192.

4. Fred Lawrence, "The Fragility of Consciousness," 72.

5. Taylor's philosophical anthropology is best evidenced in his *Sources of the Self* (Cambridge, MA: Harvard University Press, 1989); "Overcoming Epistemology," *Philosophical Arguments* (Cambridge, MA: Harvard University Press, 1995), 1–19; and "Rorty in the Epistemological Tradition," in *Reading Rorty*, ed. Alan Malachowski (Cambridge: Basil Blackwell, 1990), 257–75.

6. Doing so was the primary aim of my doctoral dissertation, "From the Disengaged Subject to the Subject as Subject in Taylor and Lonergan" (Saint Louis University, 2000), the fifth chapter of which has been revised into this current form. This article marks the second half of the published critical integration begun in my "Lonergan and Taylor: A Critical Integration," *Method: Journal of Lonergan Studies* 19 (2001): 143–72.

7. Cf., Taylor, *Sources of the Self.* "'Disengagement' here is a term of art, meaning a stance toward something which might otherwise serve to define our identity or purposes, whereby we separate ourselves from it by defining it as at best of instrumental significance." Charles Taylor, "Inwardness and the Culture of Modernity," in *Philosophical Interventions in the Unfinished Project of the Enlightenment*, eds. Axel Honneth, Thomas McCarthy, Claus Offe, and Albrecht Wellmer, (Cambridge, MA: MIT Press, 1992), 98.

8. Charles Taylor, *The Ethics of Authenticity* (Cambridge, MA: Harvard University Press, 1991).

9. Ibid., especially 13–41.

10. Ibid., 14.

11. Ibid., 41.

12. Ibid., 55–69.

13. See Taylor, *The Ethics of Authenticity*, 13–41, and Lonergan, *Method in Theology* (Toronto: University of Toronto Press, 1971), 104.

14. See Taylor, *Sources of the Self*, 526–7, n. 20.

15. Taylor, *The Ethics of Authenticity*, 40.

16. Thus Taylor's claim that "acknowledging the transcendent means being called to a change of identity." See James Heft, *A Catholic Modernity? Charles Taylor's Marianist Award Lecture* (Oxford: Oxford University Press, 1999), 21.

17. Taylor, *The Ethics of Authenticity*, 72–3.

18. Ibid., emphasis his.

19. See Charles Taylor, *Philosophical Papers*, vol. 1, *Human Agency and Language* (Cambridge: Cambridge University Press, 1985), 3–5, and 76. As such, self-interpretation pertains to what Ruth Abbey identifies as the ontological, as opposed to the historicist, dimension of Taylor's approach to human subjectivity. Ruth Abbey, *Charles Taylor* (Princeton, NJ: Princeton University Press, 2000), 55–100.

20. Charles Taylor, "Overcoming Epistemology," in *Philosophical Arguments* (Cambridge, MA: Harvard University Press, 1995), 11.

21. See Bernard Lonergan, *Notes on Existentialism* (author's notes for lectures given at Boston College, July 1957, reprinted by Thomas More Institute, Montreal), 15.

22. Bernard Lonergan, *Lectures on Existentialism* (lectures delivered at Boston College, July 15–19, 1957), 126, emphasis his.

23. Lonergan, *Notes on Existentialism*, 15.

24. Bernard Lonergan, *Collected Works of Bernard Lonergan*, ed. Frederick Crowe and Robert Doran, vol. 3, *Insight* (Toronto: University of Toronto Press, 1992), 434, as well as *The Subject* (Milwaukee: Marquette University Press, 1995), 7: "[The study of the subject] attends to operations and their center and source which is the self."

25. Lonergan, *Lectures on Existentialism*, 154.

26. Bernard Lonergan, "*Existenz* and *Aggiornamento*," in *Collected Works of Bernard Lonergan*, ed. Frederick Crowe and Robert Doran, vol. 4, *Collection* (Toronto: University of Toronto Press, 1993), 223.

27. Lonergan, *Method in Theology*, 8.

28. Bernard Lonergan, "Philosophical Positions With Regard to Knowing," in *Collected Works of Bernard Lonergan*, ed. Robert Croken, Frederick Crowe, and Robert Doran, vol. 6, *Philosophical and Theological Papers 1958–1965* (Toronto: University of Toronto Press, 1996), 222.

29. See Bernard Lonergan, "Christ as Subject: A Reply," *Collection*, 152–84, where Lonergan draws this crucial distinction between *conscientia-experientia* and *conscientia-perceptio*.

30. Lonergan, *Method in Theology*, 95.

31. Ibid., 83.

32. Thus "the aim of *Insight*, self-appropriation, is a movement to the world of interiority." Bernard Lonergan, "Time and Meaning," in *Philosophical and Theological Papers* 1958–1965, 114.

33. Bernard Lonergan, *Collected Works of Bernard Lonergan*, ed. Elizabeth and Mark Morelli, vol. 5, *Understanding and Being* (Toronto: University of Toronto Press, 1990), 15. The significance of this rich description of the subject as subject as a response to Derrida's critique of logocentrism is considerable. I will return to the closely related postmodern critique of self-presence in the final section of this paper. See Jacques Derrida, *Of Grammatology*, trans. Gayatri Spivak (Baltimore: The Johns Hopkins University Press, 1976), 12.

34. Lonergan borrows this phrase from Arnold Toynbee and first mentions it in his *Lectures on Existentialism*, 26–7.

35. See Lonergan, *Method in Theology*, 83.

36. Ibid., 85.

37. Ibid., 265.

38. Lonergan, *Understanding and Being*, 14.

39. Lonergan, *Method in Theology*, 20.

40. Ibid., 53.

41. Ibid., 14.

42. I have explored this trap and its consequences in greater detail in "The Surpassing Subject," a paper presented at the 17th Annual Fallon Memorial Lonergan Symposium, Loyola-Marymount University, Los Angeles, CA, March 2001.

43. Charles Taylor, "Inwardness and the Culture of Modernity," 95.

44. Abbey further explains what Taylor means by a "two-place relation" when she writes, "Much of Taylor's inspiration for thinking about the self in this way comes from the hermeneutical tradition and its concern with the meaning and interpretation of texts. A self resembles a text in that there is a meaning to be understood and in the way that new interpretations can supersede earlier ones. But when it comes to selfhood, the self is not just the text to be interpreted but also the interpreter of that text." Ruth Abbey, *Charles Taylor*, 60.

45. Jerome Miller, "'All Love is Self-Surrender,'" 78.

46. See Lonergan, *Method in Theology*, 265.

47. As Jerome Miller rightly notes, given the fact that transcendental method is animated by and only culminates in the *donative* ecstasis, which Lonergan himself refers to as "self-surrender," it is anomalous that he terms the procedure whereby we heighten our consciousness of this process as self-*appropriation*. The possessiveness this locution suggests is the very antithesis of the animating spirit behind the whole of transcendental method. This anomaly thus suggests that despite his deep commitment to self-transcendence, Lonergan simultaneously hopes we remain centered in the very way appropriating one's consciousness of oneself rather than the self one is conscious of promises. See Jerome Miller, "'All Love is Self-Surrender,'" 78–9.

48. Ibid., 19–20.

49. Although it is not as detailed as Lonergan's account of the structure of interiority, Taylor's account of inwardness includes an appeal to understand subjectivity "in the life of the subject," or qua subject, an appeal which nicely parallels

Lonergan's appeal to the presence we have to ourselves as subjects, and the insistence that our experienced awareness as subjects "is the common reality all philosophical views have to recognize," an insistence which similarly parallels Lonergan's insistence upon *conscientia-experientia*. Taylor, *Human Agency and Language*, 60, and "Consciousness," in *Explaining Human Behavior*, ed. Paul Secord (London: Sage Publications, 1982), 41, respectively.

50. Hence, as Joel Anderson notes, the double meaning of Taylor's title, *Sources of the Self*. See Joel Anderson, "The Personal Lives of Strong Evaluators: Identity, Pluralism, and Ontology in Charles Taylor's Value Theory," *Constellations* 3, no. 1 (1996): 17.

51. Taylor, *Sources of the Self*, 481.

52. Ibid., 465.

53. See Elizabeth Morelli, "The Oversight of Insight," 13.

54. See Taylor, "Inwardness and the Culture of Modernity," 94–108.

Chapter 2

To Whom Do We Return
in the Turn to the Subject?

Lonergan, Derrida, and Foucault Revisited

JIM KANARIS

In 1997 I addressed myself to the issue of "the death of the subject" in contemporary Continental philosophy.[1] The concern there was to show that "the subject" in the more radical stream of that tradition is very much alive, even if diagnosed by many as not very well. In this essay I revisit that issue and the main figures I focused on in 1997: Lonergan, Derrida, and Foucault. The concern here is to pinpoint in greater detail the notion of the subject in these figures and at what points they converge and diverge on this issue. I also explore the issue of critical reciprocity, which is an important one for someone like myself who wants to remain in the tension between their varying yet respectively powerful views. Lonergan's 1968 Aquinas Lecture "The Subject" is my point of departure.[2]

"The Subject"

The penultimate paragraph of "The Subject" is perhaps the most significant for those grappling with Lonergan in the context of present philosophical concerns. He cautions against "a new neglect of the subject, a new truncation, a new immanentism" more insidious than versions he explicitly treats in the paper. Presumably these counterpositions are more insidious because they undermine any hope of answering the value question affirmatively, that is, whether something is good or worthwhile. For

Lonergan such questions are grounded finally in an affirmation of God's existence, omnipotence, and goodness.[3] Counterpositions he has in mind presume the loss of such a ground owing to the experience heralded by Nietzsche's "death of God." Perhaps it would be good to quote Lonergan in full here:

> It is, then, no accident that a theatre of the absurd, a literature of the absurd, and philosophies of the absurd flourish in a culture in which there are theologians to proclaim that God is dead. But that absurdity and that death have their roots in a new neglect of the subject, a new truncation, a new immanentism. In the name of phenomenology, of existential self-understanding, of human encounter, of salvation history, there are those that resentfully and disdainfully brush aside the old questions of cognitional theory, epistemology, metaphysics. I have no doubt, I never did doubt, that the old answers were defective. But to reject the questions as well is to refuse to know what one is doing when one is knowing; it is to refuse to know why doing that is knowing; it is to refuse to set up a basic semantics by concluding what one knows when one does it. That threefold refusal is worse than mere neglect of the subject, and it generates a far more radical truncation. It is that truncation that we experience today not only without but within the Church, when we find that the conditions of the possibility of significant dialogue are not grasped, when the distinction between revealed religion and myth is blurred, when the possibility of objective knowledge of God's existence and of his goodness is denied.[4]

Evidently this "new neglect of the subject" stems from existentialist-type philosophizing. Put positively, it emphasizes the primacy of existence or experience over essence, "thinking" life relationally over thinking "systematically," totalistically; it condemns "the old questions" Lonergan mentions as remote from real life and for that reason inherently alienating. It also predetermines truths one arrives at or has to arrive at. Put otherwise, it is a reaction to "system" in the bad sense, where system takes over questioning and no questioning of system is permitted. I agree with Walter Kaufmann that this accounts for Nietzsche's distaste for system, one element among many that existentialists have inherited from him.[5] System is equated with a particular form of philosophizing whose set of premises constitutes the system. Granted this definition, system becomes bad when closed off to the questioning of its premises, when no longer able to see beyond the grid of its own making.

Lonergan, too, of course, distances himself from system conceived along these lines. That, at first glance, is what is so curious about his negation. Why would he condemn a movement that denounces system in favor of life, reality, and subjectivity as neglectful of the subject? The question is completely rhetorical. Those familiar with Lonergan know why. Existentialist and postexistentialist philosophy is the opposite extreme of—albeit a needed corrective to—objectivist consciousness, the view that takes truth to be so objective that it can get along without the mind that thinks it.[6] The danger with existentialism, then, would be that it takes truth to be so subjective that it can get along without that which makes talk of the subject intelligible. There is no escaping talk of the object in talk of the subject; their meanings are interdependent. Of course, Lonergan appreciates much in existentialism and phenomenology, their emphasis, for instance, on the practical flow of experience and the prepredicative, the preconceptual.[7] The danger with existentialism, however, is the license it offers to subjectivity in overemphasizing the subject. He praises the phenomenological reduction, offering a variant of it in his own philosophy, but condemns its hope for absolute certainty.[8] He sees such hopes as leading inevitably to skepticism and perhaps with a bit of interpretation could be seen as agreeing with Nietzsche that they lead to nihilism. This basically amounts to a neglect of the subject, even if subjectivity is emphasized. Nor does he feel that Heidegger surmounts this issue in his emphasis on Being. There may in fact be a sickness intrinsic to conceptions of the subject-object relation, which Heidegger has diagnosed as the forgetfulness of Being. But to subvert that primordial relation by an even more primordial notion is only partially remedial. The danger is that what one thinks is absent by virtue of the nature of the discourse is merely prolonged, namely the forgetfulness of subject. This constitutes Lonergan's fundamental philosophic critique of Western consciousness.

No less odd, but anticipated now given this background, is that Kant is still considered a problem, irrespective of our Nietzschean and Heideggerian sensibilities: "Heidegger contains potentialities of getting beyond Kant, but he can't push through. He's never written the second part of his *Sein und Zeit*. Kant is still a problem."[9] Ricoeur says the same thing without explicit reference to Kant.[10] In "The Subject" the Kantian problem is identified in a footnote, which Lonergan briefly engages in his treatment of the "immanentist subject." After enumerating philosophers to whom we owe the contemporary emphasis on the subject, he notes the following about Kant: "One should, perhaps, start from Kant's Copernican revolution, which brought the subject into technical prominence while making only minimal concessions to its reality. The subsequent movement then appears as a series of attempts to win for the subject acknowledgement of its full reality and its functions."[11]

Why Lonergan believes Kant makes only minimal concessions to the reality of the subject doubtless owes itself to his transferal of the Kantian problematic as regards knowing the object to knowing the subject. Just as our judgment and reasoning give us only mediate knowledge of what intuition "knows" immediately, and what intuition knows immediately is of a sensitive nature, phenomena, not noumena, so too our judgment and reasoning about the human subject reveal only a phenomenal subject, a representation of a representation. A merely phenomenal subject grasped mediately through judgment in mediate relation (again through judgment) to a merely phenomenal world amounts to minimal concessions to the reality of both for Lonergan. His response is classic.

> It is just as much a matter of judgment to know that an object is not real but apparent, as it is to know that an object is not apparent but real. Sense does not know appearances because sense alone is not human knowing, and because sense alone does not possess the full objectivity of human knowing. By our senses we are given, not appearance, not reality, but data. . . . Further, while it is true enough that data of sense result in us from the action of external objects, it is not true that we know this by sense alone; we know it as we know anything else, by experiencing, understanding, and judging.[12]

The same applies to the subjective field, except that what is given in it is not the result of any external action but the condition of the possibility of external action being present to us. Needless to say, this sine qua non, the data of consciousness, is an item of this "anything else" known through itself qua experiencing, understanding, and judging.

What of this "subsequent movement" then, which seeks "to win for the subject acknowledgement of its full reality and its functions"? For Lonergan, it does indeed provide, from various angles, correctives to Kant but it does so without reversing what is flawed or counterpositional in Kant. As a result, its correctives are half-baked, incarcerating us in a world of concepts whose reality can be as intangible and questionable as the distinction it is founded upon. With the exception of Hegel, Lonergan would interpret this as a rush to the existential without genuine insight into insight and hence appreciation for the reality value or "objectivity" of knowing. In so far as it rejects the questions of cognition, epistemology, and metaphysics, it is a flight from reality potentially more dangerous than the commonsense rejection of such query seeking.

We get to the reality of the subject and what it knows, for Lonergan, through rigorous self-analysis of cognitional operations vis-à-vis actual instances of insight. I need not recount the familiar procedure of *Insight*. Suffice it to say inadequately here that for Lonergan it boils down to the precedence of insight over concept. Insight is our link to reality mediated through concepts and (dis)confirmed through judgments—through grasp of the virtually unconditioned. Judgment connects us to a reality that is not posited as being more real than what is or can be known. "It is just as much a matter of judgment to know that an object is not real but apparent, as it is to know that an object is not apparent but real." "Ens iudicio rationali cognoscitur."

Assume here, for the sake of argument, the uniqueness of Lonergan's position. It's not a claim for the subordination of reality to knowing, which is the intention in Kant's limit concept (*Grenzbegriff*) of noumenal reality. It is, rather, a claim for the isomorphism that obtains between reality and knowing at the level of judgment—incidentally not at the levels of either experience or understanding. For Lonergan, it is unlike the alternative of Hegel, which merely collapses the distinction on the side of the subject.[13] There is no such collapse in Lonergan thanks to the unconditioned, which "connects judgment with the absolute."[14] The underlying claim, then, in the closing paragraph of "The Subject" is that subsequent radical movements in philosophy are radical relative to Kant and Hegel while remaining Kantian and Hegelian in their negations. To put it in the terms of *Insight*, they still "function under the shadow of the principle of immanence."[15]

Itineraries of Re-turn

Procedurally not a great deal separates Lonergan from, say, Nietzsche or Heidegger. They all approach these giants of modern philosophy on their own terms and from different methodological perspectives: Nietzsche: historical philosophizing or genealogy; Heidegger: fundamental ontology; Lonergan: cognitional process. The difference, at least for Lonergan, is that these radical thinkers thwart systems as Kant's and Hegel's by assuming their relative legitimacy, the legitimacy of their categories. Nietzsche and Heidegger think within Kantian and Hegelian frameworks as they look for internal inconsistencies via new means of thinking. In a sense, they leave everything as is in their destruction. "Kant," we are reminded, "is still a problem."[16] By contrast, we are told, cognitional theory assumes the legitimacy of the task of these philosophers without assuming the legitimacy of their categories. It discovers internal inconsistencies but through analysis of insight into insight, a means of thinking that engages Kant and Hegel head on in the pattern of experience according to which they think. Nietzsche and Heidegger do not think according to their pattern but introduce concerns that are patterned differently in their move to a higher viewpoint.[17]

Some describe Lonergan's tactic as radical. It is radical in a moderate or etymological sense of getting to the root of a problem. Few, however, understand the term so benignly. What qualifies Nietzsche and Heidegger as radical for many is that they uproot Kant and Hegel; they make a guarded break with that tradition. To forward their positions and reverse their counterpositions, it is usually held, does little, if anything, to negotiate the sickness diagnosed by Nietzsche and Heidegger; it merely prolongs what requires overcoming. It is worth noting, however, that not even Derrida, who functions under different philosophic constraints, is convinced by the programmatic of escape valued by so many today. Thus he can say:

> [Nietzsche, Freud, and Heidegger] worked within the inherited concepts of metaphysics. Since these concepts are not elements or atoms and since they are taken from a syntax and a system, every particular borrowing brings along with it the whole of metaphysics. This is what allows these destroyers to destroy each other reciprocally—for example, Heidegger regarding Nietzsche, with as much lucidity and rigor as bad faith and misconstruction, as the last metaphysician, the last "Platonist." One could do the same for Heidegger himself, for Freud, or for a number of others. And today no exercise is more widespread.[18]

Alternatives always function concentrically with what is critiqued, however radically. Indeed, their intelligibility depends to a large extent on what they distance themselves from. The issue is not to escape the circle but to colonize it and then to blast it, creating fissures for the emergence of new meaning. The point is not that Lonergan supports Derrida's understanding of the function and critique of meaning. Who would be so silly as to state this without endless qualification? I make two points, the first being somewhat innocuous. First, radicality is not what it always seems. One may think one has severed all ties with a tradition, only to reflect it back in negative terms. Derrida is a master at showing this. Second, Lonergan may not agree with the spin Derrida puts on our entrapment in a tradition, but he certainly appreciates what introducing another language into one's critique does not mean. It does not mean that one has annulled a tradition or, more significantly for Lonergan, the importance of a tradition's questions and concerns, in their particular patterning. Destabilizing a ready-made world to allow for the emergence of another, one that is different, novel, strange, and intimate[19] is fine. But one must return finally to matters immediately pertinent to what necessitated alternatives in the first place.

Return to Kant. Re-turn Kant. That is the plea. Return to the subject. Re-turn the subject. That is the task; it was Kant, after all, who "brought the subject into technical prominence." What are we to make of this itinerary of return? How does it differ from present returns? Is it fair to understand "present returns" as returns? Finally, how might we understand present returns, if they are returns, in the light of an appreciation of Lonergan's itinerary?

For practical reasons, I limit the field of present returns to Foucault and Derrida. They offer a form of thinking that for me radicalizes the subsequent movement Lonergan talks about in a way that captures the Zeitgeist. And they do so while tempering what I see as the triumphalism of negation inherited from Nietzsche and Heidegger. We glimpse this, for instance, in the quotation cited earlier from Derrida. So much for the aspect of "present" in present returns. What about the aspect of "return"? Can Derrida and Foucault truly be seen as returning to what is supposedly overcome in Nietzsche and Heidegger? Obviously not, if by "return" we understand the circumvention of the "death of God," which for these figures implies the "death of man." Return for them *is* a question of revisiting that which was once thought. What is avoided, as is well known, is the way in which that something was or presently happens to be thought, that something here being the subject. The sense of return, then, is one of returning what is overturned. This, I suggest, is a meaning one may draw from Derrida's question: Who comes *after* the subject?[20] The subject ("who") is still a question, is still an identity in question ("who?"), to be thought after the subject, that is, in the strictly temporal sense of "after that which has been overturned" and in the deconstructive sense of "thinking after an interminably deferred identity." The re-turning of the subject for the reinvention of ever-new subjectivities in Derrida involves rethinking the subject *"in a certain way,"*[21] his way. That way assumes a structuralist understanding of language that Derrida radicalizes in his critique of logocentrism, the privileging of presence over absence, the spoken word over the written word, the signifier ("sound pattern") over the signified ("concept"), and so forth. The history of western thought for him is one long getaway narrative, an attempt to escape language, language as written, by disparaging it in the hopes of something more real, more extratextually, extraconceptually present. It is a getaway, too, in the sense of language "gone on holiday." The language user thinks he or she may attain the full presence of that which is outside the play of signs, oddly unaware or reluctant to accept the only outside there is: the one proclaimed by the inside play of signs. In this way what is outside is truly inside, where speaking of an inside or privileging an inside over an outside becomes equally pointless.[22]

The subject that Derrida re-turns is such an outside. Returning to it has to be a question of re-turning it indefinitely in a close reading of texts, a deconstructive reading of texts from which we have inherited dichotomies requiring radical rethinking. The subject is textuality. Glimpsing the trace of this textuality, traces of its trace, is the proper task of deconstruction. Derrida doesn't hope for more. Indeed, the hope for more he feels is overrated and finally misguided. It is based on honoring extratextual presence over that in which presence is said to be absent: writing. According to Derrida, neither presence nor absence applies to the surplus of textual meaning. For taking writing seriously involves a breakdown in understanding things in terms of binary structures, inside/outside, presence/absence, subject/object, and so on: "Il n'y a pas de hors-texte."

I think it is important to be clear that not only Lonergan would find Derrida's appreciation of the sign unsettling, but semioticians do as well. The move nowadays seems to be one of disengaging semiotics from philosophic presuppositions about semiosis as specifically or exclusively linguistic or textual.[23] The luxury of space to enter that debate eludes us. I merely offer it as a suggestion for future research. It seems to me that something along these lines needs to be implemented if dialogue between Lonergan and Derrida, which is both fruitful and critical, is to develop. For now I limit myself to Lonergan's assessment in "The Subject" and offer a few suggestions as to what the dynamics of such a future project might look like. But before I do that, I would like to comment briefly on the re-turning of the subject in Foucault.

Foucault is more accessible than Derrida on the subject. He is more historical, too, in the sense that he situates his thought more explicitly vis-à-vis other movements in the philosophy of the subject. Methodologically, of course, he ascribes to the overturned subject of Nietzsche, which poses the question of the historicity of the subject. Thus Foucault distances himself from Husserl's philosophy of the subject, which "set as its task *par excellence* the foundation of all knowledge and the principle of all signification as stemming from the meaningful subject."[24] He also distances himself from the Marxist alternative, which "put itself forward as a humanistic discourse that could replace the abstract subject with an appeal to the real man, to the concrete man."[25] He is poststructuralist but in a way and for reasons that differ from Derrida's. Incidentally, Foucault himself had some issues with Derrida's emphasis on textuality. According to one commentator, "[Foucault] declares that such work is pedagogically dubious, teaching falsely that the text is all and the philosopher is its supreme commentator."[26] Whether or not that is true is beside the point. I only mention it here as another example of how a poststructuralist, who does not in the least share Lonergan's convictions about mental acts of meaning, can have strong reservations about the ubiquity of the text.

Foucault is not interested in the subject as an originating act of meaning. For him this amounts to philosophy that prefers the subject without history. Specifically he has in mind the phenomenological method and the cogito. He wouldn't flinch, of course, from indicting similarly any other method that rethinks knowledge vis-à-vis a transcendental subject. Still, he wants to avoid an air of dogmatism. "I do not deny the cogito," he says, "I confine myself to observing that its methodological potential is ultimately not as great as one might have believed and that, in any case, we can nowadays make descriptions which seem to me objective and positive, by dispensing with the cogito altogether."[27] It pivots on the issue of totalization. Must knowledge of the self as rational be reduced to that which accepted forms of rationality tell us about ourselves? Foucault doesn't think so.

What about originating acts of meaning? Although interesting, that is, if one scrutinizes the social conditions that allow us to value such questions, he prefers to leave philosophy of knowledge to philosophers of consciousness. For him such questions are of a lesser urgency today. More urgent, if not simply more interesting, is analysis of the discursive formations providing for an understanding of ourselves. The domain of such analysis he calls "technologies," techniques and certain kinds of discourse about the subject. Its articulation is put forward as a diagnosis of the present: "to say what we are today and what it means, today, to say what we do say."[28] As a task, it sets itself against the Heideggerian "obsession with *technē* as the only way to arrive at an understanding of objects that the West lost touch with Being."[29] Foucault reverses the question and asks, "[W]hich techniques and practices form the Western concept of the subject, giving it its characteristic split of truth and error, freedom and constraint?"[30] Finally, in a way that sounds uncannily like Lonergan, Foucault thinks of this archaeology of the subject in terms of another kind of critical philosophy, "[n]ot a critical philosophy that seeks to determine the conditions and the limits of our possible knowledge of the object, but a critical philosophy that seeks the conditions and the indefinite possibilities of transforming the subject, of transforming ourselves."[31]

Again, the matter is conceived of as a task. The concern is not with the general structure of the subject, as in Husserl and Lonergan, but with the specific historical instantiations of the subject and their conditions of possibility. He himself has provided what he would only too readily see as an initial sketch of this task, his early work, for instance, on the subject vis-à-vis techniques of domination and signification, and his later work on sexuality and the subject. In a word, a contextual diagnostic must remain open ended. Ironically, there can be no end to analysis of the subject after the subject, after the end of subjectivity. This is as true for Foucault as it is for Derrida, however much they differ from one another.

Placing Re-turns

One can find much in Lonergan that resonates with this disenchantment with the subject. The diagnostic that it boils down to the myth of the given is basically correct. Like Derrida Lonergan is equally critical of the out-there-now-present, let alone the analogous in-here-now-present. Like Foucault[32] he wants to mine the "already there" subject, the analysis of which does indeed limit the field of knowledge to absolute apodicticity based on immodest desires. Where the equivalency breaks down is in the trajectory of return. Derrida and Foucault are left with no other alternative—know no other alternative, it seems—than to follow the trail from the subject that has been overturned to the overturned subject, which they re-turn in their own unique ways. The problem for Lonergan is simple enough. A deficiently attained subject will inevitably muddy the trail from an overturned to re-turned subject. The diagnosis may be correct but it is restricted to that of which it is a diagnosis, oversights and all. That, I take it, is the verdict of "The Subject." The re-turning of the subject by Derrida and Foucault is under the same shadow of the principle of immanence that pervades the thought of the masters of suspicion upon whom they critically rely. Just as one needs to point this out with regard to the agents of the overturning, one needs to do the same with regard to the agents of the re-turning.

It is my understanding that the Lonergan community has well emphasized this aspect of the contemporary re-turn. What the agents of the re-turn misunderstand, it is rightly argued (if not a little overemphasized, in my opinion), is how object constitutive the subject of the overturned subject is. As a result, these experts of suspicion bypass what was bypassed (and, incidentally, authentic) in the overturning. An added result, which I agree is unfortunate, is the barring of all attempts to make this stop as repetitive and selfsame. Suspicion becomes hypersuspicion on account of an omission. "The shortcomings of system are not an irremediable defect,"[33] nor is the subject-as-subject who seeks to bring these shortcomings and overcomings into the noontide light. Whereas the objectives of Lonergan and the experts of suspicion are different, their intention is really quite similar: not "to determine the conditions and the limits of our possible knowledge of the object," that is, not only to do this, but also, primarily, fundamentally, to seek "the conditions and the indefinite possibilities of transforming the subject, of transforming ourselves."[34] Why this addition of a "not only . . . but also"? The retrieval of the subject-as-subject requires it, grounds it cognitionally, I should say, as its condition of possibility. This is not as radical perhaps as a radical hermeneutics would like, but it is certainly as alert and, dare I say, more cautious about being performatively consistent.

Are these grounds for bypassing contemporary methodologies of return as illegitimate? One gets the impression that it is. Derrida and Foucault, but especially Derrida, are off the mark and so too, necessarily, are their critiques. It is a comfortable position, however nervous we might be holding it. Is it mere frivolity to push the boundaries of language, to determine the limits of present language, its binary oppositions, in language, in a language where binary oppositions no longer hold? Why ground questions of the subject, questions of religion even, in a groundless "space" (*chora*) of language without "horizon of expectation and without prophetic prefiguration"?[35] Why remove questions of the subject from the domain of discovery?[36] Both Derrida and Foucault have their reasons. Allow me to offer a summary solely for the purpose of our discussion.

Derrida wants to think the condition of the possibility of binary oppositions such as subject/object, presence/absence, transcendence/immanence. He does not believe we can get along without them or that such binary oppositions must necessarily be overcome. The issue, rather, is one of thinking that which serves as the very opening of the space that provides for the thinking of such matters (subject, object, God, and so on). And that which serves as the very opening of binary oppositions is not subject to the categories of those oppositions. The strategy is to find grounds for situating claims, particularly impervious and extravagant claims, which base themselves on such oppositions. In its critical moment, the strategy is to free up discourse, to keep in check our totalizing tendency to freeze discourse. That is Derrida's grievance with logocentrism. It appeals to a universally accessible presence beyond the world of the text, in which this presence is supposedly absent. The problem—which Derrida does not envisage as a problem of course—is that this universal is really quite particular, a product of language and a community of language users who have and wish to promote their various beliefs. Again, this is not a bad thing. Suspicion enters once such claims are proclaimed to be neutral, so present, in fact, to the unbiased questioner that anyone with a modicum of reason cannot fail to see it. Mention has already been made of the manner in which Derrida unravels such claims. In its more constructive moment, deconstruction, as a means of thinking the very opening of the space of centralizing claims, provides other means of thinking, not presence per se but traces of constant presencing—for Derrida, in language, in texts, in the grapheme. For him, this entails a heuristic without horizon of expectancy, that is, a heuristic that "exposes itself to absolute surprise."[37] He wants to rethink our pledge to tell the truth without pledging to tell the truth about what is expected.[38]

Whereas Derrida situates issues of the subject in the spaces of textuality, Foucault situates them in the "discursive practices" that have invented us, subjects with a history, subjects who are history. Like Derrida, he problematizes claims based on universal givens. He is not offering a critique of presence so much as a critique of philosophy as the discursive practice that prefers the subject without history. In that way it can do without the historical conditions and all the problems, infinitesimal problems, associated with a thoroughly, inescapably contextual subject—or rather: subjectivities. The implications of this on our theorizing about the subject are significant vis-à-vis issues of power, in which we are always already implicated. Thus he states in an interview, "[T]he 'best' theories do not constitute a very effective protection against disastrous political choices; certain great themes such as 'humanism' can be used to any end whatever."[39] He wants us to get a critical hold on the risk of applying rationality, whether grounded in a subject or somewhere else, empirically in a completely arbitrary way. This he believes is based on positing an absolute value inherent in reason. He is willing to grant only an instrumental and relative meaning to rationality and the subject upon which it has been traditionally based.[40] In other words, he is not interested in playing "the arbitrary and boring part of either the rationalist or the irrationalist."[41] Our stance with regard to rationality, he would say, should be one of ambivalence. That it does not become an irrationality, as quickly as rationality is invoked, is not guaranteed by anything inherent in the structure of rationality: "There is nothing 'scientistic' in this (that is, a dogmatic belief in the value of scientific knowledge), but neither is it a skeptical or relativistic refusal of all verified truth. What is questioned is the way in which knowledge circulates and functions, its relations to power. In short, the regime of truth [*savoir*]."[42]

Again, the objective, as in Derrida, is not to discover that which lies before, under, or hidden in the subject, to discover and retrieve the subject that has always been, the powers of its rationality, and so forth. Rather, it is to retrace our steps in the history of the subject, to reinvent ourselves as subjects in and through and despite that history.

Lonergan would doubtless view these methods, particularly Derrida's, as extreme—understandable perhaps, given the flagrant or incomplete conceptions of subject against which they are reactions, but extreme nonetheless. As a result, their response to objectivity is skewed, the product of an overbearing rationality.[43] Let us not forget, too, that neither Derrida nor Foucault is a theologian, and that their individual tasks are set firmly within the procession that leads from the death of God and the subject to something beyond. Derrida wants to think religion at the limits of reason alone, in a word, to think religion without religion *"opposed to 'dog-matic' (dogmatische) faith."*[44] For the same reasons that Lonergan was dis-satisfied with existentialism he would be equally dissatisfied with positions like this. Thinking religion at the limits of reason alone will not get one very far in thinking the determinants of Christian religion along the lines of Nicea and Chalcedon, Trent, and the other Councils. Derrida would agree, of course, but maintains the need to think religion without religion for reasons I will explain in a moment. For now, I will simply echo Kevin Hart's sentiment about dismissing Derrida's position as atheism: "Derrida himself inclines to atheism—'I quite rightly pass for an atheist,' he says— and this is consistent with his argument. It would be equally consistent, though, for someone who believes in God not to convert to atheism on finding Derrida's case valid."[45] Deconstruction is not about converting individuals to atheism or theism. It is all about getting atheists and theists to think the condition of the possibility that forms their respective posi-tions, and to do so openly in a self-critical way.

There is nothing new in the incongruities I mentioned. Most Lon-ergan scholars would be able to point them out in a flash. However, the possibility of "appropriation" exists, and this, too, Lonergan scholars would be able to quickly point out. As Lonergan was able to accommodate the insights of Heidegger, albeit a Heidegger (he would say) pruned of immanentist ontological oversights, he is able to accommodate Derrida and Foucault, under similar conditions. Fair enough. I myself have almost argued the same.[46] Nevertheless what one does not encounter too often is an openness to a reciprocated and steady critique from Derrida and Fou-cault to Lonergan. True, the provocations of postmoderns seem to neces-sitate this reflex. Barred before an authentic understanding can be suggested is the very hint of transcendental arguments. If I may quip back Foucault's words, I was never interested in playing the arbitrary and boring part of either the transcendentalist or the deconstructionist. Surely those of us who have learned much from Lonergan can tolerate being displaced from time to time from his paradigm of thinking, even if he has taught us to associate that of which his paradigm speaks with ourselves. The associ-ation, however, is quite complex, as Derrida would only too eagerly show. At any rate, perhaps like King David, whatever his intentions, we may see such displacements as gifts (see 2 Sam. 16:11), time out, as it were, for the emergence of a higher viewpoint.

Even if we grant that Lonergan's notion of the subject is not that which is overturned by the masters of suspicion and re-turned by the experts of suspicion—and I realize for many this is granting too much—does it follow that their critiques of transcendental subjectivity are off the mark? Is "deconstructive reduction," as detonator of precipices on which we comfortably settle after interminably wrestling with the demands of another reduction, phenomenological reduction (*à la* Lonergan), not just what the doctor ordered? We may be as unconvinced as Gadamer by the significance of etymologies.[47] But the tendency to autoimmunize ourselves against the so-called limits of language does require, it seems to me, a good dose of our inextricable relation to language. As I said earlier, the question whether we are to view that relation as radically as Derrida is an open one. Still, I don't see this as affecting the general thrust or the utility of deconstruction.

Linked to this is the corrective of Foucault's analysis that accounts for the constitution of the subject within a historical framework, that is to say, "without having to make reference to a subject that is either transcendental in relation to the field of events or runs in its empty sameness throughout the course of history."[48] Again, the call is not to irrationality, nor is it antitranscendental. The point is to include rationality and transcendental analysis of the subject among the conditions of historical emergence. I have already used the term "ambivalence" as Foucault's recommendation regarding what our stance should be toward rationality and its basis in subjectivity. I might introduce another term, from Foucault himself: "dangerous." In warning against taking his own genealogical analysis cynically Foucault states that it "is not that everything is bad, but that everything is dangerous. . . . If everything is dangerous, then we always have something to do."[49] If everything is dangerous, then we always have to be on our guard. Epistemic modesty is necessary. I am reminded of an indictment brought against the Lonergan community by Fred Lawrence:

> How many of us know students of Lonergan who use Lonergan's panoply of terms and relations to serve the power goals either of individuals or of groups? How many of us have experiences of so-called Lonergan people who assume the Romantic pose of having worked so much harder, or suffered so much more or become so much deeper than everyone else? Perhaps postmodernism under hermeneutic, deconstructivist, and genealogical auspices can offer an astringent for Lonergan scholars who may have missed the radically postmodern challenge posed by Lonergan's thought.[50]

I concur, but I think Lonergan is partly to blame. His compelling analysis of human knowing is grounds for his sanguinity, which he expresses in the most self-effacing of terms in the introduction to *Insight*.[51] However, one notices in him the tendency to see everything in terms of the structure of knowing, particularly as patterned intellectually, although his thought certainly accommodates other forms. Like Derrida and Foucault, he has his reasons for this. I think he expressed this wonderfully at the International Lonergan Congress in 1970: "I cannot regret the way I wrote *Insight*. My purpose was not a study of human life but a study of human understanding."[52] Still, one senses that the questioning of that structure on some other grounds is greatly disturbing to Lonergan. His impatience with Heidegger is an example that springs immediately to mind. This may be wrapped up with an overemphasis on self-presence as wholly beyond language and thus as the best means for finally testing truth. In this way it can remain unscathed by other means of discourse that would seek to relativize its ground. (This process of relativization, by the way, is not one in which other grounds offered are proclaimed as superior. Nor is it a means of dispensing with that of which it is a critique.) I see this as a problem, not as something decisive in terms of where the hammer falls. Moreover, I think it is a problem evidenced far more in students of Lonergan, as Lawrence has diagnosed, than in Lonergan himself. Still, traces of it can be detected in Lonergan, which is reason enough to maintain some sort of ambivalence about his position on the matter. Because "everything is dangerous," we must be vigilant, with regard not only to our appropriation of Lonergan but to Lonergan himself.

Conclusion

I have sought to situate Lonergan's contribution on the question of the subject in the context of present re-turns of the subject. That context is one in which it is thought that the subject, bequeathed to us as an objectified topic by Kant and Hegel, must be re-turned on the basis of the overturning of the subject introduced by Nietzsche and Heidegger. The real issue of this re-turn, as I see it, is to create new ways that allow for the emergence of ever-new thinking on the subject. Lonergan provides the cautionary note that there is a subject yet to be overturned, the authentic subject bypassed by the overturn and contemporary re-turns. It is still a task, in other words, to come to terms with this return which, incidentally, does not close the door on the critical interaction between this turn to the subject and current attempts to think the subject *after* the subject. I have also provided suggestions as to how this contemporary re-turn may prove useful in, even if critical of, our understanding of the return to the subject in Lonergan.

To whom, then, do we return in the turn to the subject? The polysemy of this question pivots for us on the term "whom." The sense of "return" is one in which it is acknowledged that we are always already implicated in the turn to the subject. The identity of "whom" regards the subject we are always already returning to. That is one meaning of the term in the question. There is another.

The identity of "whom" also regards the individuals we have been considering. To whose notion of the subject are we to turn in the return— Lonergan's, Derrida's, or Foucault's? Can we decide once and for all? There is a sense in which I can fully embrace Lonergan's itinerary. It purges the notion of the subject of immanentist connotations, providing for a dynamic basis in ourselves to gauge concepts of reality and to live rationally self-consciously in that understanding. There is also a sense in which I feel a need to remain ambivalent, and that is when other forms of knowing become marginalized through a totalistic tendency to view all things through cognitionalist lenses. Because it is a subtle tendency in Lonergan I think we are greatly aided by the diagnostic procedures and understandings of Derrida and Foucault; they help keep this innate tendency in us in check. To whom, then, do we return in this sense? It depends.

Notes

Paper presented at the 17th Annual Fallon Memorial Lonergan Symposium: West Coast Methods Institute/Lonergan Philosophical Society 2001 in Los Angeles (Loyola Marymount University) on April 22. The topic of the conference was "Returning to the Subject."

1. See Jim Kanaris, "Calculating Subjects: Lonergan, Derrida, and Foucault," *Method: Journal of Lonergan Studies* 15, no. 2 (1997): 135–50.

2. Bernard Lonergan, *The Subject* (Milwaukee, WI: Marquette University Press), 1968.

3. Bernard Lonergan, *A Second Collection*, ed. William F.J. Ryan and Bernard J. Tyrrell (Toronto: University of Toronto Press, 1974), 85.

4. Ibid., 86.

5. Walter Kaufmann, *Nietzsche: Philosopher, Psychologist, Antichrist*, 4th ed. (Princeton, NJ: Princeton University Press, 1974), 78–85.

6. Lonergan, *A Second Collection*, 71–2; Lonergan, *Philosophy of God, and Theology: The Relationship Between Philosophy of God and the Functional Specialty, Systematics* (London: Longman & Todd, 1973), 13.

7. See Lonergan, "Notes on Existentialism," author's notes for lectures given at Boston College (Montreal: Thomas More Institute, 1957), photocopy.

8. In *Insight* (p. 440) Lonergan further dismisses Husserl's phenomenology as a purified empiricism. Francis Schüssler Fiorenza notes that this applies only to the Husserl before 1913, "when he conceived of philosophy in a more ontological manner." See Francis Schüssler Fiorenza, introduction to *Spirit in the world*, by Karl Rahner, trans. William Dych (New York: Continuum, 1994), xlv, n. 41.

9. Lonergan, *Philosophical and Theological Papers 1958–1964*, vol. 6 of *Collected Works of Bernard Lonergan*, ed. Robert C. Croken, Frederick E. Crowe, and Robert M. Doran (Toronto: University of Toronto Press, 1996), 242.

10. See Paul Ricoeur, "The Task of Hermeneutics," in *Paul Ricoeur: Hermeneutics and the Human Sciences: Essays on Language, Action and Interpretation*, edited by John B. Thompson (Cambridge: Cambridge University Press, 1981), 59.

11. Lonergan, *A Second Collection*, 70, n. 2.

12. Lonergan, *Collection*, vol. 4 of *Collected Works of Bernard Lonergan*, ed. Frederick E. Crowe and Robert M. Doran (Toronto: University of Toronto Press, 1988), 218.

13. For my own critical commentary on Lonergan's interpretation of Hegel see Kanaris, *Bernard Lonergan's Philosophy of Religion: From Philosophy of God to Philosophy of Religious Studies* (Albany: State University of New York Press, 2002), 53–7.

14. Lonergan, *Understanding and Being: The Halifax Lectures on "Insight,"* ed. Elizabeth A. Morelli and Mark D. Morelli, revised and augmented by Frederick E. Crowe with the collaboration of Elizabeth A. Morelli, Mark D. Morelli, Robert M. Doran, and Thomas V. Daly, vol. 5 of *Collected Works of Bernard Lonergan*, ed. Frederick E. Crowe and Robert M. Doran (Toronto: University of Toronto Press, 1990), 119.

15. Lonergan, *Insight: A Study of Human Understanding*, vol. 3 of *Collected Works of Bernard Lonergan*, ed. Frederick E. Crowe and Robert M. Doran (Toronto: University of Toronto Press, 1992), 440.

16. Lonergan, *Philosophical and Theological Papers 1958–1964*, 242.

17. On "the pattern of experience" according to which thinkers like Nietzsche and Heidegger are said to think see Kanaris, "Lonergan and Contemporary Philosophy of Religion," in *Explorations in Contemporary Continental Philosophy of Religion*, ed. Deane-Peter Baker and Patrick Maxwell (New York: Rodopi Press, 2003), 65–79; "Calculating Subjects," 135–50; "Engaged Agency and the Notion of the Subject," *Method: Journal of Lonergan Studies* 14, no. 2 (1996): 183–200.

18. Jacques Derrida, *Writing and Difference*, trans. Alan Bass (Chicago: University of Chicago Press, 1978), 281–2.

19. Lonergan, *Philosophical and Theological Papers 1958–1964*, 216.

20. Derrida, *Points . . . : Interviews, 1974–1994*, ed. Elisabeth Weber, trans. Peggy Kamuf et al. (California: Stanford University Press, 1995), 255.

21. Derrida, *Writing and Difference*, 288.

22. Derrida, *Writing and Difference*, 279.

23. See Marcel Danesi, introduction to *Signs: An Introduction to Semiotics*, by Thomas A. Sebeok (Toronto and Buffalo: University of Toronto Press, 1994); Umberto Eco, *A Theology of Semiotics* (Bloomington: Indiana University Press, 1976); Murray Jardine, "Sight, Sound, and Epistemology: The Experiential Sources of Ethical Concepts," *Journal of the American Academy of Religion* 44, no. 1 (1996): 1–25; Walter J. Ong, *Orality and Literacy: The Technologizing of the Word* (London: Methuen, 1982).

24. Michel Foucault, *Religion and Culture: Michel Foucault*, ed. Jeremy R. Carrette (New York: Routledge, 1999), 159.

25. Ibid., 160.

26. Roy Boyne, *Foucault and Derrida: The Other Side of Reason* (London and New York: Routledge, 1990), 74.

27. Foucault, *Religion and Culture*, 95.

28. Ibid., 91.

29. Ibid., 161, n. 4.

30. Ibid., 161, n. 4.

31. Ibid., 161, n. 4.

32. See Foucault, *Religion and Culture*, 95.

33. Lonergan, *A Second Collection*, 83.

34. Foucault, *Religion and Culture*, 161, n. 4.

35. Derrida, "Faith and Knowledge: The Two Sources of 'Religion' at The Limits of Reason alone," in *Religion*, ed. Jacques Derrida and Gianni Vattimo (Stanford, CA: Stanford University Press, 1998), 17.

36. Foucault tells us that his examination of the self is "not at all a question of discovering the truth hidden in the subject. It is rather a question of recalling the truth forgotten by the subject . . . [W]hat the subject forgets is not himself, nor his nature, nor his origin, nor a supernatural affinity. What the subject forgets is what he ought to have done, that is, a collection of rules of conduct that he had learned" (*Religion and Culture: Michel Foucault*, 165).

37. Derrida, "Faith and Knowledge,"17.

38. Derrida plays on the judicial sense of *respondeo* (to reply, to answer) as a key, pragmatic ethico-political act of *religio*—religion, that is, at the limits of reason alone. He deconstructs dubious etymological treatments of *religio*, which tie the term to determinate religious faith. This provides him with latitude for a broader, pragmatic understanding of religion as "the promise of keeping one's promise to tell the truth—and to have already told it!—in the act of promising. To have already told it . . . and thus to consider it told" ("Faith and Knowledge," 30). Eliminated, then, from this "messianic" is the horizon of expectation and prophetic prefiguration that go hand in hand with doxological faith, messianisms. Among Derrida's aims is to allow for the possibility of a universal culture of faith whose universal rationality and political democracy provide a foil for autoimmunization.

39. Foucault, *The Foucault Reader*, ed. Paul Rabinow (New York: Pantheon Books, 1984), 374.

40. Foucault, *Religion and Culture*, 229.

41. Ibid., 328.

42. Ibid., 330–1.

43. See Kanaris, "Calculating Subjects," 139–40.

44. Derrida, "Faith and Knowledge," 10. For a brief comment from Foucault on the death of God see *Religion and culture*, 84–5. He is in basic agreement with Nietzsche.

45. Kevin Hart, "Jacques Derrida (b. 1930): Introduction," in *The Postmodern God: A Theological Reader*, ed. Graham Ward (Oxford: Blackwell Publishers, 1997), 165.

46. See n. 17 above.

47. Hans-Georg Gadamer, "Dialogues in Capri," in *Religion*, ed. Jacques Derrida and Gianni Vattimo, 201.

48. Foucault, *Power*, ed. James D. Faubion, trans. Robert Hurley et al, vol. 3 of *Essential Works of Foucault 1954–1984*, ed. Paul Rabinow (New York: New York Press, 1994), 118.

49. Foucault as quoted in Merold Westphal, *Suspicion and Faith: The Religious Uses of Modern Atheism* (Grand Rapids, MI: Wm. B. Eerdmans, 1993), 287.

50. Fred Lawrence, "The Fragility of Consciousness: Lonergan and the Postmodern Concern for the Other," *Theological Studies* 54 (1993): 211.

51. See Lonergan, *Insight*, 24.

52. Lonergan, "Bernard Lonergan Responds," in *Language, Truth, and Meaning: Papers from the International Lonergan Congress 1970*, ed. Philip McShane (Notre Dame, IN: University of Notre Dame Press, 1972), 310.

Chapter 3

Self-Appropriation

Lonergan's Pearl of Great Price

JAMES L. MARSH

There are many philosophers who have proposed one of their ideas as a key to understanding the world. Examples that come to mind are Plato's theory of forms, Aristotle's account of the good, Kant's transcendental deduction, and Hegel's *Begriff*. But for my money, Lonergan's self-appropriation is the most valuable of all keys. One reason for Lonergan's superiority is that he draws on and incorporates into a new, higher synthesis aspects of all these thinkers. But his own contribution is significant and important too.

Yet one can easily miss the centrality of self-appropriation in Lonergan's work, especially in his work *Insight*, reading it as a treatise in epistemology or philosophy of science or metaphysics rather than seeing the book's main purpose as self-appropriation, the cognitive and existential taking possession of myself as a knower, chooser, actor, and lover in relation to being. Such enterprises as philosophy of science or metaphysics only have relevance in *Insight* as effects and implications of self-appropriation.

I propose in this essay, therefore, to discuss self-appropriation, first by articulating and reflecting on some basic Lonerganian texts on the issue, then in the context of contemporary philosophy, showing how such self-knowledge can illumine and resolve perplexities arising from inadequate self-knowledge, then reflecting on my own work as an instance of self-appropriation, and concluding with some reflections on the subject. Who and what is the subject, and how is the subject related to self-appropriation?

One reason for reflecting on my work in this context is that in thinking about the issue, I have been led to discover or rediscover an autobiographical or individual element in the notion of self-appropriation. Self-appropriation enables me as a knower and chooser and actor to discover and create myself as a unique and transcendentally universal self. Consequently, my own work is an expression of my own unique self-appropriation, and it might be of interest to reflect on my work in that light. Different people can do different things and become different people as a result of self-appropriation, and the effect on a community of self-appropriated selves can be complementary, mutually enriching, and enabling fruitful mutual and individual self-criticism. Different self-appropriated knowers can mutually illumine and enrich and criticize one another in a negative and positively constructive manner.

Lonergan on Self-Appropriation

Clues to the centrality of self-appropriation in Lonergan are given in the introduction to *Insight*. Here Lonergan says that this book "is not about mathematics, nor a book on science, nor a book on common sense, nor a book on metaphysics; indeed, in a sense, it is not even a book on knowledge. . . ."[1] On a first level, the book contains sentences about mathematicians or science or common sense. On a second level, their meaning and significance are to be grasped "only by going beyond the scraps of mathematics or science or common sense or metaphysics to the dynamic, cognitional structure that is exemplified in knowing them."[2] On a third level, "the dynamic cognitional structure to be reached is not the transcendental ego of Fichtean speculation, nor the abstract patterns of relationships in Tom or Dick or Harry, but the personally appropriated structure of one's own experiencing, one's own intelligent inquiry and insights, ones' own critical reflection and judging and deciding."[3] Already we see Lonergan emphasizing the personal and unique in relation to the transcendental and universal.

Lonergan goes on. The crucial issue is an experimental one, and the experiments will be performed not publicly but privately: "It will consist in one's own rational self-consciousness clearly and distinctly taking possession of itself as rational self-consciousness. Up to that decisive achievement, all leads. From it, all follows."[4] Here we see further evidence for the private, individual aspect of self-appropriation, linked to universal aspects. No one else, no matter what his knowledge, eloquence, logical rigor, persuasiveness, can do it for me. Nonetheless, the act has public antecedents and consequences. The private and individual are linked to the public and universal. And just in case we have not gotten the point, Lonergan drives it home: "In the third place, then, more than all else, the aim of the book is to issue an invitation to a personal, decisive act."[5]

Self-Appropriation and Contemporary Philosophy

One major aspect and consequence of self-appropriation is transcendental method, the experiencing, understanding, judging, and choosing of myself as an experiencing, understanding, judging, and choosing being. In transcendental method, self-appropriation takes explicit, full possession of itself. As he articulates this concept in the first chapter of *Method in Theology*, in my opinion one of the most important chapters Lonergan ever wrote, we see a more explicit emphasis on, and articulation of, the so-called fourth level of freedom, decision, and love, already present in *Insight*, of course, in the insistence on rational self-consciousness, as distinct from the rational consciousness of reflection and judgment. But this emphasis on freedom and choice as essential to method invites comparison with thinkers such as Heidegger in *Being and Time*, in which freedom and authenticity are also essential to Heidegger's version of the existential phenomenological version of the transcendental project.[6] And Lonergan is also implicitly critical of Heidegger insofar as the full story about intentionality in relation to being is not simply finitude but infinitude, and a dialectic between limitation and transcendence.[7] Moreover, this conception of transcendental method overcomes the dichotomy in Gadamer between truth and method. Method, Lonergan insists, is not the automatic grinding out of results like sausage from a sausage machine, but rather "a normative pattern of recurrent and related operations yielding cumulative and progressive results."[8] Method is not, as Gadamer seems to think, a set of rules that can be followed blindly by anyone as on an assembly line.[9]

Self-appropriation as a project of self-knowledge is a modern project which, for Lonergan, has its antecedents in Descartes, Kant, Hegel, and Kierkegaard, but which also has affinities with Ricoeur, Heidegger, Sartre, and Husserl. As such, it is a philosophical pearl of great price that one ignores and rejects at one's peril. Various postmodern interpretations of reason, for example, as identitarian, technocratic, logocentric, disciplinary, or one-sidedly conceptual reveal themselves to be one-sided, undifferentiated caricatures of reason. Lonergan emerges as the true or truer friend of difference.[10]

In Lonergan's account of knowing, there is a movement from pre-conceptual to conceptual, question to answer, insight to concept, particular experience to universal conceptual formulation. In the magnificent chapter 1 of *Insight*, for example, Lonergan traces the genesis of the definition of a circle from data to question to preconceptual guess to insight to definition. In chapter 10, on reflective judgments, there is a similar genesis of judgment from evidence to questions about its sufficiency to grasp of the virtually unconditioned to judgment. Again, there are active and passive aspects on each level of knowing. On the level of experience, I have to be attentive to data, allowing the appropriate images to emerge. On the level of understanding, I have to be intelligently receptive to the emergence of insights, going where the preconceptual hints and guesses seem to lead. On the level of judgment, I have to be open to all of the evidence, and if the evidence is not there or contradicts my hypothesis, to recognize that. Human knowing, as Lonergan conceives it, is not one-sidedly conceptual or judgmental or active, imposing itself on a recalcitrant field of experience. Such conceptions show themselves, in Lonergan's account, to be one-sided caricatures of reason.[11]

Because data can be of two kinds, data of sense and data of consciousness, there are two kinds of science and method, empirical science and generalized empirical method, or in the later language of *Method*, transcendental method. Because philosophical judgments can be verified in data of consciousness, philosophy can be regarded as scientific in a way different from, and yet similar to, empirical science. There is an affinity of Lonergan's approach to Husserl's in *The Crisis of European Sciences and Transcendental Phenomenology* and *Formal and Transcendental Logic*, in which Husserl argues that if the basic orientation of logic and science is judgments grounded in evidence, then transcendental phenomenology and transcendental logic fulfill that orientation more adequately and rigorously and with greater certitude than empirical science and formal logic. Indeed these disciplines receive their adequate ground and basic premises from transcendental phenomenology and transcendental logic.[12]

Like Husserl, then, and against postmoderns, Lonergan can say, "Be logical" or "Be scientific." These are legitimate enterprises. If one does that, then formal logic requires a grounding in transcendental method, and empirical science in generalized empirical method. The premise underlying both enterprises—that being is intelligible—is grounded and justified in transcendental method and in the metaphysics flowing from it.

Moreover, because philosophy is most fundamentally method and not logic, logic is relativized as merely a product of understanding. Because empirical science is distinguished from, and grounded in, generalized empirical method, knowing cannot be legitimately equated with empirical science or technology. I am not tempted, therefore, in a postmodern manner to look for a postrational, postconceptual, postmetaphysical alternative outside of reason or knowing or metaphysics.[13]

Because knowing is fueled by desire, it is not neutral or value free as some modernists and postmodernists are inclined to say. Rather, knowing is passionately interested in the truth, guided intrinsically by the transcendental precepts, scientifically by the canons of empirical method, and hermeneutically by the canons of hermeneutics. Knowing is disinterested in the sense that it is, or should be, free from the influence of bias. Because such is the case, Lonergan can distinguish, in a way analogous to Habermas, between knowledge-constitutive interests and those that are extrinsic to, or nonessential to, knowledge. But in a way that is deeper than Habermas, enterprises like science or hermeneutics or ethical-political liberation, Habermas' three knowledge-constitutive interests are more like Lonergan's patterns of experience, which require for their grounding and unity cognitional theory and transcendental method articulating the structure common to all patterns of experience.[14]

Because knowing therefore is essentially internally value-laden, because objectivity is the fruit of authentic subjectivity, there is not the consequence of relativism that haunts thinkers like Nietzsche or Foucault who make claims about the value-laden character of knowledge. Lonergan rejects, as they do, the notion of purely neutral, value-free, objectivist reason, but unlike them this is not a reason for rejecting reason or modernist reason. Rather their accounts are a postmodern caricature of reason. Because reason is essentially value laden and not value free, he avoids the pitfalls of a purely objectivist, disinterested concept of reason rooted in the idea of knowing as looking. Because he can distinguish between values, norms, and desires intrinsic and those extrinsic to reason, postmodernist relativism can be avoided. Scientists, logicians, or philosophers will do good science, mathematics, or philosophy to the extent that they are genuinely authentic, guided by the transcendental precepts and canons of scientific and hermeneutical method.[15]

Moreover, because being is the known unknown towards which the desire to know heads, there is an awareness of, and orientation to, mystery on a psychic, emotional, intellectual, and spiritual level. I respond in felt wonder to a universe that is perceived as wonderful, worthy of questioning, worthy to be responded to in gratitude for the gift of being. Lonergan's conception of metaphysics and theology based on self-appropriation is not closed to mystery and devoted to mastering it, but open to it, accepting it, and valuing it. For this reason, dicta of the late Heidegger, such as that questioning is the piety of thinking and thinking as thanking, have a place within philosophy, theology, and metaphysics, not outside them. Because Heidegger's concept of metaphysics is so narrow, conceived it as closed to mystery and oriented to mastery, he thinks one has to go beyond metaphysics to incorporate and practice such dicta. Contemplative, wondering appreciation of the world is a foundation and consequence of self-appropriation. Self-appropriation begins with a question, "What and who am I?" or "Why is there something rather than nothing?" and ends in a kind of second immediacy, a wondering, appreciative response to mystery, in which my answers have inspired only further questions about the known unknown.[16]

The active receptivity of the four transcendental precepts finds its proper completion in a surrender to God as mystery, a "falling in love with God."[17] And because of the vertical movement downward of such surrender, occurring in such a way as to influence the activities of experiencing, understanding, judging, and deciding on more mundane levels, then that surrender to divine mystery in the fourth level intensifies the receptivity already functioning in these levels and expressed in the transcendental precepts. The religiously converted philosopher, as a result of religious conversion, is able in his own daily, mundane work of philosophy to engage in a kind of Lonerganian "thinking as thanking."

My Own Work as a Consequence of My Self-Appropriation

Now I come to the third part of my essay, which is to reflect on my own work as an expression of self-appropriation. This expression is most clearly present in my three-volume trilogy, which begins with cognitional theory and phenomenology in *Post-Cartesian Meditations* (PCM), moves into an ethics and social theory in *Critique, Action, and Liberation* (CAL), and concludes in metaphysics, philosophy of religion, and theology of liberation in *Process, Praxis, and Transcendence* (PPT). Thus, the trajectory of the work follows, in its own way, Lonergan's description of cognitional theory as the basis and pronouncements on ethical, metaphysical, and religious issues as the expansion.[18] PCM is the basis of my philosophy and CAL and PPT are its horizontal and vertical expansions.

In addition, in each work there are specific ways in which Lonergan's influence is present: in chapter 3, on objectivity, in PCM, in the grounding of critical theory in self-appropriation in CAL, and in the discussion of intellectual, moral, and religious conversation as radical conversion in PPT. This last point suggests what is perhaps my main, most original, and controversial expression of self-appropriation, namely that its aim implies a radical critique and overcoming of capitalism. Even this move, I have become recently convinced, has its undeveloped roots and antecedents in Lonergan, such as the remark in *Insight* about going beyond the liberal thesis and Marxist antithesis and in works written after *Method* which claim that there is a necessity to go beyond the reign of the multinational corporation and that the basic principles of capitalism are flawed. Fidelity to both Lonergan's theory and to a contradictory, social reality demand that radical self-appropriation be completed by a radical, liberationist ethics, politics, and theology.[19]

Another way of putting this point is to say that I, along with Lonergan and such thinkers as Matthew Lamb and Robert Doran, argue for a plague on the houses of both late capitalism and state socialism. In the context of such agreement, there is still room for fruitful discussion, agreement, and disagreement among self-appropriated Lonerganian knowers, choosers, lovers, and doers on such issues as the status of Marxism. Is it all or mostly counterpositional, as Lonergan seems to say, or a contradictory unity of position and counterposition as Lamb and Doran are inclined to say, or mostly or totally positional as I am inclined to say and argue exhaustively in my three volumes? Here such issues come up for discussion as to whether and how much Marx is to be distinguished from Marxism-Leninism as a reductionistic aberration (and this I am inclined to say is counterpositional, both bad Marx and bad social theory) and from a non-reductionistic Western Marxism, including such thinkers as Herbert Marcuse, the late Jean-Paul Sartre, and Antonio Gramsci as a fruitful development. I am inclined to make this move and I sense Lamb and Doran are up to a certain point, but Lonergan is much less inclined to do so.

The discussion among us would be guided by the canons of hermeneutics. Among us we'll agree that self-appropriation leads to a radical, ethical, political, and theological critique and overcoming of the capitalist New World Order and agree also about the importance of a culture influenced by the scale of values—vital, social, cultural, personal, and religious—and three conversions radiating downward into the politics and economics of our current situation and transforming these. Even this point, I think, is somewhat present in Marx but is underdeveloped and is more thoroughly developed by later Western Marxism, for which economy, polity, and culture interact in a reciprocal way, not in a one-way, deterministic manner.[20]

My own conviction, about which I confess to being pretty confident, is that while such a radical critique and overcoming will and should draw on sources that are non-Marxist, as I do myself, we deprive ourselves of a precious resource if we ignore Marx and Western Marxism. Such an attempt strikes me as similar to attempts to think about transcendental philosophy while ignoring Kant, physics while ignoring Einstein, or biology while ignoring Darwin. All of these represent forward moves in the learning of the human race that we ignore at our peril. And I am inclined to think that because the capitalism of which he was the first, deepest, and most comprehensive critic is now virtually world-wide, Marx is not dead but is more relevant than ever. As Derrida puts it in a recent book, there is no decent, humane future without Marx. His ghost hovers over our current, somewhat uneasy, quasi-manic celebration of the New World Order. Maybe he is right about the irrationality of the capitalist system.[21]

Self-Appropriation and the Subject

I turn now to my fourth main point, the status of the subject and its relationship to self-appropriation. First of all, the subject is the agent of self-appropriation. Self-appropriation is or leads up to the decisive personal act that no one can do for me. Second, the subject is the object of self-appropriation, in the sense of explicit objectification and in the sense of intended result or goal. Third, the subject is the conscious dynamism of self-appropriation as it moves from starting point to goal. Fourth, the subject is the dynamic, dialectical unity of opposites such as sensible and intellectual, cognitive and existential, psychic and spiritual, transcendental and historical. Fifth, the subject is a unity of "what" and "who," universal and individual. In self-appropriation, I become my own original, unique, authentic man or woman, philosophically and existentially, but not in such a way as to sever individuality and uniqueness from the transcendental and universal.

Indeed, self-appropriation helps to overcome unenlightened attempts to sever these opposites, and other sets of opposites as well. Self-appropriation leads to an intellectual and existential overcoming of one-sidedness. Consequently, my self-appropriated presence is similar to, yet different from, Lonergan's, Doran's, Meynell's, Byrne's, Elizabeth Morelli's, or Mark Morelli's. As a result, there is a basis for affirmation and celebration of difference not present in postmodernism, which tends undialectically to split apart difference from sameness, individuality from universality. As self-appropriated persons, we can legitimately claim, against postmodernists, to be the true or truer friends of difference.

Conclusion

A final way to view self-appropriation is to see it as a pathway to, and achievement of, personal freedom. In a real sense, *Insight* and *Method in Theology* are the "introduction to the non-Fascist life," in a way different from and yet similar to and superior to Foucault's description of Deleuze and Guattari in an introduction to *Anti-Oedipus*. In being my own man or woman, I am joyfully and rhapsodically "anti-oedipal," free from any external or internal fathers or masters. Indeed, in a certain sense, I become non-Lonerganian in the sense of being able and willing to move or try to move beyond his thought, read and learn from thinkers he did not read or to whom he was unsympathetic, avoiding excessive reliance on Lonergan's doctrine, and refusing to rely excessively on his authority. The move to philosophical enlightenment demands, finally, kicking away the Lonerganian ladder and slaying all internalized fathers, even Lonergan himself.[22]

And here I am inclined to think about and affirm the way in which Bob Doran, in a move apparently endorsed by Lonergan himself, has explored psychic conversion as a necessary complement to intellectual, moral, and religious conversion. Full self-appropriation, then, is about the whole self, psychic as well as spiritual, feeling as well as thought, unconscious as well as conscious. Liberation is not only political but also personal, not only from external victimization of unjust social structures but also from the internal victimization of a violated psyche. Coming to accept and empathize with my violated psyche opens me up to identification with external victims, the poor, the exploited, and the oppressed and vice-versa. Radical psychic conversion, mediated by intellectual, moral, and religious conversion, leads to radical political conversion.

The way up is the way down. Moving to the heights of intellectual, moral, and religious conversion implies moving down into the depths of solidarity with the oppressed. In opposition to the inauthentic upward mobility of a mind, heart, and spirit "capitalized" and colonized by the New World Order is the downward mobility of someone who has recognized his or her own solidarity with the victim both in the psyche and in the current oppressive social order. This downward mobility rooted in full psychic and spiritual freedom is the final manifestation and fruit of self-appropriation.[23]

Notes

1. Bernard Lonergan, *Insight: A Study of Human Understanding* (London: Longmans, Green & Co., 1958), xviii.
2. Ibid., xviii.
3. Ibid., xviii.
4. Ibid., xviii.
5. Ibid., xix.
6. Martin Heidegger, *Being and Time*, trans. John Macquarrie and Edward Robinson, (New York: Harper and Row, 1962).
7. Lonergan, *Method in Theology* (Toronto: University of Toronto Press, 1990), 3–25; *Insight*, 472–9.
8. Lonergan, *Method*, 4.
9. Hans-Georg Gadamer, *Truth and Method*, trans. Garrett Barden and John Cumming (New York: Seabury, 1975). See also Lonergan, *Method*, 5–6.
10. See James L. Marsh, *Critique, Action and Liberation* (Albany, NY: State University of New York Press, 1995), 59–74, 219–34, for a fuller discussion and critique of postmodernism.
11. Lonergan, *Insight*, 3–32, 271–316.
12. For a fuller discussion of Husserl, see James L. Marsh, *Post-Cartesian Meditations* (New York: Fordham University Press, 1988), 13–23, 210–12. See also Marsh, *Critique, Action and Liberation*, 226–8.
13. Lonergan, *Insight*, 276–8.
14. Lonergan, *Insight*, 70–102, 348–56; *Method*, 262–5. For a fuller discussion of Habermas on this issue, see Marsh, *Post-Cartesian Meditations*, 72.
15. For a fuller discussion of Nietzsche on this issue, see Marsh, *Post-Cartesian Meditations*, 75–81.
16. Lonergan, *Insight*, 530–49. For a fuller discussion of Heidegger on this issue, see James L. Marsh, *Process, Praxis, and Transcendence* (Albany: State University of New York Press, 1999), 10–19, 26.
17. Lonergan, *Method*, 101–7.
18. Lonergan, *Insight*, 387.

19. Ibid., 241. See Marsh, *Post-Cartesian Meditations*, 75–91; *Critique, Action and Liberation*, 3–16, 43–5,174–6; *Process, Praxis, and Transcendence*, 21–9. See also Lonergan, *The Lonergan Reader*, ed. Mark Morelli and Elizabeth Morelli (Toronto: The University of Toronto Press, 1997), 569–71.

20. See Robert Doran, *Theology and the Dialectics of History* (Toronto: University of Toronto Press, 1990), 355–470; Matthew Lamb, *Solidarity with Victims: Toward a Theology of Social Transformation* (New York: Crossroad, 1982); Marsh, *Process, Praxis, and Transcendence*, 192–4, 230–46; *Post-Cartesian Meditations*, 201–7.

21. See Jacques Derrida, *Specters of Marx*, trans. Peggy Kamuf (New York: Routledge, 1994), 569–71.

22. See Gilles Deleuze and Felix Guattari, *Anti-Oedipus: Capitalism and Schizophrenia*, trans. Robert Hurley, Mark Seem, and Helen R. Lane (Minneapolis: University of Minnesota Press, 1983), xiii.

23. See Doran, *Theology and Dialectics of History*, 232–53.

Chapter 4

Subject for the Other

Lonergan and Levinas on
Being Human in Postmodernity

MICHELE SARACINO

There has been little attention to, understanding of, and responsibility for the Other in the history of Western civilization. In the global context, we only need to remember the Shoah, the African slave trade, and the Crusades to realize how the human subject has devalued and denigrated the Other. On the North American front, the apathy toward the poor today exemplifies how the subject continues to disregard the Other. Without a doubt, the history of the Other has been a history of suffering. Some may wonder why suffering still occurs, especially in light of the social (that is, political, economic, and technological) progress made since the Enlightenment. Is it possible that humanity has become anesthetized to suffering, forgetful of the anguish of the past, and blind to that of the present?[1] Or is it more the case that humanity continues to repeat the mistakes of the past by consciously ignoring the facts and, hence, rationalizing suffering. Whatever the reason, this cycle of decline cannot continue.[2] In our postmodern context, even if we want to, we cannot avoid the suffering of the Other. Graphic images of the tumultuous world communicated via the Internet and satellite, combined with the expansion of transcontinental travel, bring the cycle of decline to the forefront, and call us to reflect on what it means to be human toward others in the postmodern world.

Any reflection on being human in postmodernity is painstaking, because of the seemingly disparate ways in which contemporary

65

Continental theorists and Christian theologians interpret subjectivity. On the one hand, contemporary Continental thinkers are most attentive to suffering and decline; moreover, they apprehend the subject in society as fragmented and decentered because of such decline. Related to the fragmented nature of this postmodern subjectivity is humanity's inability or refusal to make accurate judgments about what is good and true.[3] So where contemporary Continental thought is quite valuable in pinpointing the problems in society, at the same time, it can be problematic in not attempting to remedy these problems through decision and action.

Christian theology, on the other hand, interprets subjectivity as being capable of and responsible for acting decisively in the face of the Other who suffers. Similar to contemporary Continental theory, Christian theology maintains that human beings have distinctive experiences, come from various social locations, and are in complicated relationships with God and others. However, unlike contemporary theorists, theologians maintain that such contingencies need not lead to fragmentation, for fragmentation is not normative, but the result of sin and alienation, a consequence of the fall of humanity.[4]

Still, the concrete suffering of the Other, which is stressed so emphatically in contemporary Continental thought, prohibits theologians from interpreting the fragmented dimension of subjectivity as a result of individual sin only. Fragmentation is the confused identity born of the subject's lived experience in relationship to others. Hence, to the extent that the cycle of decline encompasses the effects of the social sins of colonialism, racism, sexism, and classism, theologians need to take the fragmented life of the human person quite seriously.[5] Affirming the belief that critical attention to decline and fragmentation is indispensable to contemporary theological interpretation of being human, this chapter brings Christian theology and Continental theory into dialogue through a study of the work of Bernard Lonergan and Emmanuel Levinas.

To many, the Canadian Jesuit theologian, Lonergan, and the Continental Talmudic thinker, Levinas, are very unlikely interlocutors. Reading Lonergan and Levinas through a commonsense lens, one could certainly claim that they have little in common. Casual conversation in the academy is grounded in the assumption that Lonergan is thoroughly modern and Levinas is definitively postmodern. Nevertheless, from a critical engagement of these two thinkers, it should become apparent that Lonergan and Levinas are indeed grappling with similar problems of modernity.[6] Both

Lonergan and Levinas find a conceptualist or thematizing attitude toward others problematic; both reject a naïve interpretation of freedom. Both uphold some variation of the notion of intersubjectivity; both renew an ethics of openness to others from their respective religious traditions. In the dialogue between Lonergan's and Levinas's perspectives, contemporary theologians can grapple with some of the pressing questions of the times, such as how to engage others without perpetuating bias and causing violence.

Lonergan on Being Human in the Midst of the Other

Unlike Levinas, Lonergan does not offer an explicit theory of the Other. What Lonergan does extend to theologians, nonetheless, is a method for an ethics of thinking and an invitation for self-appropriation—both of which encourage the subject to responsibly engage other people and cultures. Below, we will uncover how Lonergan's responsible subject is open to alterity in three ways. First, the human person, according to Lonergan, is opened and shaped by a dialectical encounter with the Other, specifically through various patterns of experience. Second, the subject's experience is complicated by the subject's attitude toward history and culture. Lonergan's theory attempts to underscore the nuance of culture; moreover, his notion of the transcultural anticipates many of our contemporary concerns about historical context, difference, and cultural diversity. Third, Lonergan's account of subjectivity, specifically his emphasis on understanding and conversion, resonates with the postmodern desire for a deconstructed subject, that is, someone open to and attentive to otherness.[7]

To begin, Lonergan's understanding of the subject's relationship with the Other is rooted in the dynamic process of interpersonal encounter. In *Method in Theology*, Lonergan defines encounter as dialectical, in which the subject's "meeting persons, appreciating the values they represent, criticizing their defects, and allowing one's living to be challenged at its very roots by their words and their deeds" opens the subject for others.[8] We can locate dialectical encounter similar to this in our own lives. Most of us have had the rich experience of meeting someone new and being challenged and shaken to our core by the feelings evoked in us through that encounter. During such a scenario, Lonergan would urge us to reflect on those specific feelings of challenge and conflict. By struggling with those feelings evoked by the Other, we can realize our potential to move to a higher viewpoint, to authentic subjectivity. According to Lonergan, being attentive to our experience during the dynamic process of encounter opens us to the possibility of conversion for God and others.

However, being attentive to experience is a difficult task, especially since experience, in general, is an illusive notion. Nevertheless, Lonergan helps us gain understanding of the complexity of experience by categorizing our general experience into specific patterns. These patterns include, but are not limited to, the biological, aesthetic, intellectual, dramatic, social, psychological, and religious patterns of experience.[9] His categorization of the patterns of experience is not meant to limit the depth of the human subject, but to better understand it. Indeed, patterns of experience are not directives for how humans should live, but possibilities for humanity to be open to authentic living. Lonergan writes, "I'm not attempting an exhaustive account of possible patterns of experience. I'm trying to break down the notion that man is some fixed entity. . . . Human lives are not all the same."[10] For our purposes, the way in which the subject deals with the Other in an interpersonal encounter brings to the forefront the dramatic pattern of experience.

When encountering another, it is particularly through our dramatic pattern of experience that we feel various sensations, such as love, fear, jealousy, anger, or attraction. More often than not, however, we deal with these feelings in inappropriate ways. For instance, when we feel fear toward someone, we often avoid that person instead of attempting to realize the underlying reason for our trepidation. A better approach, according to Lonergan, would be to figure out whether or not this stranger actually poses any danger by questioning if there exists another plausible reason for our fear, such as bias. If bias is the reason for our fear, we ought to acknowledge how that bias prevents us from engaging the stranger in life-affirming ways. Only when we are attentive to how we engage others through the dramatic pattern of experience can we come to terms with some of the challenges and conflicts that surface during dialectical encounter.

Clearly, the outcome of our dialectical encounter with the Other is a result of our attentiveness or inattentiveness to our dramatic pattern of experience. Put another way, the quality of our engagement with the Other hinges not merely on our experience of the Other, but more importantly, on how we process our experience of the Other. Like so many contemporary and poststructural theorists, Lonergan acknowledges the ambiguity regarding the process of experiencing the Other.[11] Even so, he would insist that through questioning and answering, one can understand such experience at a higher level of consciousness.

Lonergan does not conclude his analysis of the subject's experience of the Other at the level of dialectic; on the contrary, as the subject is engaged and challenged by the Other during an encounter, the subject has the potential to move from dialectic to dialogue. Whereas dialectical encounter encompasses the process by which the subject is challenged by another's position, dialogue is an event in which the subject and Other can move from conflict to friendship, "from a conflict of statements to an encounter of persons."[12] Without question, the conflict of dialectic should not result in interpersonal estrangement or violence, because behind every statement and proposition, there is a concrete, embodied person who has dignity and demands respect. Dialectic, hence, creates an opportunity to move toward friendship and love.

Up until this point we have been discussing the complexity of personal experience when encountering another in a dialectical and hopefully dialogical manner. Still, the intricacy of experience and the challenge of being attentive to difference cannot remain at the level of the individual, for people belong to social structures, such as families, schools, businesses, political groups, and the media, and are influenced by diverse people, including parents, teachers, entrepreneurs, politicians, and journalists. It becomes clear that human beings are not isolated individuals, but social subjects who belong to communities. According to Lonergan, the social pattern of experience traces the human person's concrete relationships as the person moves into the larger community.[13] As a member of society, the social subject is encouraged to make serious decisions, being called particularly to participate in political institutions, develop the economic well being of the community, and think ethically about the employment of various technological discoveries. Ultimately, the way in which the social subject engages these three spheres of society (politics, economics, and technology) effects either progress or decline. Lonergan explains: "The dramatic subject, as practical [that is, the social subject], originates and develops capital and technology, the economy and the state. By his intelligence he progresses, and by his bias he declines."[14]

Upon moving into society, effecting either progress or decline, the social subject is faced not only with issues of politics, economics, and technology, but also with the question of cultural diversity. Lonergan explains how historical and cultural context influences the subject's relationship with others through his notion of the transcultural.[15] Here, the term "transcultural" does not mean that all humans are the same regardless of their experience or context, but that the structure of human knowing is present in every human being, throughout all periods and cultures. Thus, that which is known is not transcultural; instead, the structure for knowing is transcultural—the potential for experiencing, understanding, judging, and deciding is the transcultural. By appropriating these operations, humans have not only the capability but also the obligation to be attentive and open to the insights, feelings, and values of different people. In sum, this human potential for understanding transcends the closed dialectical and dialogical encounter between subject and Other previously discussed, and embraces the plurality of cultures throughout the world.

By emphasizing the fact that human beings can understand other cultures, Lonergan calls our attention not only to the Other in our midst, but also to the complexity of cultural diversity on the global scale. In this way, Lonergan avoids any attitude of "provincialism" when dealing with difference across cultures.[16] What's more, Lonergan rebukes those people and cultures who read themselves as normative, while they assume that "the rest of the world is made up of strangers and the strangers are totally strange, totally odd . . . 'inscrutably Oriental.'"[17]

Following Lonergan's lead, Matthew Lamb worries that when we deem some human cultures as impossible to understand, we end up neglecting, ignoring, fictionalizing, or "treating [these] cultures as if they were specimens in a modern zoo."[18] One contemporary instance of such cultural neglect can be identified in the way in which Americans and many other Westerners act toward the Islamic community. We often treat Muslims as less than human, harbor bias against them, or even worse, forget their existence altogether. In order to be authentically human, nonetheless, Lonergan and Lamb would urge us to actuate our potential to understand those who seem different from us by engaging them in dialectic and dialogue. For only when we enact the transcultural and relate to those different from us, for example Muslims, as fully human, do we become authentic subjects.

It is not too strong to suggest that the transcultural potential to know other beings and cultures is that which marks us as authentically human. The transcultural is that which enables us to move from a position of dialectical conflict to dialogical love. But when we ignore the transcultural potential and refuse to strive toward understanding, the end result is our alienation from God and others. Alienation reflects the subject's inability to convert from a position of bias to a position of authentic subjectivity, to being for others. Yet when human beings positively enact their transcultural potential to know, conversion for others can occur in three ways: intellectually, morally, and religiously.

According to Lonergan, intellectual conversion can occur when we realize how our bias regarding a certain person or group prohibits us from understanding them. For instance, in American culture we often make assumptions about people without taking the time to understand who they really are. To return to the previous example, many Christians, Jews, and atheists in America have a negative perception of Muslims, most probably because they have a limited understanding of the Islamic tradition. Any information that is relayed by the media regarding Muslims usually relates to their supposed connection to terrorist activity or their seemingly negative treatment of women. Instead of focusing on the negative, biased portrayal of Muslims, it would be beneficial if people were more attentive to the Islamic tradition by finding out, both through personal contact and research, the actual beliefs and practices of Muslim communities. Only once a more sophisticated intellectual grasp of the Islamic worldview is obtained will we be free to relate to Muslims in more humane ways. A change in one's understanding, therefore, can lead to a change in one's moral horizon, that is, to moral conversion. Moral conversion occurs when a shift in understanding leads a person to have a shift in value. Once it is realized that all Muslims are not a threat, then the person can value them as complete persons, and eventually act in friendship toward them.

By extension, moral conversion further opens the subject to the possibility of falling in love with God and others. Arguably being in love with God is the highest form of self-appropriation, for when in love with God, the subject is drawn out of a closed world and reoriented to a stance of right relationship with others.[19] Lonergan scholar Frederick Lawrence explains that "within Lonergan's framework, then, the decentering, detotalizing, and becoming heterogeneous of the self can be reinterpreted as the basic and radical displacement of the subject that occurs most paradigmatically in religious conversion."[20] Hence, inasmuch as we become repositioned for others through intellectual and moral conversion, it could be argued that only when we fall in love with God do we become complete, authentic beings for others.

At this point, one could make a case that Lonergan's normative subject is open to diversity and oriented toward God and others, in fact, is already "deconstructed."[21] In employing the phrase "already deconstructed," Lawrence does not imply that the subject is self-sufficient or perfect as is, but rather that the subject is positioned by the presence of God and others. This notion of being positioned by alterity is present most explicitly in contemporary Continental theory, such as in the work of Derrida, Lyotard, and, most importantly, Levinas. By typing Lonergan's anthropological subject as already deconstructed, Lawrence compels us to focus on the way in which Lonergan understands being human as being accountable to others. A postmodern subject in the best sense of the word, Lonergan's subject is graced in openness to alterity.

Even as Lawrence attempts to demonstrate that Lonergan's work yields a reverence for otherness, Lawrence argues that unlike some contemporary Continental theories, Lonergan's cognitional theory demands that we not only describe otherness, but also judge and decide in the face of alterity. In this way, Lonergan's cognitional theory repudiates an insidious relativism that is present in so much of contemporary Continental thought. Lawrence writes, "[I]n the posture of sensitivity to otherness and difference that goes together with agnostic pluralism, radical pluralists fail to come to terms with the way in which it takes correct judgments adequately (if never exhaustively) to come to terms with the other as other."[22] Contrary to the thought of the radical pluralists (and relativist contemporary theorists), Lawrence shows us that alterity and intersubjectivity are only maintained when subjects attend to the sense data of the Other, grapple with their own preconceptions of the Other, and act reasonably and responsibly toward the Other. Notice that these activities perform the operations in Lonergan's transcultural structure of knowing.

By interrogating Lonergan's reading of subjectivity and otherness, we discovered several points. We learned that even though Lonergan values experience per se, he is more concerned with our being attentive to that which complicates our experience, such as bias. Our attentiveness to the complexity of experience, nevertheless, is only the initial step in the rigorous process of understanding our relationship with others. Openness to alterity extends beyond the subject's individual world to the subject's social pattern of experience. Chronicling the social dimension of being human required us to reflect on the transcultural potential in all of humanity not only to know self or another, but also to engage and understand other cultures. As we reflected on Lamb's exposition of the transcultural, contemporary questions about diversity and pluralism surfaced. Finally, Lawrence's analysis helped us to understand that Lonergan's authentic subject is already deconstructed, already open to otherness. Below we will learn how Levinas's subject, similar to Lonergan's anthropological subject, defers to the Other.

Levinas on Being for the Other

Levinas's writings about alterity are numerous. Here, however, I will detail only two, albeit extremely significant, threads in Levinas's reading of the Other. I will begin by tracing his roots in both Talmudic and Cartesian thought, demonstrating how the Other is neither someone who can be thematized, nor the object of positivist ontology. Rather for Levinas, the Other is precisely the unthematizable, the noncorrelative, and the unutterable trace that calls the subject into being through the ethical relation of facing. Then I will delineate the way in which this unthematizable alterity is illustrated through the heuristic of heterosexual love. This gendered and spousal imagery is not meant to reduce the Other to a specific persona, but to emphasize the open and mysterious qualities of the Other, as well as the obligatory stance of the subject in the face of the Other.

Levinas commonly distinguishes between his confessional and philosophical works. As Jill Robbins has observed, "[T]he confessional writings are the place in Levinas's work where he makes explicit the reference to Judaism that is largely implicit in the philosophical works."[23] Nowhere is his Jewish religiosity written more largely than in his description of the ethical relation for the Other[24] in terms of facing. As his writings on the Jewish tradition and the Talmud in *Difficult Freedom* make apparent, the heuristic of covenantal obligation informs Levinas's ethical notion of the face.[25] Specifically, the notion of facing or being faced by the Other is rooted in the theophany in Exodus 33.[26] There, God initiates a face-to-face, that is, personal encounter with Moses, while never showing his actual face to Moses's naked eye. Levinas comments on this encounter, "The Old Testament honours Moses as the greatest of the prophets. Moses had the most direct relationship with God, described (in Exodus 33:11) as 'face to face.' And yet, the vision of the divine face is refused, and according to Exodus 33:23, only God's 'back' is shown to Moses."[27] From this brief excerpt, we can infer that Levinas reads Exodus 33 as signifying two paradoxical moments in our being in relationship with others: intimacy and distance. In terms of intimacy, God's proximity summons humanity to obligation. Surely, one cannot escape the overwhelming obligation demanded by the nearness of the Other. At the same time, ironically, within the theophany there is an aspect of distance, which evokes awe in the subject. This distance caused by God's hidden visage accentuates the separation between divinity and humanity, and causes the subject to defer to the Other.

Quite poetically, Levinas's thought on the ethical relation of facing brings to the surface the ambiguity and complexity of being human in relation to others. In regard to the Mosaic theophany, the tension between God's proximity and distance leads to a paradoxical predicament in which God's revelation is interpreted as intimate and comprehensible, and at the same time, as separate and mysterious. Whereas the intimacy of this relationship underscores the intersubjectivity between subject and Other, the distance highlights the distinctiveness of both parties. We can relate to this religiously charged trope of facing within our own lives. Being human for others emerges in the tension between *being close and similar to* and *being separate and different from* another person. When faced or encountered by another, we are commanded to be responsible for that person. But being responsible for another does not mean dominating or controlling that individual's life, for the distance between us and the Other overdetermines the particularity of each party. Hence, even though there is a definitive feeling of intimacy when facing another, the otherness that imbues the relationship is cause for respect and responsibility. According to Levinas, the vacillation between the proximity and distance determines the relation of the subject to the Other and calls the subject to be responsible for the Other.

Facing the Other need not be an esoteric, misunderstood concept of postmodern theory, for a concise understanding of facing gets at the heart of Levinas's project. The ethical relation of facing between subject and Other can be interpreted clearly in two ways: primarily, as a fleeting trace of the Infinite (nonthematizable God) and, secondarily, as a mark that people embody in their interpersonal relationships. Even though God passes in the face, the presence of the Infinite is not Levinas's primary concern. His main concern, in fact, is the responsibility of the subject that is called forth by the trace or passing of the Infinite. The trace cannot be conceptualized as a presence; instead, like an ethereal visitation, the trace enters and withdraws at the command of the Other, as a nonpresence of the Infinite. The fleeting trace of the Infinite should cause people to be struck by awe and to move toward justice—convert them to being subjects for the Other.

Much of Levinas's understanding of Infinity would appear to be tied to Jewish religious experience, and specifically to that paradoxical intimacy with that which is distant, the revelation of Infinity in Exodus 33. Yet if much of Levinas's theory stands between two worlds—Jewish thought and Western philosophy—it is also necessary to trace how Western philosophical theory, specifically the work of René Descartes, influences Levinas's reading of the Infinite. To begin, Levinas laments the absence of a responsible person, "someone who is no longer agglutinated in being, who at his own risk, responds to the enigma and grasps the allusion. Such is the subjectivity, alone, unique, secret, which Kierkegaard caught sight of."[28] This enigma that Levinas refers to is the incomprehensible, noncorrelative Infinite: an idea that he retrieves from the thought of Descartes.[29]

Reflecting on Descartes, Levinas claims that contrary to positivist readings of it, the Infinite is not an object that can be thematized or conceptualized. He asserts:

> The idea of the infinite is not an intentionality for which the infinite would be the object. Intentionality is a movement of the mind adjusted to being. It takes aim and moves toward a theme. In the theme, being comfortably accommodates itself. . . . Being is the unconcealed, the thematized—that on which thought stumbles and stops, but which it straightaway recovers. The idea of the infinite consists in the impossibility of escaping from recovery; it consists in the impossibility of coming to rest and in the absence of any hiding place, of any interiority where the I could repose harmoniously upon itself.[30]

From Levinas's perspective, the Cartesian notion of the Infinite counters any act of thematization, which reads of the Other in terms of the same. Infinity calls the subject out of the subject's self into an asymmetrical relation with and obligatory stance toward the Other. Notably, the anthropological problems associated with the philosophical stance of immanence are checked by the transcendent demand of Cartesian Infinity: "Descartes shatters immanence thanks to the idea of the infinite."[31] Furthermore, according to Levinas, the Infinite calls the subject back to an immemorial past with the Other, that is, to an "always already" relationship with the Other. Hence, as Descartes claims "that there is manifestly more reality in infinite substance than in finite—to wit, the notion of God before that of myself," Levinas argues that a human being's attachment to the Infinite precedes any reflection upon the self.[32]

Obviously the notion of Infinity is inextricably connected to being human, for it is the dazzling presence of the Infinite placed within the subject that actually opens the subject for the Other—an opening that marks transcendence. Again, the Infinite is not a static object or essence; rather, it is the mystery that incites humanity's desire for goodness, and goodness here might be thought of as the parallel content of Infinity. Goodness is not an ambiguous or catchall notion, but rather the seed of humanity's transcendence: "Goodness, a childish virtue; but already charity and mercy and responsibility for the other, and already the possibility of sacrifice in which the humanity of man bursts forth."[33] Infinity calls forth goodness by demanding subjectivity of being for the Other.

Similar to Lonergan's warning against provincialism is Levinas's assertion that subjectivity is not based on stereotyping or thematic reflection on the Other's situation. Instead, being for the Other or "the putting into question of the I by the Other is an *ipso facto* election, the promotion to a privileged place on which all that is not-I depends."[34] Notice that a Jewish notion of chosenness prevails in which there is a covenantal responsibility that is prior to all deliberation and reflection, in accordance with a predisposition of the heart.[35] Chosenness here is not only a privilege, but also an obligation. Thus, even before questioning and consciousness, there exists obligation for the Other. Levinas clearly states, "[A]ll reflective self-critique already takes place after responsibility."[36] Ultimately, the face of the Other and the trace of the Infinite reverse the order of human action, from a voluntary situation in which the subject acts toward the Other in naïve freedom, to a hostage situation in which the Other's demand for justice precedes the subject's self-centered use of freedom.

A vital dimension of Levinas's project is not merely what he states, but also how he states it. Thus, one would be remiss to ignore Levinas's erotically charged description of the hostage situation between subject and Other. By way of what I call a *discourse of desire*, Levinas further illustrates the Mosaic trope of facing. Through a critical reading of Levinas's work, it becomes apparent that this discourse of desire unfolds on two levels. On one level, otherness is analogized in feminine imagery; and on another level, the subject's attraction for the Other is imagined within the drama of heterosexual love.

On the first level, Levinas explains alterity by exploiting the rhetoric of femininity. According to Levinas, "[T]he Other whose presence is discreetly an absence, with which is accomplished the primary hospitable welcome which describes the field of intimacy, is the Woman."[37] Here, Levinas attempts to emphasize the hospitable, receptive dimension of the Other—an Other who calls and welcomes the subject into the ethical relation of facing. In addition to accenting the hospitable aspect of alterity, Levinas highlights the mysterious quality of the Other by employing such terms as "overflowing" and "voluptuosity." Voluptuosity refers to the subject's enjoyment of and desire for the hiddenness of the Other. This voluptuosity "transfigures the subject himself, who henceforth owes his identity not to his initiative of power, but to the passivity of the love received."[38] Similar to that of the Mosaic trope of facing, the erotic term "voluptuosity" marks the ethical relation of facing between subject and Other, in which intimacy and distance are maintained. As receptive and mysterious, the Other calls the subject into relationship, but refuses to be totalized, thematized, or controlled.

As one would imagine, explaining alterity within the rhetoric of femininity is not without problems. Some feminist scholars have accused Levinas of an underlying sexism, associating otherness with the feminine sentiments of receptivity and mystery. French feminist thinker Luce Irigaray, for example, worries that Levinas's thought leads to an insidious gender essentialism in which women become reduced to their biological and cultural affinities for mothering, caring, domesticity, and hospitality.[39] Like Irigaray, we would be wise to question Levinas's gendered discourse, and ask why in this age of postmodernity, when we are cognizant of the implications of sexist language, does Levinas use this tired trope of femininity to highlight the intricacy of alterity?

Nevertheless, in response to feminist criticism, Levinas refutes the accusation that he is sexist, as well as rejects the facile conflation of the feminine with otherness and the masculine with subjectivity.[40] What's more, through a critical reading of Levinas's work, one can verify that he does not uphold an essentialist bias in which he regards all women as passive and all men as active. Levinas's theory, instead, assumes that being human involves not only the active, traditionally masculine dimension of relating to others, but also encompasses a passive, traditionally feminine dimension of being for others. In fact, when facing others, we are enmeshed in a delicate balance of listening (feminine) and responding (masculine). Hence, being human for others demands both our receptive and active capabilities. Undoubtedly for Levinas, in being for the Other we become "cogendered."[41]

As Levinas genders the Other in feminine imagery, he romanticizes the relationship between subject and Other. This is the second level through which his discourse of desire unfolds. Specifically, Levinas describes the ethical relation between subject and Other in terms of heterosexual love. In an effort to provide an alternative to the biblical notion of facing, Levinas imagines the intimate and distant relationship between subject and Other in terms of a romance—a relationship so powerful that it has the potential to create new life. He speaks about the ethical relation between subject and Other as fecund in that it leads to more relationships, in the same way that the desire between two lovers results in a child.[42] This notion of fecundity, which epitomizes the potential of the ethical relation of facing, has two important aspects: a maternal dimension and a paternal dimension. Maternity accentuates the nearness of the Other, while paternity emphasizes the distinctiveness between subject and Other. Let me explain further.

In an effort to deepen our understanding of our obligation to the Other, Levinas plays with the notion of maternity. In fact, he privileges maternity as the "ultimate sense of this [closeness and] vulnerability," of being for the Other.[43] In such a relationship, the mother is a hostage of the child and substitutes herself for the welfare of the child. One could argue metaphorically that by performing or mimicking the substitution between mother and child, the human subject is hostage to and postured for the Other. The notion of maternity, however, like the gendering of the Other, is not without problems. While not devised to be understood literally, maternity does denote a particular role: mothering. The metaphor of motherhood for interpreting the subject as for the Other is limiting on two levels: primarily, because only women can physically bear children, and secondarily, because women can bear children only during their fertile years. The figure of maternity excludes other people, including men, children, and the elderly, from imagining themselves as open, receptive, and responsible.[44] Consequently, feminist thinker Catherine Chalier argues that the generosity of being for the Other must transcend the metaphor of maternity, because while maternity is a significant way in which women are open to otherness, openness goes beyond one act, function, or set identity, such as motherhood.[45] The notion of mother, moreover, is rooted in spousal imagery, which is inextricably connected to sexist assumptions about marriage and sacrifice.[46] Arguably, for some, maternity as a metaphor for subjectivity for the Other is myopic.

With this said, it is important to understand the other aspect of the ethical relation of facing, paternity. As Levinas employs the notion of maternity to capture the subject's proximity to the Other, he utilizes the idea of paternity to concretize the separation between subject and Other. Recall from our discussion of the theophany that Levinas is concerned with maintaining a distance between subject and Other in order to respect the Other's particularity. Levinas's play with the notion of paternity secures the ethical space of separation. Accordingly, Levinas imagines the father as different from his offspring, and at the same time, the bond of paternity solidifies the obligation between them.

Significantly, from both aspects of the ethical relation of facing, maternity and paternity, the fruit of the encounter between subject and Other is fecundity. Nevertheless, fecundity materializes not merely in the metaphorical production of a child, but more importantly in the concrete proliferation of additional relations and responsibility. This is where I think Levinas's use of the discourse of desire is most helpful. The notion of fecundity captures the excessiveness of our obligation to the Other. To be sure, the multiplicity of relations that develops through fecundity does not diminish the subject's responsibility: on the contrary, fecundity magnifies one's obligation. Levinasian translator and scholar Alphonso Lingis explains, "To find that the one before whom and for whom I am responsible is responsible in his turn before and for another is not to find his order put on me relativized or canceled. It is to discover the exigency for justice, for an order among responsibilities."[47] Thus, the language of fecundity points to the complexity of interpersonal relations—to the way in which human bonds are never singular, but rather continually produce more connections and responsibilities.

By mapping the way that Levinas's theory develops out of Jewish and Cartesian worldviews, it becomes apparent that Levinas's interpretation of subjectivity is second to his discussion of the priority of the Other. It is the face of the Other or the trace of the Infinite that actually calls humans into being subjects. This activity of being is not for self, but directed by and for others. Significantly, the social dimension of Levinas's subject echoes

Lonergan's thoughts on authentic subjectivity. Still, Levinas's theory is distinct in that he contextualizes being human for others not within the cognitional process, but within the trope of heterosexual love. Navigating among the problems of gender essentialism, Levinas writes about being human through a discourse of desire in order to underscore the fecund nature of responsibility. Relationship breeds more relations, responsibility fuels larger obligation.

Our Future of Living with Others: Lonergan's and Levinas's Contributions to Constructive Theology in the Twenty-First Century

The distinct worldviews of Lonergan and Levinas should never be confused. The alterity between their individual histories and personalities must be respected. Still much can be gained from putting them into dialogue. From the perspective of Catholic theology, an encounter with Levinas's contemporary Continental thought is advantageous in a number of ways. Alternatively, Levinas's argument could be strengthened by the foresight of a broad thinker such as Lonergan. In the following paragraphs, then, I will outline what contemporary theologians could gain by appropriating Levinas's thought, ways in which Lonerganian thought could contribute to Levinasian scholarship, and areas in which Christian theology in general could be strengthened by the dialogue between Lonergan and Levinas.

Levinas's confidence in the demand of the Other to bring about the best in the subject is the most that postmodern theory can offer the theological enterprise. Levinas never doubts the integrity, particularity, ability, and gift of the Other. Such a positive attitude toward diverse persons and cultures might facilitate more life-affirming missionary strategies, in which people are not colonized and totalized into the faith, but welcomed and invited.

What's more, this Jewish thinker's intricate analysis of social relations helps bring to light the ephemeral and positional character of otherness. For instance, the way in which Levinas explains alterity, not merely in terms of gender (or race or class), but in terms of desire, could facilitate a more nuanced notion of solidarity. Even as Lonergan is attentive to otherness, Levinas's complex notion of the ethical character of being, that is, the always already obligatory stance to the Other, can refine Christian notions of solidarity. Solidarity is the acknowledgment that we are already connected and responsible for others. By integrating Levinas's thought into Christian theology, one could argue more strongly that being human is about being for others first.

Levinas can strengthen Christian discourse in even more ways. The way in which he links the gendered, embodied subject to the site of justice is an appealing way to address the legacy of an insidious mind/body dualism in theology. Moreover, the manner by which he plays with corporeality in his discussion of being human ought to enliven theologians to better define their interpretations of the relation between biological accident (such as sex and pigment) and spiritual destiny.

Lastly, theologians, particularly Lonergan scholars, could benefit from Levinas's writing style. Levinas's vigilance to the call of the Other is present not only in his theory, but also in his writing technique. His language has been described as "evoking"—a term that captures Levinas's beautiful blending of biblical narrative, philosophical question, romance language, and personal journey.[48] His evocative style of discourse invites the reader into a disposition of being for the Other. Anxiously awaiting his next linguistic turn, his reader learns what it means to wait for the command of the Other. Indeed, Levinas's theory is performative in the best (nonfaddish) sense of the word.

Scholars appropriating Lonergan's thought could learn from this evocative style. Arguably, Lonergan's cognitional theory would have been received more readily if he had changed his rhetorical style; however, at this point, it is up to the next generation of scholars to interpret Lonergan's writings more performatively. For the content and aim of Lonergan's work is clearly valuable: being human is inextricably connected to the potential to know and love others. Still this concise axiom is burdened and somewhat obscured by the static discourse through which it is communicated. What's more, to our current postmodern sensibility, Lonergan's theoretical approach is off-putting, even alienating.[49] Obviously, the discourse through which a message is communicated is extremely important. If the rhetoric that relays the message is alienating, then the message could be misunderstood or lost altogether. Realizing how important the process of understanding is to Lonergan's interpretation of authentic subjectivity, I firmly believe that the sensual and affective language in Levinas's theory could help to articulate not only the head, but also the heart of Lonergan's anthropological subject.

In all fairness to Lonergan, it is not as if he would have nothing to say to Levinas's strand of contemporary Continental thought. Indeed, if

Levinas had encountered Lonergan's person, Levinas would have been also challenged. First and foremost, Lonergan could have asked Levinas a painful, yet necessary question: *Why are you so illusive on the questions of reason and being?* This is a strange problem to pose to Levinas because his entire project is grounded in debunking the totalizing gaze of ontology. Nonetheless, I think theologians, before they blindly embrace Levinas's thought, need to think about his rejection of being. In other words, after reading Lonergan one wonders whether Levinas's emotive reaction against the primacy of being actually needed to be so dramatic. Indeed, in Levinas's writing of the ethical structure of for-the-Other, is not being for the Other implied? Levinas's thinking could be better utilized if he had explained more clearly the connection between nonbeing or beyond being and human agency.

Related to this question of human agency is Levinas's seemingly seamless transition from the hypothetical face to the situation of justice. One should wonder how Levinas accounts for the subject's enactment of justice, the use of reason, and the human motive for goodness. Here a larger framework or context for understanding Levinas's overall goals would prove helpful. More strongly put, I think that Levinas's ethics would be improved by Lonergan's method. Michael Purcell makes a similar claim about the need in Levinas's thought for a method; however, Purcell employs the work of Rahner to extend Levinas's claims.[50] I think a more fitting match for this task is Lonergan, with his refined strategy for moving toward authentic progress and realizing the human good. Lonergan does not confuse method with abstract ideas and rules, but discerns method in our own operations.

This leads us to the final way in which Lonergan's project can influence future thought on Levinas. Whereas Levinas's work opens Christian theology to many important questions, he never really answers any of them because he has neither a well-defined method nor a structured anthropology. Levinas describes the limits and issues surrounding anthropology, yet never constructively envisions one. In this respect, Lonergan's anthropology of the authentic subject provides Levinas with the structure he needs to move forward in his efforts at justice and solidarity. To be sure, Levinas's writings are evocative, but Lonergan's thoughts are constructive. In order to develop Christian community, one needs both questions and answers, deconstruction and construction. Accordingly, Levinas's weaknesses, in terms of his ambiguous notions of freedom, agency, and justice and his lack of method are indicative of his descriptive rather than explanatory anthropology. In other words, whereas Levinas describes the problems in Western philosophical anthropology in relation to both the biblical milieu and his own experience, Lonergan attempts to explain what it means to be human in relation to other humans. Being human means developing and engaging the potential to experience, understand, judge, and act in the face of others.

From this posthumous dialogue between two very important thinkers of the past century, theologians can note several important factors when constructing theology in the new millennium. First, otherness in our diverse, global context is a reality. Given the destructive ways of dealing with otherness in the past, theologians need to reframe the notion of difference positively in order to avoid the same mistakes. Lonergan and Levinas can help with the project of reframing otherness, quite ironically by using traditional religious and philosophical terms. Second, otherness is related to questions of body, gender, and race. While these topics were not fully explored here, we cannot ignore the experiential, affective, and incarnate character of being in relation to others. Levinas's use of gendered, sensual language overdetermines the concrete, embodied character of being human. Moreover, Lonergan's discussion of the patterns of experience emphasizes the corporeal nature of being human. Theology in the twenty-first century would be wise, then, to address Christian anthropology by way of feminist theory and critical race theory. Third, the discussion of being needs to be further explored, even if critically. Still, ontological debate might be better received in aesthetic rhetoric, rather than in scholastic language, for performative language is not faddish but suits the sensibility of our times. Fourth, this shift in language should not ignore the consistent need for theological method and moral judgment and decision. Too often contemporary Continental thought seems to avoid the problem of relativism. And fifth, in order for Christian theology in the new millennium to engage the concerns of people from culturally diverse backgrounds, interreligious and interdisciplinary projects such as this one need to be pursued. For only in the dialogue between these two seemingly disparate thinkers could one hope to further the study of being human in a postmodern world.

Notes

1. Since the faces of those suffering, murdered, and tortured are available continuously on television (public and cable networks), Internet sites, films, music

videos, compact disc jackets, and so on, we could argue that humanity has become oblivious or anesthetized to pain. Moreover, some may be comforted by the fact that there is a reality somewhere of pain and suffering. Jean Baudrillard, in his work, *The Perfect Crime*, (trans. Chris Turner [London: Verso, 1996]), upholds precisely this argument. He implies that the West's identity and foothold in reality is secured by suffering elsewhere (134).

2. Systematic theologian M. Shawn Copeland, evoking Bernard Lonergan, asserts that in the United States of America, "the present existential situation in which we live, unhappily, can be defined as a cycle of decline, that is, a distorted situation that is the result of our religious, moral, and intellectual deformation" (Copeland, "Memory, Emancipation, and Hope: Political Theology in the 'Land of the Free,'" *The Santa Clara Lectures* 4, no. 1 [1997]: 5).

3. Cultural theorist Kate Soper further expounds on the challenge of acting as agents in postmodernity: "[A]s we acknowledge ourselves to be de-centered and fragmented subjectivities, the gendered constructs of patriarchy and mouthpieces of a discursive ventriloquism, we also seem to rediscover a centre, the existential, angst-ridden self who must make sense of it, and seek to reorganise desire, re-read the world, adjust behaviour, and so on, in light of this awareness. As anti-humanist approaches present us as splintered, we feel a very humanist splintering between the self who acknowledges the Freudian or feminist challenge to autonomy, and the self who feels called upon to act as a morally responsible agent of self-change" (Soper, "Postmodernism, Subjectivity and the Question of Value," in *Principled Positions: Postmodernism and the Rediscovery of Value*, ed. Judith Squires [London: Lawrence & Wishart, 1993], 25).

4. Some may wonder whether the fragmented postmodern subject is, in fact, the fallen human person. Walter Benjamin, in his work on language before and after the fall, engages this issue (Benjamin, "On Language as Such and On the Language of Man," in *Critical Theory Since Plato*, ed. Hazard Adams, revised edition [Orlando, FL: Harcourt Brace Jovanovich, 1992], 743–9). For a contemporary Christian interpretation of the relationship between fragmentation of the human person and sin, see Robert R. Williams, "Sin and Evil," in *Christian Theology: An Introduction to Its Traditions and Tasks*, ed. Peter C. Hodgson and Robert H. King (Philadelphia: Fortress Press, 1985), 194–221. Williams explains a Christian interpretation of the self before the fall: "According to this natural order [of creation], selves are most free and fulfilled when they grasp and are ruled by the highest good, God. The self is unified, centered" (199). Moreover, according to Augustine's account of freedom, Williams claims, "When the self turns from the eternal good, the original righteousness of the human constitution is lost, and the self is plunged into disorder" (202).

5. Copeland, "Memory, Emancipation, and Hope," 5.

6. Both Lonergan's invitation to theologians to engage historical method and scientific inquiry in order to bring theology up to the level of the times, as well as his consideration of subjectivity, are thoroughly modern objectives. Furthermore, his emphasis on correctly understanding the notions of being, objectivity, and reality is consonant with the aims of modernity. Philosopher James L. Marsh

comments on the modern underpinnings of Lonergan's project in "Post-Modernism: A Lonerganian Retrieval and Critique," *International Philosophical Quarterly*, 35 (1995): 159. Yet other scholars have emphasized the connection between Lonergan and contemporary Continental theory, see Jim Kanaris, "Calculating Subjects: Lonergan, Derrida, and Foucault," *Method: Journal of Lonergan Studies* 15 (1997): 135–50. Arguably it is unfair and inaccurate to label Lonergan as blatantly modern. For Lonergan is not modern in the sense that he blindly embraces rationalism; rather, he is modern in that his work is grounded in a concrete struggle to adequately engage human reason in order to achieve the common good. Levinas, on the other hand, often is categorized in a commonsense manner as primarily postmodern. His clear concern for otherness and his stark rejection of the modern notions of being, objectivity, and reality locate him in the school with such contemporary Continental thinkers as Jacques Derrida and Jean-François Lyotard. Moreover, his engagement of the Hebrew Scriptures, employment of the language of disruption and alterity, and rejection of the primacy of ontology color his work as thoroughly postmodern. Still, labeling Levinas as postmodern is somewhat unhelpful, for even as he seems to perform many postmodern theoretical moves, his intention is that of achieving justice, not of wavering in an abyss of relativism. Obviously what is most significant about bringing these two thinkers into dialogue is not the confusion over the tags of "modern" and "postmodern" but their orientation for the Other.

7. See chapter 6 by Fred Lawrence in this volume, where Lonergan's subject is described as a deconstructed subject.

8. Lonergan, *Method in Theology* (Toronto: University of Toronto Press, 1971), 247.

9. Lonergan provides the most detailed information on the subject's patterns of experience in *Collected Works of Bernard Lonergan*, ed. Frederick E. Crowe and Robert Doran, vol. 3, *Insight: A Study of Human Understanding* (Toronto: University of Toronto Press, 1992), 204–14. Nonetheless, in other works, such as *Method in Theology* (27–55) and "The Human Good as the Developing Subject," in *Collected Works of Bernard Lonergan*, ed. Frederick E. Crowe and Robert Doran, vol. 10, *Topics in Education* (Toronto: University of Toronto Press, 1993), Lonergan integrates the patterns of experience into levels in the structure of the human good (79–106). The biological pattern can be understood as unfolding at the vital level, while the dramatic and social patterns emerge on the social and cultural levels of the human good.

10. Lonergan, "Discussion 3," in *Collected Works of Bernard Lonergan*, ed. Elizabeth A. Morelli and Mark D. Morelli, vol. 5, *Understanding and Being, The Halifax Lectures on INSIGHT* (Toronto: University of Toronto Press, 1990), 320.

11. Poststructuralist thinkers, using a different discourse than Lonergan, also express concern about how some people tend to ignore the complexity of experience, often by reifying it. Social scientist Joan W. Scott summarizes one such position: "*Experience* is not a word we can do without, although, given its usage to essentialize identity and reify the subject, it is tempting to abandon it. But *experience* is so much a part of everyday language, so imbricated in our narratives that it

seems futile to argue for its expulsion. . . . Given the ubiquity of the term, it seems to me more useful to work with it, to analyze its operations and to redefine its meaning. This entails focusing on processes of identity production, insisting on the discursive nature of 'experience' and on the politics of construction. Experience is at once always already in interpretation *and* something that needs to be interpreted" ("The Evidence of Experience," in *Questions of Evidence: Proof, Practice, and Persuasion Across the Disciplines*, ed. James Chandler, Arnold I. Davidson, and Harry Harootunian [Chicago: University of Chicago Press, 1994], 387).

12. Lonergan, "Natural Right and Historical Mindedness," in *A Third Collection: Papers by J. F. Lonergan, S.J.*, ed. Frederick E. Crowe, S.J. (Mahwah, NJ: Paulist Press, 1985), 169–83. This work was presented at the annual meeting of the American Catholic Philosophical Association in 1977. In the short period between when *Method in Theology* was published and when this essay was prepared, Lonergan's thought on dialectic and encounter matured significantly. In *Method in Theology*, dialectic seems to encompass both interpretative and interpersonal conflicts; but in this essay, Lonergan further distinguishes between interpretative and interpersonal relations in terms of dialectic and dialogue (182).

13. For a glimpse into Lonergan's thought on the practical and social aspect of the subject's experience, see the chapter "Common Sense as Object" in *Insight*, esp. 237–42, 261–9.

14. Lonergan, *Insight*, 61.

15. Lonergan, *Method in Theology*, 282.

16. Lonergan, "Time and Meaning," in *Collected Works of Bernard Lonergan*, ed. Robert C. Croken, Frederick E. Crowe, and Robert M. Doran, vol. 6, *Philosophical and Theological Papers 1958–1964* (Toronto: University of Toronto Press, 1996), 95. It is important to note that while some scholars maintain that Lonergan is thoroughly modern, his attitude against provincialism resonates with the postcolonialist and postmodern thought of Frantz Fanon and prefigures that of Edward Said, bell hooks, and Jean Baudrillard.

17. Lonergan, "Time and Meaning," 95.

18. Matthew L. Lamb, "The Notion of the Transcultural in Bernard Lonergan's Theology," *Method: Journal of Lonergan Studies* 8, no. 1 (1990): 69. For more on the connection between perverse understandings of difference and the social sins of racism and sexism, see Lamb, *Solidarity with Victims: Toward a Theology of Social Transformation* (New York: Crossroad, 1982).

19. Lonergan addresses the subject's intrinsic desire to understand, an orientation that reaches toward God, in "The Natural Desire to See God," in *Collected Works of Bernard Lonergan*, ed. Frederick E. Crowe and Robert M. Doran, vol. 4, *Collection* (Toronto: University of Toronto Press, 1988), 81–91. Being in love with God is an important affective dimension of intentionality that until recently has not been explored in any depth. For an investigation into the significance of affective intentionality, see Andrew Tallon, *Head and Heart: Affection, Cognition, Volition as Triune Consciousness* (New York: Fordham University Press, 1997).

20. Lawrence, "The Fragility of Consciousness: Lonergan and the Postmodern Concern for the Other," *Theological Studies* 54 (1993): 91. For an analy-

sis of how Lonergan's notion of religious conversion fosters ethical relations toward others, see Walter E. Conn, "The Desire for Authenticity: Conscience and Moral Conversion," in *The Desires of the Human Heart: An Introduction to the Theology of Bernard Lonergan*, ed. Vernon Gregson (Mahwah, NJ: Paulist Press, 1988), 36–56.

21. See Lawrence's chapter 6 in this volume.

22. Lawrence, "Fragility of Consciousness," 81.

23. Jill Robbins, *Altered Reading: Levinas and Literature* (Chicago: University of Chicago Press, 1999), 43. For a discussion of Levinas's interaction with biblical text, see 32–8.

24. Throughout this essay, I employ the phrase "for the Other" to signify Levinas's idea of responsible subjectivity. Levinas claims that subjectivity is not rooted in the world of the self (which he names *ipseity*); rather, it is grounded in obligation and opening for the Other. He employs the phrase "for the Other" in some texts, including the essay "God and Philosophy," in *Of God Who Comes to Mind*, trans. Bettina Bergo (Stanford, CA: Stanford University Press, 1998). In his most comprehensive work, *Otherwise Than Being or Beyond Essence*, trans. Alphonso Lingis (Pittsburgh, PA: Duquesne University Press, 1988), Levinas refers to this same approach as the "one-for-the-other."

25. Levinas, *Difficult Freedom: Essays on Judaism*, trans. Seán Hand (London: Althone Press, 1990).

26. For an analysis of the practical implications of this Exodus text, see Levinas's "Revelation in the Jewish Tradition," in *The Levinas Reader*, ed. Seán Hand (Oxford, England: Basil Blackwell, 1989), 190–210.

27. Levinas, "Revelation in the Jewish Tradition," 204.

28. Levinas, "Enigma and Phenomenon," in *Basic Philosophical Writings*, ed. Adriaan T. Peperzak, Simon Critchley, and Robert Bernasconi (Indianapolis: Indiana University Press, 1996), 76.

29. As Levinas upholds Cartesian metaphysics, he locates himself in the French Continental school of thought. His understanding and appropriation of Descartes makes sense in light of his emphasis on Platonic thinking. He states, "In agreement with Plato and Plotinus, who dare to pose, against all good sense, something beyond being, is not the idea of being younger than the idea of the infinite? Should we not concede that philosophy cannot confine itself to the primacy of ontology, as has been taught up to now and against which, in France, Jean Wahl and Ferdinand Alquié have vigorously protested? And that intentionality is not the ultimate spiritual relation?" ("Transcendence and Height," in *Basic Philosophical Writings*, 21–2). Levinas is not alone in this generous or less caricatured reading of Descartes. Charles Taylor interprets the Cartesian *cogito* in light of God (see *Sources of the Self: The Making of Modern Identity* [Cambridge: Harvard University Press, 1989], 324). Also Tina Chanter argues that Descartes was not as certain or positivist as he is caricatured to be (see "Reading Hegel as a Mediating Master," in *Levinas and Lacan: The Missed Encounter*, ed. Sarah Harasym [Albany: State University of New York Press, 1998], 4). Yet the Descartes we encounter in Lonergan's work, specifically in *The Subject* (Milwaukee, WI: Marquette University Press,

1968), is a traditional reading of Descartes, which upholds the autonomous nature of the *cogito* and the certitude associated with positivist epistemology.

30. Levinas, "Transcendence and Height," in *Basic Philosophical Writings*, 20, 21.

31. Ibid., 21.

32. René Descartes, *Meditations on First Philosophy in Focus*, ed. Stanley Tweyman (London: Routledge, 1993), 67. For a deeper analysis of Levinas's thought on Descartes's reading of Infinity, see Levinas, "The Idea of the Infinite in Us," in *Entre Nous: On Thinking-of-the-Other*, trans. Michael B. Smith and Barbara Harshav (New York: Columbia University Press, 1998), 219–22.

33. Levinas, "The Rights of Man and Good Will," in *Entre Nous: On Thinking-of-the-Other*, 157.

34. Levinas, "Transcendence and Height," in *Basic Philosophical Writings*, 18.

35. Significantly, Jewish interpretations of heart connote a conversion of the whole person (see *The Jewish Encyclopedia* 6 [New York: KTAV Publishing House, 1964], 295–7). This Jewish interpretation of heart encompasses the human capacities for knowing, feeling, and willing and refers to the "seat of the emotional and intellectual life" of a person (295). This is an interesting point because Levinas's subject is a holistic embodied subject for whom intelligibility is located in sensibility, rather than merely in the spatial configuration of the mind or head.

36. Levinas, "Transcendence and Height," in *Basic Philosophical Writings*, 21.

37. Levinas, *Totality and Infinity: An Essay on Exteriority*, trans. Alphonso Lingis (Pittsburgh, PA: Duquesne University Press, 1969), 155.

38. Levinas, *Totality and Infinity*, 270.

39. See Luce Irigaray, "Questions to Emmanuel Levinas: On the Divinity of Love," in *Re-Reading Levinas*, ed. Robert Bernasconi and Simon Critchley (Bloomington: Indiana University Press, 1991), 109–18.

40. Levinas explicitly rejects the facile conflation of femininity with otherness in *Totality and Infinity*, 256–80.

41. Levinas employs the language of being cogendered in "Love and Filiation," in *Ethics and Infinity, Conversations with Philippe Nemo*, trans. R. Cohen (Pittsburgh, PA: Duquesne University Press, 1985), 63–72.

42. Levinas, *Totality and Infinity*, 256.

43. Levinas, *Otherwise Than Being or Beyond Essence*, 108.

44. The way in which we privilege fecundity as a role and age span is evident in the North American culture which values youth, mothers, and career women over senior women. Moreover, senior women are in danger of being marginalized by a hegemonic male gaze, which renders beauty in terms of youth and fertility. Frida Kerner Furman carries out an enlightening study of the ways in which older women both internalize and externalize the dominant culture's assumptions and attitudes about age and gender in her work, *Facing the Mirror: Older Women and Beauty Shop Culture* (New York: Routledge, 1997).

45. Catherine Chalier, "Ethics and the Feminine," in *Re-Reading Levinas*, 119–29.

46. For an exploration of the problems associated with such spousal imagery in the church, see Susan A. Ross, *Extravagant Affections: A Feminist Sacramental Theology* (New York: Continuum, 1998).

47. Lingis, introduction to *Otherwise than Being*, xxxv.

48. Theodore De Boer, *The Rationality of Transcendence: Studies in the Philosophy of Emmanuel Levinas* (Amsterdam: Gieben, 1997), 147.

49. Some Lonergan scholars have even commented on their initial reluctance to continue reading Lonergan because of the somewhat ambiguous, off-putting style of writing. See R. Michael Clark, "Byway of the Cross," in *Lonergan Workshop* 12 (1996): 43–4; Jerome Miller, "All Love is Self-Surrender," *Method: Journal of Lonergan Studies* 13, no.1 (1996): 53.

50. See Michael Purcell, *Mystery and Method: The Other in Rahner and Levinas* (Milwaukee, WI: Marquette University Press, 1998).

Chapter 5

Kristeva's Horror and Lonergan's Insight

The Psychic Structure of the Human Person and the Move to a Higher Viewpoint

CHRISTINE E. JAMIESON

The emergence of women in the public realm signifies important progress for humanity. Multiple historical factors played significant roles in fostering this progress.[1] Paradoxically, an outcome of this progress is the greater availability of evidence of violence and dehumanizing treatment of women. This evidence indicates that despite important advancement for women, misogynous behavior has not abated and may, in fact, be escalating.[2] Juxtaposing humanity's progress and decline in relation to women leads one to wonder about the relationship between the two. The growing presence of women in the public realm and a worsening of the bias of misogyny suggest a lacuna regarding attempts to promote the former and abolish the latter. Psychoanalyst and linguist Julia Kristeva (1941–) explores a pattern within the psychic structure of the speaking subject which sheds significant light on this lacuna. However, Kristeva's work has been criticized as being either essentialist and ahistorical or deterministic which, according to her critics, makes it difficult, perhaps impossible, for women to escape an oppressed and determined existence.[3]

Kristeva elicits an understanding of the human psyche that reveals the underlying dialectical condition of the speaking subject. For Kristeva, there is a link between this dialectical condition and the marginalization and oppression of women. This is what is meant in the title of this chapter by "Kristeva's Horror."[4] It is horrifying because it pushes us to the limits of our condition as speaking subjects. For Kristeva, there is an inherent structure within the psyches of speaking subjects that facilitates the repression—indeed, the abjection[5] of women. This insight facilitates our understanding of the lacuna that exists when attempting to explain the persistent tension between humanity's progress and decline in relation to women.

While Kristeva pushes us to the limits of our condition as speaking subjects, Bernard Lonergan provides an insight that one might draw on to channel Kristeva's horror into liberation. The insight I am referring to is Lonergan's recognition of the emergence of a higher viewpoint when confronted with the limits of intelligible horizons. In drawing on this insight, Lonergan might help one to grasp why Kristeva's thought is determining yet liberating. The human desire to understand facilitates development beyond the limits of horizons. Although Kristeva confronts us with a seemingly inescapable human condition, one might draw on Lonergan to move beyond the limits of that condition.[6] Kristeva provides an understanding that pushes our thinking concerning women's rights to a deeper level. By linking her penetrating analysis with Lonergan's insights, one can begin to understand the paradoxical experience of determinism and liberation when confronted with Kristeva's work. Lonergan's insight concerning the need to shift to a higher viewpoint when confronted with an experience (liberation within a determined horizon) which cannot be explained within the range of the present intelligible horizon provides the necessary heuristic to assist us in beginning to formulate what that higher viewpoint might be. In what follows, I will sketch Kristeva's theory of what she terms the "split subject" and follow this with a few remarks on how Lonergan might assist us in grasping the full import of Kristeva's contribution concerning the further progress of women.

The Split Subject

In describing the experience of the human person, Julia Kristeva unearths a deep, pervasive dialectic[7] that constitutes the foundation of the "speaking subject." This dialectical condition of speaking human beings has roots in the initial relationship between mothers and infants. In order for an infant to achieve an identity, a separation process must take place. The child and the mother *must* separate. Separation in fact begins at the origins of the human person. Consequently, Kristeva posits a dialectic at the very foundations of the human person. What is this dialectic?

Kristeva refers to two processes within the human person, the semiotic process and the symbolic process. The mature human person embodies these two processes. The dialectic between them produces the speaking subject. Kristeva equates the semiotic process with the infantile experience that is pre-subject/object, before the child differentiates between itself and its mother. The semiotic is identified with the instincts, drives, and needs which, in the beginning, prior to development in conjunction with the psyche and the intellect, are all that constitute the human person.[8] However, the semiotic is not left behind as the child develops into a speaking subject—rather, the semiotic process engages in a dialectical relationship with the symbolic process. The symbolic process emerges with the entrance of a "third" to disrupt the undifferentiated experience (from the child's perspective) of the mother-child relationship. In a sense, what interrupts the mother-child relationship is the mother's distraction away from the child toward another person or thing.

The beginning of differentiation is the beginning of language. It is the time in the child's development that signifies a repression of the undifferentiated maternal relationship where drives and needs are given full reign. It is a time that facilitates the emergence of the initial stages of the formation of the child's identity, that is, of the possibility and capacity of the child to become a speaking subject, to become an "I"—one who distinguishes between "I" and "other" through language. So the symbolic refers to the restraints put on the child through "the establishment of sign and syntax, of grammatical and social constraints."[9] For Kristeva, this deep underlying structure constitutes the speaking subject. Consequently, Kristeva defines the speaking subject as a "split" subject. Although the repression of the semiotic or maternal relationship is absolutely necessary for the human person to achieve an identity, we are counselled to be aware of the dialectical relationship between the semiotic and symbolic. If we, as individuals and societies, repress too severely any one of these two processes that constitute who we are, it can lead to totalitarian (there is only law and constraint but no creativity) or psychotic (there is no meaning) states.

It is important to note that the relationship between the infant and the mother is not constituted by a harmonious bond underlying the complete satisfaction of the child's desire. Prior to the entrance of the "third" or prior to the beginnings of language and identity, the infant experiences separation through drives and impulses. Separation is not *generated* by the entrance of the symbolic realm, rather, the symbolic realm serves to *complete* the separation. Separation is already part of the child's experience through oral and anal activity, introjection and expelling. The body, according to Kristeva, is never a unified body; it is a "divided body," a body made up of drives and pulsions, instincts and energies. It is inaccurate to assume that the infant's defining *experiences* of separation[10] necessarily presuppose an original experience of unity or harmony. The infant *is* divided. Division constitutes the infant even before it is born. Division of matter and biological drives constitute the human creature: "Even before birth, there is already 'a certain dehiscence at the heart of the organism, a primordial Discord.'"[11] Thus, to reiterate, separation begins at the very origins of the human being. Separation/division *is* the origin of a human being.

The dynamic between the body of the mother and the body of the infant is crucial in facilitating the beginning of the ordering of the infant's drives. Kristeva draws on the Platonic term *chora*[12] to assist in explicating this ordering. Kristeva associates the chora with 'woman.' This is because the semiotic chora, seen in full display in a newborn infant, displays itself in the intimate connection between the infant's body and the body of the mother. Thus, the semiotic *chora* is, for Kristeva, "a specifically bodily and distinctively female space within which language and subject come to be."[13] The chora is a space, a container that holds the "unlimited and unbounded generating process, [the] unceasing operation of the drives toward, in, and through language; toward, in, and through the exchange system and its protagonists—the subject and his institutions."[14] Yet, the chora is a rhythmic space; it is not fixed or situated: "Neither model nor copy, the *chora* precedes and underlies figuration and thus specularization, and is analogous only to vocal or kinetic rhythm."[15] The mother's body orders the chora through the drives of the infant, specifically through "the oral and anal drives both of which are oriented and structured around the mother's body."[16] These drives are ambiguous. They are both productive and destructive. They bind and orient the infant to the mother's body. They are constant movement, "both positive and negative in the degree to which they settle into a pattern but also destroy the stability of that pattern's new movements."[17] It is this dualism within the body itself that "makes the semiotized body a place of permanent scission."[18] The oral and anal drives, those sensory-motor impulses, create a constant movement within the infant. These bodily drives create a force that Kristeva, following Freud, insists is predominately destructive. Kristeva draws here on Hegel's term "negativity." Distinct from "negation, which is the act of a judging subject,"[19] "[n]egativity . . . is the fourth term in the Hegelian ternary dialectic. . . . It is, in effect, the very movement or 'ground' of the dialectic."[20] Prior to thought or knowledge, it is the primary instinctual trait upon which all drives and impulses operate. The oral and anal drives, constituting the primary material introjection and rejection in the infant's body and associated exclusively with its relationship to the mother's body, are both the condition for and potential dissolution of the symbolic realm. Thus, at a preconscious level, there is juxtaposition between negativity, destruction, and the maternal body. Although preconscious, this juxtaposition plays an influential role in the experience of women and men and, subsequently, in the marginalization and oppression of women.

Kristeva asserts that all human beings are exiles. In asserting this, she is not referring to the phenomenon that we are exiled from our mothers or exiled from that place where all needs and desires are met. Rather, she is saying that the condition of exile constitutes our very identity; it is the common human experience of being "strangers to ourselves."[21] From the origins of our existence we emerge (literally) via the state of being exiles. The semiotic dimension must be repressed in order for the child to become a speaking subject. Yet it does not (nor can it) disappear. This is because our identity is constituted on the dialectic between the semiotic and the symbolic. Our identity is not constituted on a complete and irrevocable break with the semiotic. How does this work? One way to understand this is through the distinction in language between, on the one hand, the *transparency* of language and, on the other hand, its *materiality*. Kristeva's initial work in linguistics led her to distinguish between two connected yet quite distinct aspects of language. On the one hand, there is the "poetic" dimension of language, language's "materiality"—the actual physical aspect of language: the sounds, rhythms, combinations of letters, the form of texts, their articulation and style. This aspect of language underlies, on the other hand, language's capacity to convey a message—the language of "transparency," that is, "when the work is forgotten for the sake of the object or concept designated."[22] Meaning, which emerges in and through language, comes about through a dialectical relationship with the differentiation of sounds, among other things. But the materiality of language must be kept in the background if meaning is to come to the fore. Imagine focusing always on the sounds and the differences in sounds when someone is speaking. Meaning is lost. That dimension of language must fade into the background. If it becomes the focus, meaning and communication are impossible. We regress into a meaningless world, a strange world, an uncanny world where nothing is familiar.

Our lives constitute a separation. That separation is between the semiotic process where there is no constraint but fluidity without boundaries or censorship, and the symbolic process that comes about through constraints, rules, laws, and boundaries. This is the condition of being human, of being a speaking being. This is the condition with which we enter relationships. Identity is key. The boundary condition of our psyches is fragile at times. Unless we maintain a certain balance in the dialectical relationship between the semiotic and the symbolic, this fragility can lead to two possible outcomes. First, certainly people with psychosis have a very difficult time maintaining the division. The semiotic realm invades their world and they live in realities that literally do not make sense. Second, the need for identity can also create an imbalance on the side of the symbolic realm. Too severe repression of the semiotic dimension leads to a rigid adherence to constraint, to law, and to identity. We have an identity as female or male, black or white, Canadian or American, and so on. We become entrenched in these identities so that the other becomes the enemy threatening our identity. Yet, according to Kristeva, what is threatening our identity is not the other. It is the semiotic dimension of our psyches. We project our fear of the fragility of our own psyches onto the other—whatever constitutes that other. This threat of the other has particular significance concerning the perceived threat of women. At a completely bodily level, at a level that is preconscious, prior to our capacity to reflect, women threaten our very identity. Women are a threat to the symbolic realm because it is women who bear children. We are all born of women. Women's proximity to the semiotic realm makes women, at a preconscious level, a threat to our identity. It also means that women become aligned with a certain joy in the remembered absence of constraints to drives and impulses.

There are a variety of interpretations concerning systemic marginalization, oppression, and violence against women. Kristeva's theory concerning our condition as split subjects is important because it probes the origins of human identity and links abjection of women to the emergence of human identity. Although difficult to accept, Kristeva is convincing in her assessment that the pervasive problems women face are the result of deeply ingrained aspects of the human psyche. Through her psychoanalytic analysis of the common human experience of abjection, she relentlessly bridges the chasms of the psyche in order to understand what this experience is and how it emerges.

Kristeva's analysis is both a blessing and a curse. She follows the trail of abjection. It leads her to an experience that all human beings have in common—the experience of birth, of separating from the mother's body. Kristeva powerfully demonstrates how this preverbal, archaic experience is both a heartbreaking loss and a separation upon which our lives utterly depend. Kristeva's conviction is that this pivotal experience in the growth of the human psyche continues to live in us. It continues to influence us. Thus, it accounts for the strangely intertwining emotions of hatred and desire directed at women's bodies in every culture. The inescapable element in this scenario is that all human beings are born through women's bodies. All men and women are determined by this physical reality. All suffer from its consequences. Yet women particularly bear the brunt of its determining influence.

Despite Kristeva's "horror," my experience when reading her work is one of liberation, not oppression. Much of the current dialogue concerning women's issues, particularly the problem of violence against women and the problem of misogyny, is limited because, in my view, it is unable to reach the depth of understanding that Kristeva offers. This is so because the range of questions and insights has not expanded enough to address the deep and troublesome psychic dynamic that exists within all human beings. This psychic dynamic emerges dramatically in Kristeva's work.

The Emergence of a Higher Viewpoint

Bernard Lonergan can assist us, I believe, in overcoming the seeming inescapable dilemma that Kristeva's work presents us with. Lonergan's thought can contribute at two levels vis-à-vis the dilemma. First, Lonergan's notion of the emergence of a higher viewpoint could enhance Kristeva's work by providing a heuristic which explains the paradoxical experience of determinism and liberation within Kristeva's thought. Kristeva elaborates upon our determined condition as speaking subjects by intricately analyzing the dialectical relationship between the semiotic and the symbolic processes within the speaking subject. She demonstrates how this determined condition accounts for the pervasive marginalization and oppression of women throughout history. Yet, paradoxically, Kristeva uncovers a creative, transforming capacity within the speaking subject's determined existence for which that determined existence cannot account.

Second, Lonergan's notion of the emergence of a higher viewpoint helps us to understand why Kristeva's theory does not invalidate feminist theories that attempt to correct biases which lead to the subordination of women or the denigration of women's experience. Feminist theories concerning women's marginalization and oppression attempt to account for the difficulties women face in a patriarchal worldview. Two paradigms which feminist theories draw on are liberalism and social constructionism. Following Lonergan's insight into the emergence of a higher viewpoint, these theories are valid within the system of questions they address. I argue that the emergence of higher systems or higher viewpoints is necessary because these lower systems can no longer adequately deal with the questions and insights they generate. These feminist theories raise questions and pose problems which cannot be addressed within the range of their horizon of questions and answers. I suggest that Kristeva's theory tackles these higher level questions and problems. Let me elaborate on these two levels where Lonergan's insight into the emergence of higher viewpoints or higher systems of knowing can contribute to Kristeva's work.

1. There is a determinate aspect about Kristeva's theory concerning the split condition of the speaking subject. Kristeva, according to her critics, occludes options which may allow women to escape an oppressed and determined existence.[23] Kristeva is a materialist in the extreme. Her analysis of the effects of the human creature's biological condition rests on the foundation of a materialist reading of reality. Yet Kristeva provides a deep insight into the speaking subject's transforming and creative potential. The split condition of human persons constitutes not only the underlying potential for violence against the other who threatens identity (with a particular emphasis on women because of their proximity to the semiotic realm), it concomitantly is the source for creativity because of its uncensored, unrestricted potential. Thus, paradoxically, amid the very limits that Kristeva identifies, one can sense an experience of liberation and transcendence. The difficulty with this paradox is that on the lower level—the level of materiality—one cannot account for the creativity and transforming capacity of Kristeva's work. At the same time, one cannot deny its existence. Kristeva paradoxically assists her readers in accounting for a transformative, creative capacity within the human species by focusing exclusively on the determined, biological condition of the human crea-

ture's embodied psyche. I suggest that Lonergan's attention to the emergence of a higher viewpoint addresses this paradox. In *Understanding and Being*, in relation to the intelligibility of language, Lonergan states, "If you find, with regard to men, that all of the laws and schemes of sensitive psychology, which pertain to the psychic level, do not account for the intelligible talk that men carry on, you have to go on to a still higher level and posit intellectual forms that account for human behavior."[24] Lonergan's explication of the emergence of a higher viewpoint facilitates our understanding of Kristeva's ability to hold in tension the sheer determinedness of the human condition (and as a consequence, the inescapable dilemma women face) and an open-ended creativity. This creativity does not merely provide relief from our imprisoned condition as speaking subjects but can potentially shift us to a higher level. It can shift us to a level that liberates us from the constraints of the lower level. (One is reminded here of Lonergan's example of the emergence of algebra from arithmetic.)[25] In this scenario I suggest that Lonergan offers an important insight and thus an important contribution to Kristeva's work. Through the analytic tool of a higher viewpoint, one can transcend the limits one is faced with in Kristeva's theory. Lonergan's notion of heuristic helps us to understand how this is so.

The capacity of the human person to seek what is unknown through what is known is the basis of all human progress. This search involves what Lonergan calls "heuristic structure." Heuristic structure orients us (as knowers) toward what is unknown. Kristeva is astutely aware of the human capacity to progress from what is known toward, but never exhausting, what is unknown. Her own investigations into the split condition of speaking subjects demonstrate her willingness to pursue her investigations to the limits of an intellectual horizon. Concomitantly with this relentless investigation, a shift takes place.

In an interview about a novel she wrote in 1991,[26] Kristeva indicates that the thrust of the novel is positive despite its seemingly negative, pessimistic undercurrents. She writes, "[A]s long as the investigation is being carried out, the crime is challenged, and death does not prevail."[27] There is an analogy between what Kristeva indicates in this comment concerning her novel and the investigations she undertakes in unearthing the dialectical condition of all human beings. By authentically following the investigation to the end of its course, to the end of its possibilities, Kristeva experiences and allows her readers to experience a shift that opens out onto a previously unknown reality. At one level (a lower level) it appears that Kristeva has taken us into an inescapable human condition. But it is precisely because she takes us to that point that we are able to shift to a higher level. We begin to understand that the sets of questions we are addressing concerning women's rights need considerable revision. This leads us to the second level of how Lonergan's insight into the emergence of a higher viewpoint may contribute to clarifying not only the paradox but also the importance of Kristeva's theory.

2. Various feminist theories attempt to address the marginalization, oppression, and misogynistic treatment of women. For example, feminists who embrace liberalism[28] focus on the importance of equality of rights and respect for women. The important objective within the feminist liberal paradigm is the entrance of women into the public realm. Women seek equality with men at every level. The foundation for this objective is the Enlightenment's humanist creed that privileges liberation and individualism, highlighting the human person's capacity for moral reasoning. Yet the liberal paradigm poses problems for women. It relies on the basic tenant that there is a common human nature which all people (both men and women) share. Thus, differences are downplayed or bracketed. The liberal paradigm also presupposes that human consciousness has the capacity to transcend bodily and emotional forces in order to reflect rationally on reality. Thus, the liberal paradigm does not account for gaps that appear in its system of thought which may undermine its presumed transparency to itself.

Social constructionist theory has been utilized by feminists in order to draw attention to the patriarchal social structures that systemically oppress women. Simone de Beauvoir sums up this paradigm when she states, "[O]ne is not born, but rather becomes, a woman."[29] The social construction of values is the key tenant of this paradigm. The underlying assumption of social constructionism is "that something more powerful than human choice and more pervasive than individual freedom is at the root of the problem of women's lives. In particular, one may not assume that women have consented to their lot, since it has been constructed by, and reinforced in, social practices."[30] Feminists who follow the social constructionist paradigm are not determinists. They see the possibility of a reconstruction, not at the level of the individual (as with the liberal paradigm), but at the level of social life. The desire for reconstruction emerges from the discontent of the oppressed or the disenfranchised. However, reconstruction is problematic. The social structures that oppress women and that feminists seek to tear down and reconstruct are, according to Kristeva, the result of a necessary foundation that facilitates the development of the psychic structure of the speaking subject. Feminists who attempt to reconstruct these social structures with ones that are more acceptable fall into the problem of reversal. The split condition of the speaking subject necessitates, according to Kristeva, the repression of the semiotic. Social reconstruction, as with individual reconstruction, regardless of what form it takes, will always incorporate this repression as part of its necessary condition. Thus, Kristeva indicates that feminists who adhere to the social constructionist paradigm inevitably fall prey to the same "logic of power" which they seek to overcome.

The emergence of higher systems or higher viewpoints comes about because lower systems can no longer adequately deal with the questions and insights they generate. (Again, Lonergan's example of the emergence of algebra from arithmetic facilitates our understanding.) The questions and insights that feminists' theories generate but are unable to deal with clearly call for the emergence of a higher viewpoint. The concepts used by feminists who adhere to a liberal paradigm and those who draw on a social constructionist paradigm are adequate within their horizons of intelligible meaning. However, the questions and the insights generated by these paradigms but which the paradigms cannot answer or account for are addressed, as I have shown above, in Kristeva's work. Kristeva recognizes the inherent problems within the liberal and social constructionist paradigms. Through unravelling the inconsistencies in these paradigms, she takes her readers to a higher level of understanding. This higher level accounts for the unanswered questions in the systems operating at a lower level. In relation to the importance of higher systems of knowledge, Bernard Lonergan states, "Fresh data are ever being brought to light to force upon scientific consciousness the inadequacies of existing hypotheses and theories, to provide the evidence for their revision and, in the limit, when minor corrections no longer are capable of meeting the issue, to demand the radical transformation of concepts and postulates that is named a higher viewpoint."[31] In Kristeva's explication of the dialectical relationship between the semiotic and the symbolic within the speaking subject and the implications of that relationship vis-à-vis pervasive marginalization and oppression of women, she brings to our attention the inadequacies of both social constructionism and liberalism. These paradigms attempt to account for the problems women face through social influences or the absence of moral reasoning. These theories are not wrong. If one remains within the sets of questions that social constructionism and liberalism address, these theories are adequate. However, a higher system emerges with Kristeva's work because her theory facilitates the emergence of new questions which do not so much contradict social constructionism and liberalism as actually transform these lower systems. Thus, Kristeva's work has the capacity to shift our thinking. It puts us in touch with the limits of our horizons. It helps us realize that we must transcend the limits of our present intelligible horizons concerning the pervasive oppression and marginalization of women. Only then can we truly begin to address the problem of women's rights.

Finally, following Kristeva's thought, the dialectical relationship between the semiotic and the symbolic within the human psyche accounts for the revolutionary quality of poetic language and of all forms of language which push beyond the limits of referential language. It accounts for creativity in both its darker (melancholy, violence, horror) and lighter (love, ethics) dimensions. When language is used to circumscribe reality there is stability. However, that stability cannot remain. Because the speaking subject encompasses both the semiotic and the symbolic, he or she is continually disrupted. Thus, we experience fear when confronted with the other. We fear that our clean and proper identity will be soiled, fragmented, disturbed, and eventually dissolved. Our identity is fragile. It is not solid and permanent. Therein lies our greatest fear and our greatest hope.

Conclusion

Kristeva's work does not undermine or discount the importance of the continuing work concerning women's rights. Rather, her theory helps us to understand more deeply why, despite the best efforts of women and men and important advances of women on many levels, problems of misogyny and violence against women continue to escalate. Kristeva's investigations lead us to limits of the human condition that circumscribe our existence as speaking beings. At the same time, she shifts our thinking to a higher level. In my view, it is precisely because of this dialectical tension within Kristeva's work that Lonergan offers crucial tools to facilitate our understanding of why she is such an important contributor to the issue of women's rights. As well, Lonergan's insight into the emergence of a higher viewpoint promotes a shift in our thinking as we seek to understand more deeply the pervasive problems concerning women. This is because the emergence of a higher viewpoint is a crucial insight in striving to understand and transform our habitual (indeed, our instinctual) mode of operating in the world.

Notes

1. One important example is the United Nations General Assembly concomitantly establishing in 1946 the Commission on the Status of Women and the Commission on Human Rights. This historic event marked, in principle, an acknowledgment of the equal status of women and women's entitlement to all rights set forth in the Universal Declaration. It recognized the integral link between the treatment of women and the violation of human rights.

2. As part of its mandate, the United Nations monitors the progress of women vis-à-vis human rights violations. In so doing, it reveals that violence and dehumanizing treatment toward women is escalating in a variety of contexts. It is seen in the family (domestic violence, traditional practices such as genital mutilation, infanticide, incest), in the community (rape, sexual assault and harassment, trafficking in women, prostitution, labor exploitation, pornography, women migrant workers), and at the level of the state (violence against women in detention and custodial violence and in situations of armed conflict).

3. For examples of those who criticize Kristeva's work as essentialist, see Teresa de Lauretis, "The Female Body and Heterosexual Presumption," *Semiotica* 67 (1987): 259–79; Elizabeth Grosz, "The Body of Signification," in *Abjection, Melancholia and Love,* ed. John Fletcher and Andrew Benjamin (London: Routledge, 1990), 80–103. The ahistorical criticism is broached by Nancy Fraser, "The Uses and Abuses of French Discourse Theories for Feminist Politics," in *Revaluing French Feminism: Critical Essays on Difference, Agency, and Culture,* ed. Nancy Fraser and Sandra Lee Bartky (Bloomington: Indiana University Press, 1992), 177–94. Janice Doane and Devon Hodges, *From Klein to Kristeva: Psychoanalytic Feminism and the Search for the "Good Enough" Mother* (Ann Arbor: University of Michigan Press, 1992), 60, and Andrea Nye, "Woman Clothed with the Sun: Julia Kristeva and the Escape from/to Language," *Signs: Journal of Women in Culture and Society* 12 (1987): 664–86, are critical of Kristeva's determinism, which offers no hope for women to move beyond marginalization and misogyny.

4. The title of Kristeva's 1980 book is *Pouvoirs de l'horreur* (Paris: Seuil). It was translated as *Powers of Horror: An Essay on Abjection,* trans. Leon Roudiez (New York: Columbia University, 1982).

5. In *Powers of Horror: An Essay on Abjection* Kristeva presents an analysis of the phenomenon of abjection. She juxtaposes the abject and the feminine and suggests that both are threatening because both are aligned with what is "unnameable." The abject "disturbs identity, system, order." It "does not respect borders, positions, rules" (4). She describes this "unnameable" abject through its exterior

and interior manifestations. Exteriorly, abjection is manifested in what is seen as improper and unclean. It is what is thrust aside and what thrusts me aside. Interiorly, abjection emerges as the struggle to separate from the maternal body. Abjection displays, for Kristeva, the loss that my identity is founded on. The foundation of my being is not an identity, a system, or an order. Rather, "I" am founded on that which is pushed away, repressed, abjected in order that "I" may live. Kristeva observes two levels at which this is so. First, at a societal or cultural level, the human is separated from what is animal. Thus, separating marks out "a precise area of our culture in order to remove it from the threatening world of animals and animalism" (12–13). Second, at an individual level, there is the need to break away from the archaic relationship with the maternal entity. (This breaking away begins even before one exists outside the womb. Indeed, birth is perhaps the most definitive breaking away we undergo.)

6. It is important to note the strong divergences in language and methodology when juxtaposing two thinkers like Kristeva and Lonergan. Kristeva writes as a psychoanalyst and linguist. Her writing is elliptical, elusive almost in her effort to describe a human experience which, as we will see, is prelinguistic or preverbal. Kristeva evokes a response in her readers in much the same way a poem might evoke emotion and possibly transformation. Lonergan is a theologian and a philosopher who utilizes an empirical and logical style in much of his work. Thus, the differences are significant but, in my view, not mutually exclusive.

7. It is important to distinguish here the difference between Kristeva's understanding of dialectic as a condition which continually underlies the ongoing relationship between the semiotic and the symbolic and Lonergan's understanding of dialectic as dealing "with concrete positions and counterpositions—concerned with the contradictory and interested in change" (Lonergan, *Insight: A Study of Human Understanding* [New York: Harper & Row, 1978], 217). For Lonergan, the differences between the positions are irreducible, but by recognizing this, one heads for resolution through recognition of the need for a higher viewpoint and thus, the move toward a universal viewpoint. For Kristeva, there is no resolution to dialectic. The speaking subject is constituted through the dialectic between the establishment and the countervailing of a sign system, that is, through the dialectical relationship between the symbolic and the semiotic realm.

8. Kristeva accounts for her unique application of the term "semiotic" in "The Semiotic *Chora* Ordering the Drives," in *Revolution in Poetic Language*, trans. Margaret Waller (New York: Columbia University, 1984), 25–30.

9. Alice Jardine, "Opaque Texts and Transparent Contexts: The Political Difference of Julia Kristeva," in *The Poetics of Gender*, ed. Nancy K. Miller (New York: Columbia University, 1986), 109.

10. I refer here to the mirror stage and the castration stage. Briefly, the mirror stage constitutes the "spatial intuition" within the infant (usually between the ages of six and eighteen months) which enables the infant to begin to experience a separation from the semiotic realm. In this original experience of separation, the infant sees its image in a mirror. There are three phases involved in the mirror stage. First, the image the infant sees in the mirror is perceived as a real person (probably associated with the adult holding the infant if such is the case)

whom the infant tries to grasp. Second, the infant becomes aware that what it sees in the mirror is an image and not a real person. Third, the infant perceives the image as its own self. The infant, prior to control over motor skills, is able to recognize the image as itself yet different from the body it experiences. The destructive and disturbing drives and instincts are the body that the infant experiences. Yet the infant grasps an image of itself which is unified and whole. In this manner, the infant achieves its first conquest over its body. The castration stage signifies the detachment of the child from the mother. The child's exclusive desire for the mother is broken by the entry of a third term, the father, or anything that draws the mother's desire away from the child to something outside that exclusive relationship. This is the "imaginary castration" that keeps the infant from dissolving into the body of the mother. It produces in the infant its first experience of lack or absence. Hence, the mother becomes the infant's first object of desire.

11. Dawne McCance, *Posts: Re Addressing the Ethical* (Albany: State University of New York Press, 1996), 142, n. 7. McCance quotes from Julia Kristeva, "Modern Theatre Does Not Take (A) Place," trans. Alice Jardine and Thomas Gora, *Sub-Stance* 18–19 (Winter-Spring 1977), 131–4.

12. In the *Timaeus*, Plato speaks of the chora as "an ancient, mobile, unstable receptacle, prior to the One, to the father, and even to the syllable, metaphorically suggesting something nourishing and maternal" (Julia Kristeva, *In the Beginning was Love: Psychoanalysis and Faith*, trans. Arthur Goldhammer [New York: Columbia University Press, 1987], 5).

13. Michael Payne, *Reading Theory: An Introduction to Lacan, Derrida, and Kristeva* (Cambridge: Blackwell Publishers, 1993), 177.

14. Kristeva, *Revolution in Poetic Language*, 17.

15. Ibid., 26.

16. Ibid., 27.

17. Allon White, *Carnival, Hysteria, and Writing* (Oxford: Clarendon Press, 1993), 70.

18. Kristeva, *Revolution in Poetic Language*, 27.

19. Ibid., 28.

20. John Lechte, *Julia Kristeva* (London: Routledge, 1990), 133.

21. This is the title of Kristeva's 1989 publication, *Etrangers à nous-mêmes* (Paris: Fayard). *Strangers to Ourselves*, trans. Leon Roudiez (New York: Columbia University Press, 1991).

22. Julia Kristeva, *Desire in Language: A Semiotic Approach to Literature and Art*, ed. Leon S. Roudiez, trans. Thomas Gora, Alice Jardine, and Leon Roudiez (New York: Columbia University Press, 1980), 5.

23. Juliet Flower MacCannell considers Kristeva's thinking ultra conservative, complicitous with the patriarchy in suppressing any possibility of the empowerment of women. See Juliet Flower MacCannell, "Kristeva's Horror," *Semiotica* 62 (1986): 345–51. While more sympathetic to the contribution Kristeva makes to American feminists, Domna Stanton also insists that despite the seeming subversiveness of the semiotic, Kristeva "relies on a series of traditional images." Stanton asserts that "[b]y emphasizing the subject's desire to destroy the father and to (re)possess the mother, Kristeva's model for engendering the poetic does not then

deviate fundamentally from the patriarchal oedipal script" ("Difference on Trial: A Critique of the Maternal Metaphor in Cixous, Irigaray, and Kristeva," in *The Poetics of Gender*, 166). See also, "Language and Revolution: The Franco-American Dis-Connection," in *The Future of Difference*, ed. Marilyn Eisenstein and Alice Jardine (Boston: G. K. Hall, 1980), 73–87.

24. Bernard Lonergan, *Understanding and Being*, ed. Elizabeth A. Morelli and Mark D. Morelli, Collected Works of Bernard Lonergan, vol. 5 (Toronto: University of Toronto Press, 1990), 205.

25. Lonergan, *Insight*, 13–19.

26. Julia Kristeva, *Le vieil homme et les loups* (Paris: Librairie Arthème Fayard, 1991). *The Old Man and the Wolves*, trans. Barbara Bray (New York: Columbia University Press, 1994).

27. Julia Kristeva, "Interview: *The Old Man and the Wolves*," in *Julia Kristeva Interviews*, ed. Ross Mitchell Guberman (New York: Columbia University Press, 1996), 165.

28. I draw on Susan Frank Parsons, *Feminism and Christian Ethics* (Cambridge: Cambridge University Press, 1996) for my treatment of both the liberal paradigm and the social constructionism paradigm.

29. Simone de Beauvoir, *The Second Sex*, trans. H. M. Parshley (New York: Bantam Books, 1961), 249.

30. Parsons, *Feminism and Christian Ethics*, 69.

31. Lonergan, *Insight*, 76.

Chapter 6

Lonergan's Postmodern Subject
Neither Neoscholastic Substance nor Cartesian Ego

FREDERICK LAWRENCE

The Subject as Self-referential Identity

Postmodernism derives from Heidegger's critique of ontotheology. In rejecting ontotheology, postmodern philosophers and theologians such as Heidegger, Derrida, Levinas, and Marion oppose Idealism's and Naive Realism's image of the subject.

When Zorba the Greek said, "My God is like me, only bigger, crazier," he was reiterating the basic anthropological principle that the god of the person is like the person. Can we invert this thought and say that the way we imagine God will pretty much correlate with the way we imagine ourselves as a human subject? I think we can.

Thus, if we imagine substance as an underlying already-out-there-now stuff, and we imagine God to be the supreme already-out-there-now or "already-in-there-now" being endowed with the greatest possible power, then we will probably entertain an image of the human subject as already-out-there-now + consciousness, where by "consciousness" is meant exclusively the *intentional* side of consciousness. Thus, consciousness does not have to do with awareness proper, but with awareness precisely as awareness of this or that object.

For Descartes, then, consciousness is virtually synonymous with the *ego cogitans*, mental self-reflection, whose chief operation is the objectifying and reflexive one of *cogitato*.[1] Similarly, the German word for consciousness, *Bewußtsein*, highlights this object-oriented/objectifying/ objectified image of consciousness (as intentionality).[2]

Although premodern and modern Naive Realism pictures the subject-as-object in virtually the same way as Idealism, it lays greater stress on the subject's soul than on its consciousness. It declares that the soul knows reality, and insists that it ought to subordinate itself to the natural order made manifest in the laws of nature. These ideas are not wrong in themselves, but Naive Realism—unable or unwilling to ground its knowledge claims critically—is content with commonsense dogmatism.

In contrast to the Naive Realist subject-as-object the Idealist one— whether as Cartesian *res cogitans* or as Kantian transcendental ego— replaces the soul with the self. Classically, the Idealist self is out of this world; it simply presides over the world in terms of itself and on its own terms: the modern self as master and possessor of the world.

IDEALISM, NAIVE REALISM AND THE ALREADY-OUT-THERE-NOW

Both Idealism and Naive Realism picture the subject to be yet another object in the inventory of objects, to be apprehended by a later reflection on acts of perceiving and knowing other objects. However, whenever we imagine the subject as already-out-there-now and add consciousness, then consciousness is imaged on the model of a closed container: an already-in-here-now property of an already-out-there-now substance. Then the epistemological question inevitably becomes either, How does the subject escape to reach reality out there? or, How does the subject bring in here the reality that exists concretely out there?

If, in both Idealism and Naive Realism, the presiding image is that of the subject originally confined to the in here and of the object out there, the objects that are really out there of course include particular instances of people, places, and things commonly called by names or nouns. This would include all beings or entities, even the gods or god.

At least in its Kantian form, Idealism agrees with Naive Realism that the human being's sole access to reality is through sensation (*Empfindung*), sense intuition (*Anschauung*), or sense perception (*Wahrnehmung*). Deprived of the divine *intuitus originarius*, which can create or produce what it intuits, human beings more or less have to take a good look at what's out there. The Naive Realist construction of the scholastic tag *nihil in intellectu nisi prius in sensu* does not differ appreciably from this view.

Well, then, where do Idealism and Naive Realism part ways? The Naive Realist believes that knowledge and philosophy begin with the material objects in the world out there, whereas for Idealists knowledge and philosophy begin in here with consciousness.[3] In contrast the Idealist thinks that nouns and adjectival attributes are constructions—concepts or categories—which come from intellect (*Verstand*). Concepts are either determinate or indeterminate, depending on whether the materials sensed, intuited, perceived are adequately subsumed under them or not. In any case, such terms or concepts are universal. And, in the case of determinative judgments, such universals express objective knowledge of particular appearances or phenomena, but they do not cover or include the things-in-themselves, or the noumena, or the really real.[4]

For Naive Realists (at least the neoscholastic types) nouns and adjectival attributes are abstractions. They are intentional entities known as "expressed species." This means they come from species impressed pre- or unconsciously by the agent intellect on the possible intellect via materials originally, primitively, and—necessarily—correctly, derived from the senses, although they have already also been processed unconsciously by the so-called inner senses: the imagination that receives the images directly from the senses; the *sensus communis* that coordinates the data from the different sense faculties; and the cogitative power that already starts universalizing the data.

At any rate, for Naive Realism abstraction yields the vaunted universals—concepts or expressed species that emerge unconsciously as impoverished replicas or copies of particular instances received through the senses. Naive Realists are sure that universal concepts refer to reality— otherwise we could not tell truth and reality from falsehood and illusion. They tend to suppose that the very unconscious origin of concepts guarantees their objectivity, since any input of subjective constructing in concept formation would, to that extent, prejudice or compromise objectivity.[5]

It will come as no surprise that Idealism (or also Nominalism) regards Naive Realism to be uncritical for locating the objectivity of knowledge completely in primitive sensation. Concepts add to sense knowing the qualities of universality and necessity that cannot be sensed, so they must come from the constructive activity of intellect under the regulative promptings of reason: there is no abstraction without construction. This is for the most part true. But the Idealists believe that construction may never be transcended enough for us to know we know the really real.

At the end of the day, Idealism and Naive Realism agree that sense perception alone is the criterion for the objective significance of our concepts, since the ocular metaphor for knowing—"taking a look"—is clearly what human finitude requires in order to know. Idealism claims we attain objective knowledge of phenomena because that is all we can sense; Naive Realism insists we reach objective knowledge of the things-in-themselves, but uncritically or dogmatically.

Note that both Idealism and Naive Realism assume the following, and so what they actually hold in common is astonishingly greater than what separates them from each other:

1. The *primordiality* of the subject/object split: hence, a confrontationist view of knowledge;
2. *Perceptualism*: thinks of sensation as our privileged contact with reality;
3. *Conceptualism*: emphasizes the role of terms or concepts in human knowledge to the exclusion of the role of the preconceptual act of understanding.

These three assumptions lead inevitably to *abstract deductivism* and, as we shall see, to an overestimation of the importance of logic in science, philosophy, and theology.

The "Logic" Correlative to the Idealist-Naive Realist Subject-as-Object

Heidegger objects to Aristotle's exclusive emphasis in *Peri Hermeneias* on propositional discourse as *logos apophantikōs*, at the expense of those forms of discourse discussed in his *Rhetoric* and *Poetics*.[6] This kind of discourse either affirms or denies something about something (*ti kata tinos*), and so may be either true or false. One can attribute something to a subject that happens to be the case, or one can say something other than what is so. Thus, saying something about something has a dual structure that brings otherness into discourse, even the second degree otherness that is error.

Whenever we say something about something, we synthesize a subject with an attribute by means of a copula: the verb "to be," which according to Heidegger has no determinate lexical significance other than that of temporal presence. This presence has the double function of synthesis and positing. Heidegger criticizes Aristotle's analysis of propositions for so emphasizing the synthetic function of "to be" that the weight of the proposition is displaced towards the sub-ject (the *hypo-keimenon*), then declared to be the *ousia*, the substance.[7] Heidegger interprets substance or *ousia* as the subsistent and permanent basis that lasts through the changes in attributes. This may be based on the fact that in ordinary language "to be" and its derivatives connote duration, subsistence, and permanence in opposition to all forms of becoming.

According to Heidegger, Aristotle's reduction of all verbs to the copula "to be" deverbalizes the predicate. He thereby transforms all predicates into mere attributes of the subject as essential. In this way Aristotle (and his followers in the history of Western philosophy and theology) substantialize (and essentialize) our experience of the world, privileging the static now.

According to Heidegger, this is how the Western philosophic tradition canonized the image of an already-out-there-now object.[8] Modernity simply inverts this into the image of the subject-as-object, already-in-here-now.

Needless to say, perhaps, "god" is just a blow up or projection of such a subject-as-object, imagined to be either way, way out there, with the stress on transcendence (say, Karl Barth's *totaliter aliter*), or way, way in here (*à la* Paul Tillich) with the stress on immanence or depth. Take your pick!

Universals, Logic, and the Loss of the Other. Whether in terms of construction or of abstraction, both Idealism and Naive Realism can see no way that human intelligence is capable of apprehending the intelligible in the sensible, or the universal in the particular. Whatever occurs between (1) the presentation of particulars by the senses and the representation of particulars by the imagination, and (2) the apprehension of the universal as common to many remains incomprehensible to both Idealism and Naive Realism.[9] Hence, for both there is no intelligent mediation between the abstract universal and the concrete singular.

As a result, both Idealism and Naive Realism think of the rational control of reality as exclusively a matter of logic. Logic, you recall, is the science of the realities in the intentional order: concepts or terms; statements or propositions (which link concepts or terms); and inference (syllogisms and the like). This conception of the logical control of reality requires that one (a) subsume particulars under universals, (b) connect universal concepts with each other in a rigorous manner, and (c) draw coherent conclusions from such rigorously joined universal concepts.

Note well that this model for knowledge, involving the subsumption of particulars under universals, lies at the heart of the epistemologies opposed by postmodernists and labeled "foundationalist." If we generalize this subsumption model, we get the bête noire of postmodernism (whether of Emmanual Levinas's primacy of the ethical, or of both deconstructionist and genealogical approaches): *totalizing thought*. This subsumption model thus plays a central role in the postmodern struggle in behalf of the other.[10]

Postmodernists want to defend the other against the tyranny of the universal, whether as rules of law, institutions, or reigning and taken-for-granted conventions and narratives (especially if they are "master" or "grand" narratives). For postmodernists the particular remains other in the twofold sense that (a) it can never be adequately determined by a universal, and that (b) any such determination violates or does violence to that particular reality.[11]

Ontotheology as the Synthesis of These Counterpositions

Metaphysics. William of Moerbecke's translation of Aristotle's *Metaphysics* at Gamma 1 speaks of "scientia quae considerat ens inquantum est ens et quaerit prima principia entis et causas secundum quod ens" (knowledge [science] that considers being inasmuch as it is being and seeks the first principles of being and its [first] causes), and goes on to say, "unde et nobis entis inquantum entis primae causae sunt accipiendae; principia et causae quaeruntur entium, palam autem, quia inquantum entia" (wherefore the first causes of being as being must be accepted by us; and the principles and causes are sought as pertaining to beings, but obviously just in so far as they are beings). In terms of effective history, this construal of metaphysics evolves into what Jean-François Courtine calls the "Avicennist elaboration of metaphysics," which shapes the horizon of the scholastic problematic in modern times.[12] Siger of Brabant speaks of the "scientia quae speculatur ens secundum quod ens" (science which speculates about being according as it is being), and goes on to tell us that "philosophia considerat primas causas et prima principia . . . haec autem sunt principia et causae entis inquantum ens" (philosophy considers first causes and first principles . . . but these are principles and causes of being inasmuch as it is being); and "Ejusdem scientiae est considerare causas et principia alicujus et ipsum cujus sunt causae et principia" (It pertains to this same science to consider causes and principles of anything and the very thing of which they are causes and principles). Courtine stresses that this orientation to philosophy was first articulated not just outside, but even against the light of biblical revelation. Somewhat ironically perhaps, Francisco Suarez formulated this orientation quite influentially as follows: "Abstrahit enim haec scientia a sensibilibus, seu materialibus rebus . . . et res divinas et materia separatas, et communes rationes entis, quae absque materia existere possunt, contemplatur" (This science abstracts from sensible or material beings . . . and contemplates things both divine and separated from matter, and the common reasons of being, which can exist without matter). This view becomes organized into the *Schulmetaphysik* of the seventeenth and eighteenth centuries in a scheme divided into *metaphysica generalis* (*sive ontologia*) and *metaphysica specialis* (*theologia rationalis, psychologia rationalis, cosmologia rationalis*). Thus, the metaphysics/ontology (that earlier was the objective of Kant's critique, and later of Nietzsche's and Heidegger's) is a system that historically extends from Suarez to Kant.[13] But its gnoseological roots go back to Duns Scotus.[14]

The "god" of Ontotheology. In a manner that did strict historical and exegetical justice to neither Exodus 3:13 nor, in so far as it involved Naive Realism, to Thomas Aquinas, Gilson provided fodder for the postmodernist critique in his contention that in the great medieval disclosure of being, the active and energetic connotation of the *actus essendi* depends on the specifically Christian revelation of God as Creator: the actuality of the *actus essendi* reaches its highpoint in the *efficient causality* of the act of creation out of nothing.[15] The key issue here is the Naive Realist image of this kind of causality, which is naively extrapolated from the spontaneous experience of our skeletal-muscular system: the image of pushing against an object to move it.[16]

My hypothesis is that Nietzsche/Heidegger caricatured the Idealist and the Naive Realist version of efficient causality to expose the fundamental question (*Grundfrage*) of metaphysics or ontology. This is the search for the *ratio cur*, the cause of being as a whole that is reached by demonstrating the *causa sui*. It is worth noting that Aquinas rejected out of hand and as unreasonable the mistaken *démarche* of first taking some being, a substance, which for Idealism or Naive Realism is what Heidegger would term *ein Vorhandenes*, something present-at-hand or "already-out-there-now,"[17] and then asking for its ground, which is gained by performing an abstraction of reason from any and all particular beings. This procedure thereby encompasses the totality of such *vorhandenen* beings—thus arriving at being in general. We then enact a real abstraction to attain a being unaffected by materiality in any way—the Supreme Being as the highest cause.[18]

For the conceptualist, "being in general" is understood as the concept that is greatest in extension and least in intention. Nietzsche rightly and colorfully called it one of the "'highest concepts,' which means the most general, the emptiest concepts, the last smoke of evaporating reality."[19] Being in general is the ground of all particular beings, even of the being par excellence. Yet because it is the cause of being in general, being par excellence has to be the ultimate ground of being in general and thus of all other beings. It is the already-out-there-now ground of all: precisely the kind of being or entity that Kant called *unvordenklich* and incapable of being reached by reason; that Nietzsche found inadmissible as a logical principle, a universal cause, or a moral god; and that Heidegger regarded as the god of ontotheology.

Postmodern Critiques of the Subject

The most common postmodern accusations against this subject-as-object are that it is isolated, punctual, disengaged, and unencumbered. All of these adjectives correctly point out the untenability of the primordiality of the subject/object split; and they rightly stress that the subject cannot be extricated from its historical and social conditionings. They are more phenomenological ways of restating Heidegger's question to Husserl: What is the ontological status of the transcendental ego?

Most of the authors (for example, the late Wittgenstein, Gadamer, Voegelin, Ricoeur, MacIntyre, Taylor, Levinas, or Marion) whose critiques are represented by these adjectives hold perspectivist, relativist, or historicist versions of Idealism. In opposing alienation, they strive to integrate their historicism with either some version of Kantian moral consistency, or with one or another return to such premoderns such as Aristotle (Gadamer and MacIntyre), Plotinus (especially Levinas and Marion), Augustine (Taylor and Voegelin), Pseudo-Dionysius (Marion), or Aquinas (MacIntyre).

Others are engaged in a quest for a more integral form of humanity under the aegis of Nietzsche. Jacques Derrida (who aims for hospitality), Richard Rorty (for liberal democracy), and Michel Foucault (for liberty) pursued this from an alienated standpoint that nevertheless at least pretends to be benevolent. The alienation of some followers of Rorty, Derrida, and Foucault, as well as of certain—by no means all—Analytic philosophers and followers of Lonergan, however, is apparently sufficiently grave that their questing seems malevolent. They are the kind of people whose goal is to evoke "fear and trembling" in all whom they encounter: the male and female Samurai of philosophy and theology.[20]

Lonergan and Postmodern Concerns: Openness to and of the Subject as Other

To begin with, the subject for Lonergan is other because of the nature of self-transcendence.[21] The conscious human subject is only proleptically or eschatologically itself by reason of its incarnate openness; it is a polymorphic notion of being, not in the minimalist sense of the word "being" mentioned above, but in the completely universal and concrete sense of all the determinations that exist.[22] Sensitive, intentional, cognitive, real, and loving self-transcendence each demand that we go beyond the selves we have been until now, and become other than we are. The subject as other is therefore full of surprises, it is adventurous, and it is corrigible . . . or else!

Crucially, self-mediation occurs as mutual self-mediation, and we attain our sense of ourselves through others' sense of us. Hence, the self-mediation through self-transcendence of the human subject depends on meanings, emotions, and inconsistencies that are neither consciously intended nor desired by us.[23] The world has little noted nor long remembered that in Lonergan's account, the subject as other is marked indelibly by great vulnerability, mainly because it has to live before it knows how or is equipped to live. To the degree that the others are alienated from themselves, the other that we are to them is quite other than who we are in that different sense of "other" implied by the word "alienation." Moving in and through any given group of subjects, then, is the radical otherness, the objective falsity, of the social surd. Every subject as other is involved concretely in personal, cultural, and social sin.[24] So Lonergan's central project of self-appropriation demands several different kinds of reversals or conversions even to get off the ground.[25]

Conversion is a radical revolution in our personal, social, and historical horizon, involving a total reorientation or reorganization of our stream of consciousness—and, overwhelmingly, of our imaginations, memories, and feelings. Imagination propels the biological extroversion—in terms of the already-out-there-now and the already-in-here-now—that underlies both Idealism and Naive Realism. In our existential memories, false imaginings and an interpenetrating array of feelings prop up the fundamental cognitive, moral, and religious disorientation of "old Man" who is therefore in need of multiple conversions.

We notice this massively in the counterpositions of liberal capitalist individualism and in its opposite, the species-being of socialism. The possessive individualist imagines that one gains one's identity by excluding others, by purchasing exclusive goods, by living in exclusive neighborhoods, and by joining exclusive clubs; its spontaneous self-understanding overestimates the importance of mine versus thine. The expressive individualist overestimates originality and uniqueness and substitutes its passions for the normativity of inquiring human nature as a principle of motion and rest. Both kinds of individualists wager it all on what separates us from everyone else. The species-being socialists are not allowed to think for themselves, know for themselves, decide and act for themselves; they subject themselves to a false universalism that suppresses all the differences and eliminates prudence.

These are painful historical implications of the fact that the subject-as-other is always the pole of a horizon that is historical, social, and personal.[26] Today we like to articulate the historicity of horizon in terms of the narrativity of the self, since the stories in the light of which we live are the imaginal correlative of our horizons.[27] The easiest way to think about conversion, then, is in terms of a radical change in our stories, as for instance in Ricoeur's interpretations of the so-called Parables of Crisis.

These parables point to the radical experience of self-transcendence: religious conversion.[28] For Christians religious conversion is eschatological: God's interruption of the chronological time of the subject, of the memories, imaginings, and feelings of the subject because God gives us a new self. When it is receptive to the Gospel, the Holy Spirit engages human solidarity in a movement from sin through death to eternal life with the Father. This constitutes human existence "in Christ Jesus."[29] The encounter with Jesus in the Spirit reveals that the mutual self-mediation of human subjects is also radically involved with the absolutely transcendent—and so in some sense radically other, radically mysterious—God as creator, redeemer, and sanctifier.

In response to God's gift of love, moral and (perhaps more often than is generally acknowledged) intellectual conversions are called for. Such radical personal reversals have a dimension of otherness that defies adequate imagining, because they engage us not in horizontal but in vertical exercises of liberty.[30] The vertical exercise of human liberty differs from our usual choices between ordinary finite objects or courses of action within an already established horizon, because it has to do with the horizon itself. As a radical reversal enabling self-transcendence, it negotiates an engagement or commitment to what is beyond us. The new horizon is so other than our former selves that only humility in the case of moral conversion, and radical self-honesty in that of intellectual conversion can possibly come to terms with it beyond our spontaneous reliance on massive possessiveness. These conditions needing to be fulfilled in conversion feel like death to the degree that we remain unconverted, and that is why some kind of religious conversion is indispensable for their occurrence.

We may speak of the "self as other," therefore, because Lonergan's notion of self is integrally connected with conversion in the primal sense of a radical displacement of our ordinary, unconverted virtual self-images from the center of our universes.

The *historical* aspect of this revolution has to do with people's involvement in the cultural dialectic of progress and decline that can only be negotiated in light of some conversion that is religious. Christians enter into the order envisaged by God as the loving origin and end of the universe, making their own the story of Jesus, Son of the living God, and living by the breath of the living God, the Holy Spirit.

The *social* aspect of this revolution has to do with people's entanglement in technology, economy, and polity. It requires a conversion that is moral, as presented imaginally in Plato's great myths of Last Judgment, or in great works of art and literature, or paradoxically perhaps in Buddhist "sitting."

The *personal* aspect of this revolution requires a conversion that is intellectual, the radical rejection of dialectical counterpositions, such as the imaginal biases of Idealism and Naive Realism. Absent these conversions, all we have is one or another version of the narcissistic, self-centered animal on-the-make—for instance, careerists in philosophy and theology, in academy and church: self-made women and men who worship their makers.

Finally, perhaps the most basic reason why the subject is other has to do with the notion of the subject as subject.[31] Although it is objectifiable in many crucial aspects, the subject as subject can never be objectified completely. Lonergan's distinction between the proximate and the remote criteria of judgment illustrates this.[32] The proximate criteria regard directly the grasp of the sufficiency of the evidence for affirming that a conditioned or possibly relevant intelligible relationship is virtually unconditioned or actually relevant. In contrast, the remote criteria for the truthfulness of our factual and value judgments have to do with the historicity—the deep, underlying openness or closedness—of the subject: the roots of the subject's authenticity or unauthenticity. This can never be fully brought into the foreground at any given time, and so, Lonergan says, "our course is in the night; our control is only rough and approximate; we have to believe and trust, to risk and dare."[33]

Notes

A substantially different, earlier version of this article first appeared in the *Catholic Theological Society of America Proceedings* 53 (1998) entitled "The Subject as Other: Lonergan and Postmodern Concerns."

1. See Jean-Luc Marion, "Descartes and Onto-theology," in *Post-Secular Philosophy: Between Philosophy and Theology*, ed. Phillip Blond (London and New York: Routledge, 1998), 67–106.

2. Martin Heidegger always objected to Hans-Georg Gadamer's use of *Bewußtsein* as letting down the side. Paul Kidder tells me that Gadamer referred to this as his "holy sin."

3. See Etienne Gilson, *Réalisme Thomiste et Critique de la Connaissance* (Paris: Vrin, 1947).

4. This is the teaching of Immanuel Kant's *Critique of Pure Reason* and the *Critique of Judgment*. Almost all Continental philosophy and theology take Kant for granted.

5. On congeries of neo-Thomist gnoseologies see Georges Van Riet, *Thomistic Epistemology*, 2 vols., trans. Gabriel Franks (St. Louis, MO: Herder, 1963–65). In contrast to the neoscholastics, Lonergan was never very interested in universals.

6. As we learned initially from Gadamer and then chapter-and-verse from Theodore Kisiel in *The Genesis of Heidegger's Being and Time* (Berkeley: University of California Press, 1997), 221–309, Aristotle was the key to Heidegger's confrontation with the ontological tradition. In the Marburg years Heidegger established the "as-structure" as an ontological structure of *Dasein*; then the apophantic "as" becomes a theme of special criticism. Perhaps the *locus classicus* is *Being and Time*, #7.

7. Again Kisiel, 230: "In the years 1922/23, Heidegger had a 'flash of genius' (*Geistesblitz*: so in repeated conversations with Pöggeler) which he came to regard as the real beginning of his life's work: *ousía* for the Greeks means constant presence, and so is oriented toward only one dimension of time, the present, after the model of things 'present at hand.'"

8. See Jean-Luc Marion, "Question de l'être ou différence ontologique," in *Réduction et donation: Recherches sur Husserl, Heidegger et la phénoménologie* (Paris: Presses Universitaires de France, 1989), 163–210, esp. 189–98.

9. See Bernard Lonergan, "*Verbum* and Abstraction," in *Verbum: Word and Idea in Aquinas, Collected Works of Bernard Lonergan,* vol. 2, ed. Frederick E. Crowe and Robert M. Doran (Toronto: University of Toronto Press, 1997), 152–90, on the distinction between abstraction as formative and abstraction as apprehensive. The latter is omitted from conceptualist accounts.

10. Richard Rorty has demolished such a model of putative knowledge in his classic *Philosophy and the Mirror of Nature* (Princeton, NJ: Princeton University Press, 1979).

11. This seems to be the implicit cognitional-theoretic basis of the ideological concern for diversity manifest in many brands of multiculturalism.

12. Although Thomas Aquinas commented on Aristotle, "Metaphysica simul determinat de ente in communi et de ente primo, quod est a materia separatum," (At once, metaphysics makes a determination concerning being in common and concerning the first being, which is separate from matter) it is not possible to state clearly here that Aquinas's meaning is irreducible to all the other defining statements cited; we can only concede that historically, and in the present argument, it has been counterpositionally equated with the others mentioned in the paragraph above. An enviable historical treatment of this and the matters in this paragraph is now Jean-François Courtine, *Suarez et le système de la métaphysique* (Paris: Presses Universitaires de France, 1990).

13. For this argument see, along with Courtine, Jean-Luc Marion, "Metaphysics and Phenomenology: A Relief for Phenomenology," *Critical Inquiry* 20, no. 4 (Summer, 1994), 572–91; see, too, Marion's article referenced in note 1.

14. This is commonly taught by Lonergan passim in his works and lectures, but see Olivier Boulnois, "Quand commence l'ontothéologie? Aristote, Thomas d'Aquin et Duns Scot," *Saint Thomas et l'onto-théologique,* Actes du colloque à l'Institut catholique de Toulouse les 3 et 4 juin, *Revue Thomiste* 95, no. 1 (1995), 85ff.

15. See Jean-François Courtine, "Différence métaphysique et différence ontologique (A propos d'un débat Heidegger qui n'aura pas eu lieu)," *Heidegger et la phénoménologie* (Paris: Vrin, 1990), 33–53.

16. I am indebted to Joseph Flanagan for this insight into the source of this image for efficient causality.

17. Lonergan's term for *ein Vorhandenes* is the "already-out-there-now."

18. Here again, I depend on J.-L. Marion, "Metaphysics and Phenomenology," 575–9. Note the omission from this account of any mention of the "negative judgment of separation," about which early articles of David B. Burrell on the analogy of being (which departed from observations by Yves Simon and was grounded in Bernard Lonergan's retrieval of Aquinas on judgment) are helpful.

19. Nietzsche, *The Will to Power,* trans. W. Kaufmann and R. J. Hollingdale, ed. W. Kaufmann (New York: Vintage Books, 1967), 330, as cited by Marion in "Metaphysics and Phenomenology," 577, n. 8.

20. Roger Poole once used this expression about Derrida's *Glas.*

21. To start with, see the references under "Self-transcendence" in Lonergan's *Method in Theology* (New York: Herder & Herder, 1972).

22. On the polymorphism of human consciousness, see *Insight: A Study of Human Understanding, Collected Works of Bernard Lonergan*, vol. 3, ed. Frederick E. Crowe and Robert M. Doran (Toronto: University of Toronto Press, 1992), 410–12, 452.

23. See Lonergan, *Insight*, the section on "Genetic Method," 484–507, and chapter 17, "Metaphysics as Dialectic," 553–617.

24. See Lonergan, *Insight*, the section on "The Problem of Liberation," 643–56.

25. Lonergan only became fully, that is, explicitly, clear about this in *Method in Theology* in speaking of the genesis of intellectual, moral, and religious conversions. See *Method in Theology*, 122, 243.

26. On "horizon" see Lonergan, "Metaphysics as Horizon," in *Collection, Collected Works of Bernard Lonergan*, vol. 4, ed. Frederick Crowe and Robert M. Doran (Toronto: University of Toronto Press, 1988), 188–204; and *Method in Theology*, 235–50.

27. The important works of Paul Ricoeur and of his student Richard Kearney are perhaps well known. From the standpoint of a knowledge of Lonergan, see John Navone and Thomas Cooper, *Tellers of the Word* (New York: Le Jacq Publishing, 1981).

28. See Lonergan, *Method in Theology*, 283–4.

29. See Lonergan, "The Mediation of Christ in Prayer," in *Philosophical and Theological Papers 1958–1964, Collected Works of Bernard Lonergan*, vol. 6, ed. Robert C. Croken, Frederick E. Crowe, and Robert M. Doran (Toronto: University of Toronto Press, 1996), 160–82.

30. On this crucial distinction, see Lonergan, *Method in Theology*, 40, 122, 237–8, 240, 269.

31. On this notion, see Lonergan, "Christ as Subject: A Reply," in *Collection*, 153–87.

32. See Lonergan, *Insight*, 573–5.

33. See Lonergan, "*Existenz* and *Aggiornamento*," in *Collection*, 222–31, 224.

In Response to the Other
Postmodernity and Critical Realism

MARK J. DOORLEY

In his book *Against Ethics* John Caputo makes the rather bold claim that he is against the business of ethics. The "business of ethics" seems to result in more victims than the situation it seeks to address. "Victims are often victims of the Good, someone's Good."[1] Ethicists spin tales about the Good which claim to have universal appeal, yet often cover over the very victim that the tale was meant to address. The Good is so abstract a notion that it fails to do justice to the reality of the one who suffers, calling out for a response from the ethicist. The ethicist is content to sit in a university office and recount the tales of Aristotle, Aquinas, Kant, and Hegel while the poor, the widow, the stranger and the orphan continue to suffer and call to us. Ethics seems to inoculate human beings against the call of the Other.

Caputo is a thinker who shares the concerns of contemporary Continental philosophy. He puts into question all the accomplishments of modernity and its ineluctable march toward a world of universal rationality and freedom. In the wake of the Holocaust and the other genocidal acts of the last century it is very difficult to have any confidence in the achievements, or the promises of achievements, of human reason, most clearly represented by modern technological science. The overweening pretensions of modernity went up in the same flames that engulfed European Jewry in the camps of National Socialism. Who can seriously engage in the "science" of ethics, when that science justified, at least to some, the excesses of genocidal hate?

It is a challenge to be an ethicist (particularly an ethicist whose central concern is the possibility of foundations), to have a conversation with a "postmodern"[2] thinker of the caliber of Caputo. It is certainly not the case that Caputo is disrespectful or unwilling to engage in conversation. However, there is always a hint, dangerously close to the surface of the conversation, that he is above my serious concerns. He seems to view me as one who has yet to awaken from my fundamental enchantment. Operating with such a handicap, I find it difficult to proceed, to think through the issues of foundations in ethics, as a conversation partner with postmodern thinkers.

One might think that I could, or should, simply walk away from the conversation. I could take my stand and say that I am "Against Postmodernism," but that would be to retreat into intellectual malaise. It would be to sidestep a challenge to respond to the Other who calls into question my perspective, my stance, my fragile confidence in the ongoing intellectual, moral, and religious conversion that is my life. I cannot retreat from the challenge since it awakens in me a desire to understand, and to understand well, the question that has been put to my experience, understanding, judgment, and decision concerning the moral life and the discipline of ethics.

What I want to do in this chapter is to begin to respond to the concerns of contemporary Continental thinkers, particularly Immanuel Levinas and Jacques Derrida. (Caputo is a wonderful expositor of both thinkers, and his work has been full of insights for me.) The most responsible thing to do in response to these powerful voices is to struggle to understand them. That is what I attempt to do in this chapter. The "postmodern concern for the other" is, as Fred Lawrence points out in his highly articulate essay on this subject, an "astringent" for those of us who may have fallen into a dogmatic slumber in our enthusiasm for the capacities of human reason.[3] What follows is "undecidable," a central notion in Derrida's thinking. What I mean by the term is that my understanding of the postmodern position is still settling. I am not sure what to make of my conversation partner. And this conversation has disturbed my understanding of myself as a knower. I oscillate in the space between Derrida and Lonergan. This is akin to the "disaster," the dis-aster, of which Caputo speaks.[4] To be without a star, a guide, in the darkness of the abyss,[5] is where I sometimes find myself in this study.

In what follows I will explore several key notions of postmodern thought, particularly the thought of Levinas and Derrida. What I want to accomplish is the dialectic of which Lonergan writes in *Insight*: the development of positions and the reversal of counterpositions. What I have noticed, though, in my nascent study of contemporary Continental thought is that there are very few, if any, stars upon which one can rely as guides. I suggest, though, that the transcendental method is such a "star"; the question remains as to its reliability.

The Postmodern Position

In a move that recalls Kierkegaard, postmodern thinkers decry the way in which theoretical reason silences the individual, the unique, the singular. Caputo highlights this move away from the abstract by calling on us to use only "Proper Names."[6] Being, the language of metaphysics, misses the singular. This deconstruction, not destruction, of conceptualization, of distinction, of categorization is decisive for postmodern thinkers. When reason seeks to conceptualize what has been understood, it abstracts from what Lonergan calls the "empirical residue." Reason does indeed silence what is other in our experience. What is other lacks a single intelligibility; that is why it is silenced. What reason grasps as intelligible is set off from what is irrelevant to the question at hand. What is irrelevant to the case is not worthy of positive recognition by reason. It is what is left behind; it is the remnant; it does not fit into the categories of thought, categories established by the question that is asked by reason. This tendency of reason to silence what is irrelevant prompts thinkers like Caputo, following Levinas and Derrida, to want to privilege what is left behind. They want to revel in the empirical residue, the irrelevant. This residue is not necessary for grasping the intelligibility that answers a question about my experience. It can be let go, put aside, made invisible. However, it is the empirical residue that makes this thing to be the thing that it is in its singularity. A red dress worn by Eva at her prom in 1978 is conceived as a dress, but that it was "red," worn by "Eva," at a "prom," in "1978" is more meaningful than the conceptualization of the object "dress" can possibly contain. There is an excess at work in this red dress that reason in its theoretical, conceptualizing, universalizing function stumbles up against in its attempts to isolate and manipulate meaning.

What is insightful here is the limitation of theory to exhaust the meaning of an experience. Certainly it is true to assert in relation to some particular experience, such as meeting a homeless person at a soup kitchen, that to conceptualize this person as a human being is correct. However, one must also recognize, along with the limitation of theoretical forms of conceptualization, that there are other forms of conceptualization that depend for their accuracy on sensitivity to the experience. The postmodern limits the source of acts of meaning to the theoretical differentiation of consciousness. However, there are other patterns of experience which give rise to other differentiations of consciousness such that different and complementary accounts of meaning emerge from one's experience. So the story of the 1978 prom in which Eva wore the red dress is retold and, if done so well, evokes the affective dimensions of that experience in a way that theoretical consciousness cannot effect.

There is yet another accounting for the singularity of the other of experience. One has insight into one's experience. The insight is into a phantasm or image. This image is particular, singular, concrete. It is an image of one's experience, including the empirical residue. Insight pivots between the concrete of experience and the abstract of intelligibility. The pivot is important here. Insight does not abandon the concrete and singular; it needs it in order to function. However, it makes possible a conceptualization of one's understood experience which makes possible a dislocation of the subject from a world of immediacy to a world mediated by meaning in which the subject is no longer central but one of many.

This last comment is significant. Modernity's privileging of the rational subject is the object of the bulk of postmodern criticism. Since Descartes the subject has been the foundation of metaphysics. The subject's act of knowing subsumes within itself all that is other than, and different from, the knowing subject. The categorizing and distinguishing power of human reason gives the subject the ability to account for, categorize, and, ultimately, manipulate that which is different, other, wild, nonhuman, and, in the extreme, non-Aryan. The instrumentalizing power of human reason is beyond question. The technological capacity of human ingenuity is profound. Modernity has bequeathed us the idea that the universe can be understood (manipulated) in order to satisfy our wants and needs.[7] But again, is instrumental reason the only way in which reason operates? Is there not the possibility that reason can operate in a commonsense pattern, to get things done, and also operate in a theoretical pattern that is interested in how things relate to one another, a radical displacement of the subject from the center of that web of relations?

The ethical implication of this reflection on singularity is that we must resist the theoretical tendency to subsume the homeless person into a statistical accounting of the number of people who regularly attend this particular soup kitchen. Ethics as a theoretical discipline covers over the individual person who confronts me with Otherness. Ethics retreats into the realm of the abstract principle for action: respect all persons as ends in themselves or do what will promote the happiness of the greatest number. Rather than deal with people in their singularity and utter uniqueness, ethicists want to remove themselves from the pathos of the face-to-face confrontation. This movement of removal is a movement away from engagement; it is a movement back into a world that is under one's control. To give oneself over to the movement of the Other before me is to give up control and to offer oneself to the Other. In one's response to the Other one becomes a hostage.[8] It is the Other who places demands on me, the Other's demands, rather than the demands of theoretical, abstract reason. This is not the realm of classical ethical reflection. This is something different; the postmodern claims, however, that it is originary.

It is originary in that it precedes all metaphysics and ethics. "Es gibt," Caputo says, picking up a phrase introduced into the tradition by Heidegger.[9] Obligation happens when the Other confronts me with utter and unrepeatable uniqueness. Levinas asserts that prior to any questioning, any conceptualization, any metaphysical structure, there is a Face that confronts me in my isolation. As Simon Critchley puts it, "[T]he question and the questioning stance of philosophy are always a response to and a responsibility for that which is prior and over which a question has no priority."[10] Prior to any questioning, there is a responsibility. Before Being, there is the Other, the "Otherwise than Being," who places demands upon my shoulders. This is Caputo's obligation.

Zygmunt Bauman claims that morality is "non-rational," "not calculable."[11] He writes, "Moral spacing . . . engages no human intellectual capacities."[12] Our response to the Other is undecidable. We cannot make a choice that is reasonable: "The moral act itself is endemically ambivalent, forever threading precariously the thin lines dividing care from domination and tolerance from indifference."[13] One cannot figure out how to respond to the Other's call because "figuring" is a disfigurement of the Other. Reason cannot do justice to the Other; yet it is justice that one must do. The ethical relation is before reason and calls into question the claims of reason.

Levinas calls this "es gibt" the "Saying."[14] The movement toward the Said is a movement of violence to the Saying since the Said must make use of a logocentric tradition that cannot do justice to the Saying. The uniqueness of the Levinasian Face, the Saying, is covered over, bound, disfigured, by the attempt to articulate it, to define it, to set limits to it, to distinguish it, to understand it. It is this movement from Saying to Said, the movement from obligation to metaphysics and ethics, that is an act of violence. Caputo claims that such an act is unavoidable. The goal, then, would be to minimize the metaphysics, thus minimizing the violence. Whatever one does, one ends up with a disturbed sleep.[15] But must this account of metaphysics, as an overcoming of the Other by the Totalizing Same (Subject), be the only account? Is metaphysics necessarily a total account of Being? Does one mean by "account" a counting up of objects whose similarity rather than difference puts them together? Is there no other way in which to "account" for the "es gibt"?

Before we move into a more explicitly critical realist section of this paper, I would like to address the methodological approach of some postmodern thinking, particularly that of Derrida. Simon Critchley calls Derrida's approach to reading a text, "clôtural" reading.[16] This phrase recalls Heidegger's claim that metaphysics has come to a close. But it also recalls the double reading that Derrida makes of Heidegger. On the one hand, Heidegger claims that metaphysics has come to a close, but on the other hand, Derrida uncovers in Heidegger's text an opening to the Infinite, that which cannot be closed upon, or ended. Heidegger, although unwittingly, continues metaphysics, a metaphysics of presence, even as he announces the closure of metaphysics. It is Derrida's reading of Heidegger that begins a way of reading that finds a double movement or double take in the act of reading. This is evidence, as it were, that reason's Other is at work within the text undermining the tradition out of which reason speaks. This way of reading introduces undecidability as the most appropriate stance for the reader to take. Which reading is sufficient? It is undecidable. I would like to briefly look at this notion of clôtural reading.

In his reading of Edmund Husserl, Derrida agrees with Husserl's judgment that philosophical attempts to find closure are a betrayal of philosophy. Such attempts at closure represent a choice which "closes down the continuous process of comprehension or faithful description."[17] Closure implies a structure in the sense of an idea that encompasses reality; it is always finite and cannot encompass the opening to infinity that is philosophy.[18] This "opening to infinity" is the Infinite of Descartes. The incomprehensible Infinite always breaches the structure, breaking open its enclosed space. Hence, a reading that chooses an interpretation, thus closing down the process of "comprehension or faithful description," attempts to silence the Other of the reading. A faithful reading of a text ought to avoid decision about an interpretation because any interpretation is an attempt at closure, a moment that must be avoided.[19]

The deconstructive reader unmasks an odd play of movements in the text: "The pattern that deconstructive reading continually finds at work within texts is one of dislocation, where two inassemblable readings or lines of thought open up within each text. One of these readings repeats the internal exigencies or dominant interpretations of the text, while the other, which only arises out of the repetition implicit in the text, transgresses the order of commentary and shows how the text is divided against its own auto-representation."[20] A text, like Plato's *Apology*, might offer the deconstructive reader two lines of thought which undermine each other.

On the one hand, Plato is making a claim about the importance of the philosophical art in the ordering of the polis. He is distinguishing Socratic wisdom from the wisdom of the Sophists. The rule of this wisdom is undermining the integrity of Athenian society. It is imperative that the voice of reason be heard and that Socrates be free to support the integrity of the society by his role as gadfly. On the other hand, the witness to Socrates' wisdom is none other than the oracle of Delphi. Socrates claims authenticity on the basis of a myth! In the same text we have a claim to superior wisdom and a claim that wisdom rests upon myth, upon nothing more substantial than the contingent faith claims of a people. What is reason? Is it a reliable guide for choosing the good? Perhaps it is simply another opinion in the agora, which on this day, the day of Socrates' trial, simply loses the vote? A double reading opens up a fissure between the received tradition and the other of the text. The critical point to note here is that the other emerges within the repetition of the dominant interpretation. A clôtural reading will open up this fissure and allow its opposition to remain in tension. The wound worked by the text is not covered over or healed. It is merely open. But this openness is an invitation for new meanings to flourish.

What seems important here is Derrida's recognition that one must read texts within a tradition, but one must also be sensitive to the other of that tradition, as one finds it in the text. There is a double necessity here: "the necessity of lodging oneself with philosophical conceptuality in order to destroy it, the necessity of being destroyed by philosophical conceptuality—a double necessity."[21] The other is lodged within logocentrism, by which it is threatened, but simultaneously the other deconstructs logocentrism. The tension between what Caputo calls "es gibt" and the logocentric traditions crystallized in metaphysics and ethics: this is what a clôtural reading enables one to uncover in texts, any texts.

Is deconstruction anything more than critical reading? Is there something more profound than the simple caveat that one should read texts with a hermeneutic of suspicion? It is surely the case that my reading of Derrida is in its infancy stages, but I think that there is something more than mere critical reading at stake in deconstruction. What is at stake for deconstructive readers is the openness of the text to multiple interpretations. Reading ought not to be a closed event. Texts should never be robbed of their essential openness to new and different meanings. It seems that a focus on grasping the meaning of the text already implies a particular meaning such that other possible meanings are obscured or covered over. The grasp of meaning also presupposes that one can make a judgment about the meaning of the text. It is here that a crucial element in deconstruction has not yet been highlighted: the undecidable.

I cannot choose between lines of thought opened up in a text because there is no reason to make such a choice. Such a choice would be arbitrary. It would be an exercise of my power to close down one or more lines of thought that the text espouses. There are no grounds for such a choice. Derrida argues for a reading that is continually open. Why? Any reasons that suggest a particular interpretation are always undermined by the text itself. One cannot, Derrida claims, decide what meaning is dominant or controlling in a text because such a decision does violence to the text as a play of difference. There is no point from which one can speak about the meaning of the text authoritatively. One can only catch the play of traces that the text suggests.

I suggest that one can understand a text without doing violence to it. Rather than *choose*, which has ethical overtones, one can *judge* which interpretation is most reasonable. There is a standard of reason at work in critical realism. This standard is conscious intentionality under the sway of the pure unrestricted desire to know. The exigence of conscious intentionality sets the norms under which reading takes place. If an interpretation meets the demands of this exigence, then one can make a judgment. The demand of this exigence is that a possible interpretation adequately account for the meaning of the text. Is there necessity involved here? Is there some sense of a grasp of absolute truth involved here? Is there closure involved here in the sense of unrevisability? The answer to all three questions is negative. When one makes a judgment about a possible interpretation of a text one is claiming that at this point, for this person, this interpretation most adequately articulates the meaning of the text. This might change; it is always open to revision. Within a community of learners the possibility of understanding a text adequately increases in probability. One does not achieve an absolute interpretation of a text. The point is, however, that judgments can be made. The interminable play of interpretations that characterizes clôtural reading is not a necessary characteristic of reading or of knowing. Herein lies the principal conflict between the critical realist and the postmodern.

I have addressed three central postmodern concerns: singularity, the "es gibt," and clôtural reading. I have shown how they might be positional and I have raised questions about their counterpositional quality. I would like to shift my approach in this chapter to a more positive one. I would like to address two alternative approaches to the concerns raised by postmodern thinkers that may avoid a retreat into Caputo's abyss. In the spirit of clôtural reading I will also point out ways in which these alternative approaches may not be able to overcome the postmodern critique.

A First Alternative: Another Approach to Metaphysics

Thinkers like Levinas criticize the ontological thinking of people like Kant, Hegel, and some contemporary phenomenologists because their preoccupation is with the objects given to human consciousness.[22] For Kant the objects of knowledge are what appear to human consciousness as cognized in and through the regulatory concepts of human reason. The thing itself is not known; what is known is what appears to human consciousness. The object gives itself to human reason and thus betrays its alterity in favor of the totalizing function of human reason. The Other of reason, that which is known, is disfigured in the process of being known. If this construal of human knowing is correct, then the Levinasian critique of the totalizing character of ontological thinking is devastating.

Is this a correct construal of human knowing? One might raise questions about the regulatory concepts of human reason. Where did they come from? They were deduced from logic. Where did logic come from? It can be argued that logic developed on the basis of the experience of human beings. It serves a very useful purpose. Does logic solve all intellectual problems? The evidence of Newton, Darwin, and Einstein seems to indicate that logic is not the only way to understand one's experience. The concepts of human reason are rooted in human experience. The insights that ground concepts are insights into human experience. Human experience, if attended to, regularly calls into question the conclusions of logic. Questions give rise to new insights that cancel out, modify, or complement previous insights. I think it is this regular experience that Levinas alludes to in highlighting the "excess" of Descartes's idea of the Infinite, or the calling into question of the Same by the Other.

Why, though, does the calling into question overrule the tendency of logic to maintain an achieved position vis-à-vis the other that is known? Underlying the human journey is wonder. It is wonder that is the source of all questions about the world of one's experience. Wonder is capable of carrying persons beyond themselves. Transcendence, going beyond the being of the self, is rooted in the wondering of the person. What Levinas calls "exteriority" is that in response to which wondering arises. Why wonder? Why raise questions about what is beyond the self? This is the being of the human person, the one who wonders. It is the mark of the human person; it is the difference of human being.

This wonder occurs in various patterns; that is, wonder can be focused in various ways. For example, cooks wonder what they will prepare given the elements that they find in their refrigerators. Their wondering is limited to what is demanded of them as cooks in this situation with these elements. Scientists, on the other hand, who are wondering about the configuration of crystals that they have found under their microscopes, are caught in the throes of a more or less unlimited wondering that wants to understand correctly the difference that constitutes these crystals before them. There is also the mystical wondering of a Thomas Merton or the biological wondering of the starving person or the aesthetic wondering of a Pablo Picasso. Wonder occurs in a variety of patterns, patterns that place limits on the scope of the wondering.

There is a wondering, however, which is essentially unlimited. It is pure, disinterested, and unrestricted.[23] It wonders about everything about everything. It wonders not only about the practical application of some element of experience, or about the chemical makeup of some element of experience, but about everything about some element of experience. It is essentially open, transcending, seeking that which is beyond what has been thought, beyond what is known.

This wondering is a universal human experience. All human beings wonder about their lives, their experiences. Wondering, though, is often limited. The pure unrestricted, disinterested wondering, an Abrahamic wondering, is rarely celebrated, rarely held up as sacred. Hence, wondering is often Ulyssean, that is, limited to the various patterns mentioned previously, particularly the practical patterns which want to get things done. In this pattern wondering often leads to exploitation of that about which one wonders.[24] This kind of wondering leads to ontological and thus violent thinking, about which postmodern thinkers are so concerned.

However, there is this other, more primordial, kind of wondering of which each person is capable. It is evident most clearly in the wonder of children who want to know that which is different from them, in order to celebrate, to stand in awe of, that which is other than them.

The pure, unrestricted, disinterested desire to know that which is other, that which is different, is a desire for knowledge. The challenge raised by postmodernity is most evident here. The desire is for knowledge; for the postmodern thinker, the knowledge of modernity is a reduction of the Other to the Same. It is a drive to domesticate that which is different, by making it a known aspect of one's world through a process of knowing which eliminates the alterity of that which is known. If knowledge is an elimination of the alterity of that which is known, then the postmodern challenge wins the day. However, one can show that the process of knowing does not necessarily have to be a destruction of alterity. In fact, if knowledge is truly the desired end, we must do all we can to keep destruction of alterity at bay.

One might think that one knows something if one has merely sensed it. Others might think that knowing is more accurately a matter of applying the appropriate conceptual scheme to what one has sensed. However, knowing is in fact a compound activity whose elements are experiencing, understanding, and critical reflection leading to judgment. Experiencing provides the data of the five senses and the data of consciousness, including memories, feelings, and images. Understanding involves the occurrence of insights and the conceptualization of those insights. Judgment involves the marshaling of evidence that one's insights are correct, weighing that evidence, and pronouncing a judgment on the insights in question. One does not know anything unless one experiences it, understands it, and judges one's understanding to be correct. An example might be helpful.

I enter my bedroom to prepare for bed. I see an object on my bed which is not normally there. Given this sense experience, and my memories of my bedroom, I ask myself, What is it? Being an intelligent person,

I arrive at various possible answers to my question. However, I am not satisfied with a possible answer; I want the correct answer. So, I return to the evidence of my senses and my memory in order to judge which possible answer is best supported by the available evidence. I arrive at the judgment: It is a gift.

This process involved experiencing, wondering about that experiencing, understanding the possible answers that might satisfy my wondering, demanding the correct answer for my wondering, and returning to the evidence and judging which possible answer the evidence best supports. Knowing is a compound activity constituted by experiencing, understanding, and judging. These various activities are integrated by the wonder of the person who is the subject of this compound of activities. Wonder moves the person from experiencing to understanding, and from understanding to judging. Only when a judgment is asserted does the person know anything. Sense experience is not knowing; conceptual clarification is not knowing; arriving at a judgment of fact is knowing. However, judging does not occur unless there is experiencing and understanding.

It is judgment that enables the person to claim knowledge of this or that element of the person's experience. Is this knowledge a denial or destruction of the alterity of what is known in judgement? If by alterity one means merely the unknown as unknown, then yes, knowledge is a destruction of the alterity of that which is known. If, however, by alterity one means the difference and otherness of that which is known, then no, knowledge is not a destruction of alterity. The question seems to be about the meaning of knowing. To approach an answer to that question a closer look at judgment is necessary.

Judgment concerns a conditioned. A conditioned is a possible understanding of one's experience. For example, I thought the object on my bed was a gift. This is a conditioned. Judging is initiated by the question, Is it so? The "it" is the conditioned. Judgment is interested in what the conditions are and whether those conditions are fulfilled. If I understand what the conditions of a conditioned are and I understand that those conditions are fulfilled, then I make the judgment about the conditioned: Yes, it is so. In making this judgment I am claiming that the conditioned is a virtually unconditioned. An unconditioned is something that has no conditions; it is necessary and universal. A virtually unconditioned is a conditioned whose conditions happen to be fulfilled. In other words, a conditioned whose conditions happen to be fulfilled is an unconditioned by virtue of its conditions being fulfilled. However, that its conditions are fulfilled is by no means necessary: hence whatever judgment is made about some element of my experience, it is always a precarious achievement.[25] One's knowledge is not forever closed and finished. Human knowledge is eminently revisable and open to difference, to the Other.

Another way to explore the meaning of knowing is in terms of the relationship between wonder and judgment. Wonder, as we noted, initiates the process of knowing which ends in a judgment, in a virtually unconditioned. Wonder is expressed most often in the form of a question, but it is also expressed in the dis-ease one might experience in response to what one thinks one knows. It is this dis-ease that provides a measure when one is judging one's understanding of one's experience. Wonder is the source of questions, whether explicitly expressed in language or implicit in the dis-ease one might experience. Questions intend insights that might modify or complement or reverse one's earlier insights. As long as there are questions, there is the possibility of the revision of an insight. Hence, judgment cannot be made. A measure of judgment, then, is the absence of further questions. If there are no further questions, then there is no possibility for the revision of an insight, thus the insight is correct and judgment can be made. The insight is invulnerable to further revision.

The field of further questions is not unlimited. Further questions must be relevant to the issue at hand. If I am wondering about what to cook tonight for dinner, questions about Microsoft stock are not relevant, but questions about nutrition are. The relevancy of further questions is a function of one's accumulated knowledge in a particular field, one's open-mindedness, one's commitment to discovering the truth, and one's membership in a community of learners. Open-mindedness and the community of learners are prominent in this list of functions. The first demands a willingness to be attentive to the richness of experience. The second implies that knowing is not an individual adventure, nor is it the privilege of those with the proper certification. Knowing is the child of wonder and wonder is the mark of being human.

Wonder meets the Other in a relationship that precedes and conditions knowledge of that Other. The dis-ease of the wondering subject may be evidence of the primordial relationship that Levinas construes as ethical and that Caputo calls the "es gibt." It seems one could argue that the Other of knowledge (the object of the desire to know), in and through the wonder of the knower, is calling into question the understanding and limited knowledge of the knower. The subject of knowledge seems to be a knower if and only if the object of knowledge incites no further relevant questions. Is this not in some ways the kind of regard for the Other which Levinas, in particular, demands of philosophy? Of course, the relevancy of questions marks a point where one might find an opening for a deconstructive reading of Lonergan's texts. The judge of relevancy is the knower who is always conditioned by acquired expertise, by the actual community of which the knower is a member, the degree of willingness to listen and to learn, and so on. It seems rather that the Other of knowledge depends upon the knower, the Same, for its full revelation. We are back again to the disturbing quality of modernist pretensions to knowledge.

A metaphysics of presence, the target of much postmodern criticism, rests on the notion of the object as already out there now, a thing present to consciousness. A new definition of "object" is required. Knowing occurs in a context of judgments that give meaning to the terms "subject" and "object." A judgment of fact asserts the following claims: A exists, B exists, and A is not B. A more concrete derivation of this basic context might be: I exist; this desk exists; I am not the desk. What emerges in any judgment is a distinction between at least two existing things and a real relation between these two things: a subject who knows, an object which is known, and a clear distinction between the subject and object. It is only when such a constellation of judgments can be asserted that knowledge is achieved. Knowledge is not an absorption of what is other into the circle of the same. Knowledge is a guarantee that what is known is not merely a component of the circle of the same. Knowledge is an achievement of transcendence. Knowledge moves knowers beyond their world into a world not of their own making. It is knowledge construed as conceptual schematism that traps the knower in a world of immanence. However, this is not knowledge. Knowledge is achieved in judgment about the difference that constitutes the object as existing and as Other. Again, one must acknowledge that the privilege in this account is given to the subject. While subject and object are defined in and through a context of judgments, those judgments are made based on the condition of the knower, not the object known. There is yet again a covering over of the Other's difference and incommensurability.

While one might be able to argue that Lonergan provides a much more nuanced account of knowledge than anything that Hegel or Kant offered, it still seems that he is caught in the web that the postmodernists have woven. For Lonergan knowledge is a mediated complex operation. This complex operation is initiated by wonder, the pure, unrestricted desire to know that which is unknown. It is brought to a moment of rest when the fulfillment of the conditions of a conditioned is grasped. However, what the conditions are and whether the conditions that one identifies are an adequate accounting of the conditions is a function of the de facto conditions of the knowing subject. The process of knowing is at the mercy of the subject. Is there alterity at work here? An alterity that is respected all the way down?

A Second Alternative: Healing and Creating Vectors

My first response to the quandaries placed before me by postmodernity was to move from below upward. This creative vector is a source of rich insight, but it gets to ethics only after articulating an adequate cognitional theory, epistemology, and metaphysics.[26] Once an adequate account of the structure of the universe of proportionate being has been accomplished, one then asks the question of ethics, What should I do? From experience, to understanding, to judging, to deciding: this is the creative vector in human consciousness. However, ethical experience, confrontation with the Other Person, the Face of the other, happens. *Es gibt.* It interrupts the affairs of the subject. It is sudden, without warning, without announcement. Suddenly, one is Face to Face with the Other in the Other's singularity and need. This need becomes mine. I am impelled by the Face to give up my plans to be at the Other's service. The bonds of ego are loosened to be replaced by the bonds of ethics, of the Other.[27] Levinas characterizes this ethical relationship to the Other as being made a hostage of the Other.

The breaking in of the Other, the breach of the ego's journey—Is this not what Lonergan means by the grace of God? When speaking of the healing vector of human development, Lonergan talks about the "falling in love" of conversion, particularly religious conversion. This falling in love calls everything into question. It leads to new understandings and richer experiences. There is something very familiar in the postmodern characterization of the ethical relation as "before metaphysics." Prior to knowing, prior to understanding, and prior to experiencing, the human being is vulnerable to the inbreaking of the Other, of another person, of the unexpected, of the totally different. The effect of this inbreaking can be radical. Levinas thinks that it must be radical; otherwise it is not a complete sacrifice. To lose the reigns of one's life is what occurs when the Face of the Other confronts me.

What postmodernity highlights is the rupture of one's sense of knowledge and security by the advent of an Other which is surprising and beyond the circle of one's comprehension. Critchley puts the issue clearly: "What has to be continually deconstructed is the guarantee of full *incarnation* of the universal in the particular, of the privileging of a specific particularity because it *embodies* the universal."[28] The creative movement is a movement away from singularity to universality. The categorical imperative and the greatest happiness principle are the results of human consciousness in the creative vector. However, that one can apply either principle is not guaranteed, nor does having a principle release one from the responsibility to be attentive, intelligent, reasonable, and responsible.

The idea that one can guarantee the applicability of any ethical principle is wrongheaded. Nothing is guaranteed if one understands correctly human intentionality in its intelligent, reasonable, and responsible operations. However, there are many opportunities for human intentional operations to atrophy into a guarantee, privileging the conclusions of the day without remaining open to the other of one's experience. It is this atrophic character of so much of human knowing that is an appropriate target for postmodern critique. However, the solution is not to throw the baby out with the bathwater. The solution is to highlight the healing vector of human consciousness. The Other that breaks through the atrophied dimensions of human knowing and doing is a strange idea, another human being, the more-than-human others,[29] or God.

To operate in the healing vector is to fall in love, to be caught in the gravitational pull of the other which pulls one out of the norm of one's life. This experience is often mediated by one's feelings, by one's relationships, by an unexpected turn of events. It can also be conditioned by the choices that one makes and the things that one does. What is particularly important about these moments of falling in love is their utter unexpectedness, their jolting quality, their unprovoked manner. I think, also, that these moments may not be able to be conceptualized. When speaking of falling in love, Lonergan claims, "[O]rdinarily the experience of the mystery of love and awe is not objectified. It remains within subjectivity as a vector, an undertow, a fateful call to a dreaded holiness."[30] There is something Other at work here, beyond the comprehension of the Subject, which is akin to what Levinas calls the Face or the Saying. This attempt to situate the postmodern concern for the Other in the healing vector of Lonergan's analysis of history probably does not do justice to what Levinas and Derrida are after. However, it seems to me that Lonergan's sensitivity to moments of "inbreaking" is a place to begin to address the issue raised by postmodern thinkers.

Conclusion

The meaning of "conclusion" is limited only to the bringing of this text to an end, setting the conditions for an ongoing conversation. There is no possibility of "closure" in the sense that Husserl and Derrida use the term to criticize certain figures in the philosophical tradition, particularly Hegel. One needs always to be attentive, intelligent, reasonable, and responsible. What drives me to address the works of Levinas and Derrida, in particular, is my desire to understand what they are thinking. Perhaps the result of my confrontation with their work will be the judgment that nothing new is going on. Regardless of the result, the desire to understand drives me. It is that same desire that recognizes in what has gone before in this chapter a very inadequate response to the desire; there are many more questions. I think there are affinities between postmodernism and critical realism. What I have done is to stake out areas that I think might be interesting to pursue.

What I have found interesting in this process is my tendency, inculcated in me by more than twelve years of conversations with people like Joe Flanagan, Pat Byrne, Mark Morelli, Brian Braman, Mike Maxwell, Fred Lawrence, Jerry Miller, Elizabeth Morelli, Glenn Hughes, Tom McPartland, Hugo Meynell, and countless others, to interpret a text or a philosophical position in light of Lonergan's intentionality analysis. It strikes me that such a tendency to interpret out of a tradition and to limit the possibilities of meaning to those possibilities conditioned by that tradition is what Derrida in particular is concerned about. Is there such a thing as a pure reading of a text? Don't I come to a text with my intellectual baggage? Doesn't that baggage skew my reading and so do violence to the meaning of the text? Can I really listen to Derrida on his terms? Is that even desirable? If such a reading is impossible, then what is left? Does one simply stay in the backyard of one's own nest of terms and relations, pulling everything one meets into this nest? If one leaves the backyard, what is one, the next victim of a neighbor's nest of terms and relations, vulnerable to being reshaped and reformed? What does this mean for ethics?

Is one reduced to opting for a system that is as minimally metaphysical as possible, in Caputo's sense? Do I opt for the "es gibt" and leave everything else to the play of chance? Do I give up on the possibility of finding a star? Is hopelessness and the strife of the Hobbesian state of nature all that is left for reasonable people to cling to? Of course, "reasonable" has lost all meaning too, has it not?

After all those questions, leading to the abyss, I find myself still sitting at my computer, cold because my air conditioning is on too high, getting hungry and tired. What is that but an experience of the world? The terms I use to describe my experience are not just my words. They mean something to you, the reader. They communicate meaning, a meaning that can be verified by appealing to my experience. Affirming that I am getting cold and knowing that, at the very least level of moral maturity, I don't want to be cold and, at a slightly higher level, that I don't want to get sick, and finally at an even higher level, that I don't want to waste energy, I get up and turn off the air conditioner! There is a real world. I can know it. And I can act in it. I can be responsible. What is the ethical import of postmodernity? It is a reaffirmation of the prophetic witness that we have a particular responsibility for the stranger, the orphan, the widow, and the poor. To the degree that our metaphysical and ethical ruminations become barriers to this fundamental obligation then I find myself having to side with Caputo: against ethics. To be against the business of ethics, however, is not identical to being against ethics per se, ethics as the call of the Other, ethics as the struggle to be responsive to the needs of the Other who confronts me in the Other's vulnerability and need. To be against ethical living would be to cut oneself off from that which conditions the very possibility of responsibility, namely, the desire to know and to do the good.

What needs to be done in response to the critique of contemporary Continental philosophy is not a jettison of attempts to understand one's world and to act responsibly in that world but to revise those attempts in order to safeguard and make possible the fundamental obligations with which we find ourselves in this world.

Notes

1. John Caputo, *Against Ethics: Contributions to a Poetics of Obligation with Constant Reference to Deconstruction* (Bloomington: Indiana University Press, 1993), 34.

2. The term "postmodern" says much more (and much less) than is intended in this essay. Drucilla Cornell is a contemporary thinker who, in trying to

avoid too univocal a signification for the term, adopts the phrase "philosophy of the limit" to signify the movement of contemporary Continental thought. See her book of that title (New York: Routledge, 1992). For the purposes of this essay the term "postmodern" refers to contemporary Continental philosophy as represented in thinkers like Levinas and Derrida.

3. See Frederick G. Lawrence, "The Fragility of Consciousness: Lonergan and the Postmodern Concern for the Other," in *Communication and Lonergan: Common Ground for Forging the New Age*, ed. Thomas J. Farrell and Paul A. Soukup (Kansas City, MO: Sheed and Ward, 1993), 211.

4. See Caputo, *Against Ethics*, 5.

5. The abyss is what there is when Being is no longer available as a resource.

6. Caputo, *Against Ethics*, 70.

7. Francis Bacon's infamous claim that humans could "wrest" Nature's secrets from Her is a seed for our contemporary technologized society.

8. See Levinas, *Otherwise than Being or Beyond Essence*, trans. Alphonso Lingis (Boston: Kluwer Academic Publishers, 1991), 112ff.

9. See Caputo, *Against Ethics*, 6ff.

10. Simon Critchley, *The Ethics of Deconstruction: Derrida and Levinas*, 2d ed. (West Lafayette, IN: Purdue University Press, 1999), 194.

11. Zygmunt Bauman, *Postmodern Ethics* (Cambridge: Blackwell Publishers, 1993), 60.

12. Ibid., 165.

13. Ibid., 181.

14. See Levinas, *Otherwise than Being*, 45ff.

15. See Caputo, *Against Ethics*, 220ff.

16. Simon Critchley uses this term to identify Derrida's particular approach to reading. I am indebted to Critchley's analysis of this strategy of reading. See his *Ethics of Deconstruction*, 59ff.

17. Critchley, *Ethics of Deconstruction*, 63.

18. Ibid., 64.

19. When Critchley speaks of the ethics of deconstruction he is referring to the weight of the "must" in this sentence. See *Ethics of Deconstruction*, 61.

20. Ibid., 75–6.

21. Ibid., 94.

22. Levinas's critique is echoed in Derrida's critiques of all metaphysics of presence.

23. Adriaan Peperzak claims that there is no such thing as a disinterested or pure intention. All concrete intending is interested in some way. See Peperzak, *Before Ethics* (Atlantic Highlands, NJ: Humanities Press, 1997), 61. This raises a question about the possibility of a pure unrestricted desire. The issue for Peperzak—an issue shared as well by most contemporary Continental thinkers—is that there is a myth operative here that restricted human beings are capable of an unrestricted intending. On the other hand, an unrestricted intending is an intending of the unthought, the unsaid (Levinas's term). Might this not be what Levinas, Derrida, et al. mean by the "ethical relation"?

24. Ulysseian wondering instrumentalizes that about which it wonders. An Abrahamic wondering always moves into its Other as different, as mysterious, as beyond its ability to fully comprehend. This distinction between Abraham and Ulysses is a central distinction in Levinas, *Totality and Infinity*, trans. Alphonso Lingis (Pittsburgh, PA: Duquesne University Press, 1969).

25. For a clear exposition of the way in which Lonergan's several discussions of contingency in *Insight* provide answers to the concerns of Postmodernity, see Fred Lawrence, "Fragility of Consciousness," 194 ff.

26. I stopped short of metaphysics in the above account, hoping that the reader will be familiar with the Lonergan path on this question. For those unfamiliar with Lonergan's argument on this question, see *Insight: A Study of Human Understanding*, ed. Frederick E. Crowe and Robert M. Doran, vol. 3 of *Collected Works of Bernard Lonergan*, (Toronto: University of Toronto Press, 1992).

27. These bonds, of course, are never victimless. Ethics always has its victims. Every attempt to meet an obligation is an "evil," a binding. Any act of power has a victim. See Caputo, *Against Ethics*, 173ff.

28. Simon Critchley, *Ethics-Politics-Subjectivity: Essays on Derrida and Levinas and Contemporary French Thought* (London: Verso, 1999), 278.

29. I am indebted to Jame Schaefer, Ph.D., of the Theology Department of Marquette University, for this phrase, referring to the nonhuman world.

30. Bernard Lonergan, *Method in Theology* (Toronto: University of Toronto Press, 1971), 113.

Chapter 8

Lonergan and the Ambiguity
of Postmodern Laughter

RONALD H. MCKINNEY, S.J.

In the 1980s I wrote several articles arguing for the right to consider Bernard Lonergan's work in the context of what we now refer to as "postmodernism."[1] However, in 1991, I reversed myself and wrote a paper in which I tried to deconstruct the foundational character of his thoughts.[2] Perhaps it is time for me to reexamine my ambivalent stance toward Lonergan by means of a curious postmodern device: showing something marginal in a thinker's work to be quite central after all.

In *Insight*, Lonergan's attempt to deal with the problem of liberation is facilitated by his making reference to "possible functions of satire and humor."[3] His discussion here of the relevance of Kierkegaard's categories of comedy for his overall project takes a mere three pages of space in a work containing 748 pages in all. Indeed, to my knowledge, this is the only treatment of the topic of humor to be found anywhere in Lonergan's collected works. And yet I wish to argue in this chapter that it is precisely this apparently marginal issue of laughter for Lonergan that allows us to see in an intriguing way to possible postmodern dimensions of his thought.

Before attempting an analysis of these significant few pages in *Insight*, I must first provide the reader a context for understanding how crucial the topic of laughter is for understanding the postmodern project. Therefore, I will first examine the debate surrounding Umberto Eco's brilliant and successful novel, *The Name of the Rose*. This postmodern masterpiece concerns the discovery of Aristotle's lost manuscript, *Poetics II*, regarding the nature of comedy, and the murderous intrigue it provokes in

141

a medieval monastery centuries ago. This novel provides Eco the opportunity to raise, within a narrative format, the theoretical issue of the role of laughter in our postmodern culture. However, Karl-Josef Kuschel, who claims to be defending a more Christian notion of laughter, has accused him of advocating a "nihilistic" perspective on comedy. Finally, before ending with an analysis of Lonergan's work, I will consider Kierkegaard's own theory of comedy and tragedy in light of the current debate as to whether Kierkegaard himself can be regarded as a protopostmodernist. Hopefully, the reader will discover that laughter provides a very important lens for assessing the postmodern nature of Lonergan's thought.

Eco versus Kuschel

Eco's *The Name of the Rose* presents two divergent ways of assessing the therapeutic value of laughter in our postmodern world.[4] There is the view of Jorge, a Benedictine monk who denounces the dangers of laughter and desires to hide Aristotle's book on comedy from the world, and the opposing perspective of William of Baskerville, the Franciscan who champions Aristotle's affirmation of laughter.

Knowing full well that Scripture never mentions that Jesus ever laughed, Jorge follows the Benedictine tradition in his mistrust of laughter. He argues that not "everything that is proper to man is necessarily good. He who laughs does not believe in what he laughs at, but neither does he hate it. Therefore, laughing at evil means not preparing oneself to combat it, and laughing at good means denying the power through which good is self-propagating" (131). Jorge, an ardent supporter of traditional authority, claims that our proper function in life is to contemplate the truth, not to laugh at it, since laughter only fosters doubt (132).

Jorge admits that the church allows simple peasant folk their entertainment during the time of carnival as a way of purging unhealthy emotions, but still "laughter remains base, a defense for the simple, a mystery desecrated for the plebeians" (474). He opposes the world's discovery of *Poetics II*, since it would give people Aristotle's valued permission not to fear the devil: "That laughter is proper to man is a sign of our limitation, sinners that we are. But from this book, many corrupt minds like yours would draw the extreme syllogism, whereby laughter is man's end!" (474). In Jorge's mind, the discovery of this long-forgotten book would help people leap to the conclusion that what is base and marginal is actually the way to salvation; indeed, they would be likely to accept the art of mockery in place of the act of faith and forget that "there are boundaries beyond which it is not possible to go" (475-a).

William of Baskerville, on the contrary, remains true to the spirit of his religious order in his defense of Aristotle's view of laughter "as something good and an instrument of truth" (112). According to William, "[L]aughter is a good medicine, like baths, to treat humors and the other afflictions of the body, melancholy in particular" (131). He cites past spiritual authorities and gives examples whereby laughter can be used profitably "to undermine the false authority of an absurd proposition" or "to confound the wicked and to make their foolishness evident" (133). Indeed, for William laughter is a serious matter, since he "laughed only when he said serious things, and remained very serious when he was presumably joking" (425).

We shall see later just how accurate is Eco's reconstruction of Aristotle's "lost" treatise on humor. But in William's own words, comedy "achieves the effect of the ridiculous by showing the defects and vices of ordinary men. Here Aristotle sees the tendency to laughter as a force for good, which can also have an instructional value: through witty riddles and unexpected metaphors, though it tells us things differently from the way they are, as if it were lying, it actually obliges us to examine them more closely" (472).

William is appalled at the arrogance of Jorge, who has "faith without smile" and "truth that is never seized by doubt," such that Jorge appears to William as the devil incarnate (477). That William embodies Eco's own postmodern convictions is made clear in the following key insight: "Perhaps the mission of those who love mankind is to make people laugh at the truth, to make truth laugh, because the only truth lies in learning to free ourselves from insane passion for the truth" (491). Indeed, for William, the "only truths that are useful are instruments to be thrown away" (492). In an article he has written elsewhere on the nature of comedy, Eco echoes William's position in arguing that laughter can serve as an actual form of social criticism: "[Humor] gives us the feeling, or better, the picture of the structure of our own limits. . . . Humor does not promise us liberation: on the contrary, it warns us about the impossibility of global liberation, reminding us of the presence of a law that we no longer have reason to obey. In doing so, it undermines the law."[5]

Karl-Josef Kuschel considers himself, like Eco, to be a critic of the present authoritarianism that seems to reign so strongly in the contemporary world, especially in the Catholic Church, of which Kuschel is a member.[6] But he refuses to bid farewell to this church with "mocking laughter," and instead strives to remain, using a more affirmative kind of humor as his weapon. He is convinced that only such a joyful humor can serve as an antidote to the chaos of our postmodern condition that revels in a "destructive and nihilistic" kind of laughter: "A critical theology of laughter . . . will be an objection to malicious laughter: laughter at the expense of truthfulness, laughter which arises out of a delight in one's own wittiness and is ready to sacrifice all obligations to truthfulness on the altar of the good effect. It will be an objection to mocking laughter from above downwards. . . . It will be an objection to cynical laughter: the proverbial laughter of hell, which stems from the denial of truth and ethics and which feeds on Mephistophelean antifaith" (xx–xxii).

Kuschel thus sees himself as an opponent of both Jorge and William in his desire to find a middle path between the dogmatism of the one and the nihilism of the other. Kuschel agrees with William against Jorge on the need for laughter which can relativize "all manmade religious institutions, claims and moralisms" (106). He also opposes the "humorless apostles of catastrophe" like Jorge who allow no joy in their lives (96).

However, Kuschel also believes there is some truth to Jorge's perception of William's penchant for anarchy. For Kuschel, postmodernism is nothing less than a certain kind of "aesthetic of laughter: laughter at the fact that one is free from all binding ties, values and norms" (36). Consequently, Jorge seems right that William ends up serving the devil in his refusal to accept any boundaries or absolute truths. On the contrary, Kuschel argues that the Christian needs to set "limits to laughter," that we "have an ethical commitment to refuse to laugh" at certain things, for example, the poor and oppressed (122). He argues that Eco knows no such limits in his novel's absolutization of laughter: "There is no longer such a thing as the truth about God, and an attitude of irony, parody, and laughter about everything under the sun has taken its place" (127). What Kuschel would prefer is a clear willingness on the part of Eco's characters to make serious commitments, for "all aesthetic play stops when the answer must be yes or no. All irony ends when a decision is required" (131).

Thus, for Kuschel, Jorge has no appreciation for laughter at all, while William's humor is lost in a relativism of his own making. Is Kuschel's evaluation of Eco's theory of comedy a fair one? It seems to me that an examination of Aristotle would be appropriate here, since both are in fact appealing to his theory of humor to justify their own claims. However, I will be proposing an interpretation of Aristotle that diverges from the standard portrait of his theory of comedy.

Aristotle's Eutrapelia

Eco's reconstruction of Aristotle's lost treatise on comedy finds support in the work of Lane Cooper and Richard Janko.[7] They both make use of an anonymous manuscript on comedy, thought by some to be a mere Byzantine forgery, but now regarded by many scholars as an authentic reflection of Aristotle's *Poetics II*. At the heart of Aristotle's theory of comedy is his account of the long neglected virtue of *eutrapelia* (ready-wittedness), found in his *Nicomachean Ethics* IV.8.[8]

For Aristotle, practical wisdom is all about discerning the "mean" between two flanking vices for any given situation (II.6). By the "mean" he is not referring to a moderate response, but rather to whatever action and emotion is appropriate given the circumstances of a specific situation. Thus eutrapelia is the mean between the two vices of buffoonery and boorishness (IV.8). The ready-witted person is able to tactfully make and appreciate humorous jests toward others or himself in everyday conversation or in works of art themselves. The critical function of this ready wit is to fill us with delight by pointing out the "ridiculous" in human affairs. On the one extreme is the buffoon who vulgarly and improperly carries humor to excess, irrespective of how it might hurt someone else. The buffoon simply fails to see that some things, for example, tragedies, should be taken seriously, that "there are things lawgivers forbid us to abuse." On the other extreme is the boor who is incapable of making or appreciating humor, someone who is so overly serious and "finds fault with everything" as to be unable to have any patience with annoying buffoons. It is interesting to note that in *Rhetoric* II.12–14 Aristotle associates buffoonery with youth and boorishness with old age.

Later in *Poetics* I.5, Aristotle defines the "ridiculous" as "a mistake or deformity not productive of pain or harm to others." In *Rhetoric* I.12, he further makes it clear that such mistakes are those produced in our "words and deeds." These mistakes are different, however, from the *harmatia* of tragic heroes, precisely because in comedy there is no real suffering involved. Thus it follows that eutrapelia not only constitutes a virtuous mean between extremes, but it also enables its possessor to know when the mean has failed to be achieved in the words and actions of oneself or others. Indeed, the person who exercises eutrapelia performs the socially useful role of poking fun at the aberrant but harmless behavior of people in the hope that such vices might thereby be corrected in the future.

How are we to acquire this facility of making and appreciating jests in the appropriate manner? If Janko is correct in his reconstruction of Aristotle's theory, it is through the catharsis experienced by viewers of dramatic comedies that one can, in a special way, acquire the ability to appreciate appropriately the ridiculous in human affairs.[9] But of what does this appreciation consist? Robert Torrance expresses the standard position that, for Aristotle, the harmless vice laughed at in comedy is "a deviation worthy of ridicule and contempt . . . and the comic character . . . [to be] viewed as butt or scapegoat, not hero."[10] If he is correct, then laughter's sole positive aim is to mock human foibles in hopes that they might be corrected. Indeed, on this view of comedy as the satirical exposure of harmless vices, there can be no sympathetic identification with the people we laugh at, nor can there be any affection for the comic buffoon on stage, indeed, no room at all for the celebration of the comic hero. For Aristotle, Falstaff can only be someone to be pitied as the embodiment of anarchic excess.

I want to take issue here with this standard portrait of eutrapelia. First, for Aristotle the human person is one who is ever striving to live in accordance with ethical rules, as they are applicable to the particulars of each situation. However, if true justice is to be achieved, there must be allowed periodic suspensions of rules, what he calls equity (*epieikeia*). Aristotle's treatment of equity as a supplement to the written law has great implications for understanding the working of practical wisdom. In *Rhetoric* I.13–15, he argues that laws can be ambiguous, requiring clarification in accordance with the original intentions of the framers of the law or with the spirit of the law itself. Laws can conflict or even contradict themselves, requiring adjudication. New circumstances can dictate the need to make either exceptions to or reformulation of given laws, or to create new laws altogether. Finally, equity also can dictate when a clear violation of the law ought to be forgiven due to varying degrees of culpability. Thus equity is a corrective of both a legalistic literalism and an overly legalistic severity. Simply put, Aristotle knows that it is not an easy matter knowing how to achieve the mean and thus he recommends a merciful attitude.

Consider his shrewd observation, when discussing the vices flanking a virtue, that "of the extremes one is more erroneous, one less so" (*Ethics* II.9). Therefore, he argues that if we want to counter our temptation toward the graver vice, "we must drag ourselves away to the contrary extreme . . . as people do in straightening sticks that are bent" (*Ethics* II.9). This counsel is what prompts his claim, often misunderstood, "that we must incline sometimes towards the excess, sometimes towards the deficiency, for so shall we most easily hit the mean and what is right" (*Ethics* II.9).

However, Aristotle admits in this same section that "it is no easy task to find the middle," even by following his own advice regarding straightening sticks. This is why he further acknowledges that sometimes "we must as a second best, as people say, take the least of the evils." Indeed, almost chagrined, he reflects that "up to what point and to what extent a man must deviate before he becomes blameworthy is not easy to determine by reasoning." Thus only an Aristotle who is very much aware of the fallibility of our moral quest could give pardon for settling for second best.

Martha Nussbaum has been the strongest proponent of understanding Aristotelian tragedy as a vehicle for dealing with our fallibility as moral agents. According to Nussbaum, the catharsis that we are asked to undergo as spectators of a dramatic tragedy involves achieving the following insights.[11] We are to realize that we are not invulnerable to the complexities and misfortunes of life, nor should we want to be. For a life lived negotiating flexibly the conflicts we cannot avoid is a far more valuable one than a life full of perfect harmony. In such a world as ours, Nussbaum claims that Aristotle urges the spectator to form "bonds of sympathy and identification with the tragic hero," since tragedy, above all, is a "school of equity."[12]

Michael Davis lends support to Nussbaum's attempt to link Aristotle's treatments of *epieikeia* and tragedy by pointing out Aristotle's change in language regarding the "good man."[13] In the section on tragic action in Aristotle's *Poetics*, he goes from the use of *spoudaios* ("the earnest man") to *epieikes* ("the man aware of the impossibility of perfect justice"). The *harmatia* of the tragic hero, according to Davis, "seems to have to do with being too little aware of the fussiness of moral principles—they are too little *epieikeis*." We as spectators come to an understanding of this very fact that only a few tragic heroes ever achieve.

I wish to argue here that this same kind of catharsis regarding our awareness of the difficulty of achieving the mean in our moral praxis is what is realized in dramatic comedies as well. For Aristotle, it is precisely that class of harmless mistakes we all commit that is the target of most humor. Indeed, he claims in *Rhetoric* I.2 that "trifling wrongs" are usually "excused as they are those "done universally, or at least most commonly." Accordingly, ready-witted persons are not only laughing *at* themselves or others in a satirical quest for reform, but are also laughing *with* others at the unavoidable folly of the human condition we all find ourselves in. No matter how determined we are to be virtuous, the difficulties involved in such a project as summarized above inevitably result in the mistakes that become the subject matter of tragedies and comedies. Accordingly we laugh at the buffoon, not only because we perceive how the buffoon's excesses need correcting, but because we also want to celebrate this very lawlessness itself.

The comic rogue on stage revels in the lower-class rejection of hierarchical distinctions, and we, the audience, are asked to sympathize with this underdog opponent of social order, precisely because it is no small achievement to stay alive in this brutal world by the use of one's wits alone. The comic buffoon invites us to laugh *at* the boor's penchant for finding fault with everything and to laugh *with* the buffoon in his festive thumbing of his nose at all propriety. The comic hero thus serves both as an ally of virtue in his criticism of vice (boorishness) and as an enemy of virtue in his own love for anarchic buffoonery. But how can Aristotle celebrate the vice of the buffoon as comic here if he is wedded to the promotion of virtue?

Now the prominent characters in comedy are buffoons, ironists, boasters, and boors. Janko admits that for Aristotle, though "there is no emphasis on one particular character as comic hero," there is nothing "to contradict the implicit presence of such a concept."[14] It is true that Aristotle appears to disdain the buffoonery found in the plays of Aristophanes, given his remark in *Ethics* IV.8 regarding the "indecency of language" contained in the "old comedies" (which most critics take as a reference to Aristophanes). However, Lane Cooper devotes a whole chapter to his claim that Aristotle is an ardent admirer of Aristophanes.[15]

Cooper argues that Aristotle's dislike of indecent language occurs in his treatise on ethics. However, he claims that "the standard of propriety in the conduct of fictitious characters in poetry is different from the standard of conduct for the individual in his private life . . . or for men in their communal activities."[16] He cites *Poetics* I.25: "It is to be remembered, too, that there is not the same kind of correctness in poetry as in politics." Accordingly, if we are to assume an audience boorishly wedded to a misanthropic disdain for the joys of life, it is the function of Aristotelian and Aristophanic comedy to present the buffoon as a comic hero. For only by trying to make as ideal and attractive as possible the contrary vice, toward which the audience is tending, is there a chance of the virtuous mean being hit. Recall Aristotle's advice concerning the straightening of sticks and settling for second best.

Cooper thus reinforces the therapeutic understanding of buffoonery: "If Aristotle regarded the latent tendency in man either to dangerous inhibitions and repressions, or to an undue laxity of expression, as harmful, certain licenses of comedy—for example, in Aristophanes—might readily accord with his homeopathic view as to the curative value of artistic representation."[17] Thus the outrageous character played by John Belushi in *Animal House* is beloved by all, whereas in real life the anarchic love of pleasure displayed by Belushi, the actor, became suicidally destructive.

If Cooper is correct that Aristotle shares with Aristophanes a merciful attitude toward the vices of the comic hero, then modern scholars of Aristophanes should verify this. Charles Paul Segal, for one, claims that Aristophanic comedy portrays the individual's "joyful acceptance of his limitations" and is as equally educative in function as is tragedy.[18] Kenneth McLeish, moreover, examines the distinction between farcical ridicule and a comic "smile at the frailties and foibles of humanity."[19] He rejects the suggestion that Aristophanes only displays the former's lack of sympathy for its victims, simply because such a distinction was made long after Aristophanes. Indeed, according to McLeish, the comic hero in the plays of Aristophanes is a "licensed buffoon" whose function is to bring the boors of the world to their senses and to restore the "natural balance of life."[20]

Let us now summarize our conclusions regarding Aristotelian humor as a prelude for resolving the debate between Eco and Kuschel. First, for Aristotle, there is the vice of boorishness that he condemns as an excessive and harmful kind of ridicule. Then there is the virtue of eutrapelia that serves the satirical function of provoking the reform of our everyday harmless vices. Finally, there is the laughter we accord the comic hero. Not only do we appreciate his ridicule of killjoy boors, but we also celebrate his hilarious acceptance of his imperfections. For it is the comic buffoon who encourages us to pardon with laughter our own inevitable failures to achieve the virtuous mean.

I believe Kuschel would argue that the nihilistic laughter of post-modernism exemplifies the buffoonish vice of going too far with one's wit. Moreover, he would see Jorge's gloomy outlook as fitting Aristotle's depiction of the boor well, while Kuschel's own call for an affirmative, joyful humor that knows its limits would exemplify eutrapelia itself. After all, Kuschel acknowledges the need for humor to relativize and put in their place all manmade perspectives that do not have the humility to admit their own limitations. And this is what satirical ready-wittedness achieves.

However, if this is Kuschel's position, he forgets that Eco, through William of Baskerville, also advocates a humor that attempts to reveal and reform the harmless vices of which we are all guilty. The real point of contention is as regards their attitude toward the attainment of truth. Kuschel thinks that Eco's version of eutrapelia can only become a reckless buffoonery in its willingness to mock and parody everything under the sun. Eco, however, would probably argue that Kuschel's "insane passion" for truth could only rob the latter of any appreciation for the comic hero's merriment at the sheer imperfection of the human condition. Indeed, for Eco, it is precisely our awareness of the impossibility of utopia and global liberation that is so paradoxically liberating. Eco would argue that Kuschel is still wedded to the standard interpretation of Aristotle as a thinker unaware of the difficulties of attaining truth let alone the virtuous mean. Consequently, according to Eco, the lawless mirth characteristic of the comic hero is a kind of liberation that Kuschel can never appreciate. Of course, for Kuschel, such a state of affairs constitutes not liberation, but the very denial of the conditions for true freedom: the affirmation of truth, objective value, and the existence of God. It is time we explore Kierkegaard's world of thought, for he grapples with the same issues that face Eco, Kuschel, and Aristotle.

Kierkegaardian Humor

I will rely on the more authoritative readings of Kierkegaard provided by Merold Westphal, Sylvia Walsh, and C. Stephen Evans throughout this section.[21] Evans provides a pretty standard portrait of Kierkegaard's view of human development as involving three stages.[22] First, there is the aes-

thetic stage of life in which people simply live in accordance with their natural impulses in a quest for momentary happiness. Second, there is the
ethical stage of life in which people start to take responsibility for their
lives by making conscious choices to incarnate certain universal values.
Finally, there is the religious stage of life in which people learn to accept
their need to allow God to transform their lives. Irony is the boundary or
transitional sphere of life between the aesthetic and ethical stages, while
humor provides a similar transition from the ethical to the religious stage.
If enjoyment characterizes the aesthetic stage, struggle and victory typify
the ethical, and suffering the religious. Finally, the transition to each new
level of existence requires a "leap," according to Kierkegaard.

Walsh provides us with a very insightful understanding of the aesthetic stage for Kierkegaard. According to her, the aesthetic stage is best
understood as a form of "romantic irony."[23] Romantic ironists find "the
whole of existence to be inadequate, meaningless, and boring. Thus they
seek to free themselves from the historical and to set in place a self-created
actuality springing from the imagination." Their ironic negativity results
in their playful quest for the freedom of ever new experiences, a lifestyle
that does not require any kind of commitment or responsibility. She cites
Don Juan and Faust as classic exemplars of such a lifestyle.

However, according to Walsh, Kierkegaard's aesthetic stage of life
can only breed a sense of despair at the meaninglessness of all things.[24]
Every new experience simply leaves one with a sense of being fragmented
and incomplete. What is required is not just one more ironic negation of
the status quo but an act of absolute despair, a willingness to put into question one's very experimental lifestyle itself. In short, one has to quit striving to create the self and instead learn how to choose the self and take
responsibility for such a choice. Only by ascending to the ethical stage of
life can one acquire a "unified, concrete, and constant personality" that
expresses itself in moral praxis.

Walsh goes on to show, however, that the ethical life will itself lead
to its own forms of anxiety and despair.[25] Instead of being able to realize
in our actions the universal laws of ethics, we find ourselves confronted
with the reality of sin and our impotence at becoming reconciled with the
infinite. Moreover, the universal laws themselves become subject to question when, like Abraham, our religious experience would have us violate
our normal desire to be in conformity with our culture's moral code.
Indeed, the absurdity of our situation is best revealed in our confrontation

with the ultimate paradox of Christianity: our Creator chooses to become a mere creature. Another way of depicting this absurdity is the insight that our infinite striving for perfection can never be fully realized in this life.[26] This constitutes the primary reason for our "suffering" in this world.

Westphal provides an interesting reading of the transitional spheres of irony and humor.[27] For Kierkegaard, irony and humor are modes of the comic, and essential to the comic perspective is the perception of contradiction and incongruity. Westphal focuses more on the similarity between irony and humor, rather than on their differences, for both see through the relativities of our existence. They both point out the discrepancy between human performance and divine expectation. Indeed, they are both forms of ideology critique. Westphal further adds that for Kierkegaard, the ironist and humorist share the respective insights of the ethical and religious person; they just lack the "personal appropriation" of the latter: "This means that the mere humorist, while ever so close to the religious, is just as close to cynicism, just as the mere ironist, while ever so close to the ethical, is just as close to nihilism."[28]

Walsh further clarifies Kierkegaard's notion of humor.[29] She argues that both comedy and tragedy rest on the fact that we can neither actualize our quest for the infinite in this life nor give it adequate outward expression. Comedy finds this discrepancy between the actual and ideal painless, while tragedy regards it as painful, since the former knows a way out that the latter does not. Walsh never makes fully clear the precise distinction between the comic and humor itself, and so for our purposes here we will regard them as synonymous.

Walsh claims that there is a "gradation or development" in the various forms of humor. First there is an "immature," and "flippant" kind of jesting that makes light of our existential plight and is thus a mere "parody" of the religious sensibility. Then there is the "holy jest" that serves as the outward "incognito" of the religious person, protecting inward suffering from being revealed: "Thus the humorist may reflectively comprehend the various movements of the religious sphere, such as resignation, suffering, and the consciousness of guilt, but in an impatient, childlike manner revokes them in the nonserious form of jest."[30] Humor is thus the way for a religious person to gain intellectual "distance" from the divine when the commitment to living out the basic contradictions of existence becomes too painful.

Evans also makes some valuable contributions to understanding the nature of irony and humor in Kierkegaard.[31] He claims that whereas

Kierkegaard anticipates the aesthetic, ethical, and religious spheres to be open to all people, the transitional spheres of irony and humor "presuppose a specific level of intellectual and cultural development." Moreover, they make "possible" but do not "cause" the leap to higher stages. Like both Walsh and Westphal, Evans points out that irony and humor realize only an intellectual understanding, for Kierkegaard, which has not yet achieved an existential realization through committed praxis. Indeed, humor and irony preserve the "humility" of ethical and religious persons by serving as outward masks that disguise their inward achievements. Finally, Evans more clearly distinguishes the "negating" character of irony and humor than does Walsh or Westphal: "Irony is 'teasing' and 'divisive,' in contrast to humor, which is 'sympathetic' and 'profound.'"[32] The ironists see their own superiority over the crowd in their grasp of the relativity of their views and actions, while the humorists are reunited with humanity in their acceptance of the fact that we are all finite and dependent on God.

The following might best describe the relationship between Kierkegaard's categories and those of Aristotle. Kierkegaard's flippant and immature humor compares favorably to Aristotle's vice of buffoonery. The former's category of the boundary sphere of irony seems comparable to Aristotelian eutrapelia in so far as both look critically upon our failures to achieve the ideal. Finally, the Kierkegaardian category of humor as the incognito of religion appears similar to my interpretation of the laughter evoked by Aristotle's comic hero, since both involve a sympathetic identification with the finitude of our human condition.

However, an important difference between Kierkegaard and Aristotle must be noted. According to Walsh, Kierkegaard "views the production of external works of art as accidental, not essential, to the realization of the human subject."[33] Aristotle, on the contrary, sees the dramatic genre of comedy as a crucial means for educating one's capacity for humor. Indeed, for Aristotle, cognition, affectivity, and action are always interlaced, such that humorous insight inevitably leads to a change in moral praxis, precisely because emotion is the pivot between thinking and doing. Hence, for him, we not only learn ideas, but we learn our emotions in tandem as well. For Kierkegaard, on the contrary, humor remains an intellectual insight (bereft of an affective dimension) and thus cannot cause a leap to the level of ethical or religious praxis. Thus humor is but an occasional escape from the rigors of lived experience for Kierkegaard, while for Aristotle it is at the very heart of authentic human existence itself.

Indeed, Kierkegaard's association of suffering with the religious stage of life seems to suggest a necessary tragic dimension to it, while humor (comedy) is relegated to a less authentic, prior phase. For Aristotle, on the contrary, tragedy and comedy are equally significant: one deals with the painful incongruities of life, while the other deals with the everyday harmless contradictions of life. My bias is for Aristotle's way of seeing things, since this disagreement goes to the heart of whether we are to see Kierkegaard's outlook as compatible with postmodernism.

Walsh explicitly rejects the notion of Kierkegaard as a protopostmodern thinker because she claims that deconstruction is but a contemporary version of inauthentic romantic irony.[34] Westphal admits that "today's postmodern authors *usually* presuppose a world without God and without immortality."[35] However, he does not believe this nihilistic thrust of most postmodern thinkers is the only path postmodernism can take. Rather he argues for a Kierkegaardian view of the responsible self as a task and goal that is fully compatible with the postmodern concern for preserving our fallibility.[36] In such a dialogue with postmodernism, Kierkegaard's so-called individualism can be understood as "both a remedy and resistance to the false collectivism of modernity," and his irrationalism as a "protest against exorbitant claims made on behalf of human thought that wishes to deify itself."[37]

Moreover, Westphal's distinction between a nihilistic and Kierkegaardian postmodernism might also help resolve the debate between Eco and Kuschel. If an authentic postmodern point of view exists that can indeed be open to the notion of a self in relation to others and God, then perhaps there may well exist a postmodern form of laughter that cannot simply be reduced to a nihilistic kind of buffoonery. On the contrary, perhaps a religious form of humor (Kierkegaard's category revised in light of Aristotle's mingling of cognition and emotion) can also exist that helps us achieve the acceptance of our fallible human condition. It is time to look at Lonergan's contribution to resolving the ambiguity of both postmodernism and the nature of laughter itself.

Lonergan's Theory of Laughter

I have argued elsewhere that the claim that there exists an intellectualist bias in the early Lonergan of *Insight* that is only corrected in the later Lonergan of *Method* has no foundation whatsoever.[38] Consequently, I will restrict myself here to a consideration of only the arguments in *Insight*, since I believe this work constitutes the best of his thought.

In my article, "Deconstructing Lonergan," I argued that the standard interpretation of Lonergan's notion of dialectic best reveals the hierarchical logic of his foundationalist thought. In this interpretation, "dialectic" refers to "the concrete unfolding of linked but opposed principles of change."[39] Moreover, it is used only in reference to situations in human affairs in which the pure desire to know finds itself in opposition to other human desires regarding the proper direction of such affairs. This dialectic is harmonious and promotes progress when one's spontaneous desires and fallible common sense submit to the dictates of pure, disinterested intelligence, but is distorted and leads to decline when such desires refuse to be patterned by the wise suggestions of theoretical intelligence.[40] In effect, the dialectic of position versus counterposition (authenticity versus inauthenticity) is always the result of the interference of spontaneous feelings in the efforts of intelligence to order human affairs.

This constitutes a classic instance of foundational philosophizing in which, of two opposed but linked principles, one is privileged over the other. Indeed I went on to argue in "Deconstructing Lonergan" that he seems to betray again and again a preference for theory over common sense, intellect over feeling, the concept over the symbol, certainty over ambiguity, insight over its linguistic vehicle, and the permanent achievements of the past over the new developments of the present. I argued that the postmodern philosopher would want to discover a subversive logic at play in Lonergan's thought in order to demonstrate the rightful equality of both principles in a dialectical relationship.

James Marsh attempted to defend Lonergan from my charges in the following manner:

> The strong foundationalism that is the proper target of deconstruction Lonergan can claim to evade. His is a chastened foundationalism or critical modernism, claiming to steer between the Scylla of a strict Foundationalism and the Charybdis of a post-modern skepticism. . . . I think McKinney misses the extent to which Lonergan's philosophy already contains valid post-modern elements. For example, the canon of residues as Lonergan employs it in science and hermeneutics inviting and requiring us to be open to and recognize inconsistencies, anomalies, and slippages in the data or text is similar to the method of deconstruction as Derrida uses it and McKinney defines it.[41]

I have since acknowledged his criticism, but I have insisted that postmodern philosophies also exist that can steer between Marsh's Scylla and Charybdis just as legitimately as can Lonergan's thought.[42] This Marsh seemed unwilling to concede. In the remainder of this section, I want to provide an interpretation of *Insight* that does justice to Marsh's claims. Indeed, I will show how satire and humor are pivotal categories for just such a reading. The issue of whether a comparable postmodern perspective exists will be addressed in our conclusion.

That Lonergan does indeed share with Derrida a concern for negating the hierarchies involved in our thought and action is revealed in the following expansion of his notion of dialectic: "[I]ndeed, the essential logic of the distorted dialectic is a reversal. For dialectic rests on the concrete unity of opposed principles: the dominance of either principle results in a distortion, and the distortion both weakens the dominance and strengthens the opposed principle to restore an equilibrium."[43] Lonergan's description of human development must now be shown to be able to follow the dynamics of this dialectical process.

Robert Doran maintains that in *Insight* Lonergan never explicitly recognizes the primacy of existential over cognitive consciousness.[44] He thus leaves many a reader with the mistaken impression that we live in order to know instead of the other way around. Doran's position rests heavily on his citation of Lonergan's description of the "existential subject" as belonging to a state of bewilderment prior to his self-affirmation as a knower.[45] Doran, however, fails to see the different senses in which Lonergan uses this term. Elsewhere in *Insight* he defines it as "the whole man" (624) and as "the concrete, individual, existing subject" (69). Indeed, he argues here that it is the goal of *Insight* to examine this existential subject, and that is why Lonergan is concerned not just with the exploration of theoretical knowledge but with the entirety of "polymorphic consciousness" itself.

There is admittedly some ambiguity in Lonergan's presentation of the various complementary patterns of our polymorphic consciousness (biological, aesthetic, intellectual, dramatic, and mystical). But his later differentiation of the practical pattern (268, 383, 470, 580) makes clearer the significance of the dramatic pattern. Far from existing in a complementary way to the other patterns, the dramatic/practical pattern is rather the style in which people live out their lives by blending or mixing the other patterns (470). Indeed, Lonergan argues that this integrative making of one's own living into an existential work of art requires all the following: the "practical schemes" of common sense; "blueprints for human behavior" devised by "pure intelligence"; a grounding in "aesthetic liberation and artistic creativity"; and a consideration of the limitations imposed by "biological existence" (188). To these one could add the grace that comes from religious encounter with the divine, since this prior list is articulated before Lonergan's discussion of the mystical pattern itself.

Now the existential/dramatic subject and its differentiated patterns of experience need to be understood in the context of Lonergan's notion of development. According to Lonergan, "A development may be defined as a flexible, linked sequence of dynamic and increasingly differentiated higher integrations that meet the tension of successively transformed underlying manifolds" (454). Every development, moreover, reveals "an increasing liberation of serial possibilities from limitations and restrictions imposed by previous realizations" (268). Hence, Lonergan's description of overall human development in terms of the integration of organic, psychic, and intellectual development (459–79) is virtually equivalent to his earlier description of the constitution of the dramatic subject via aesthetic, practical, and intellectual liberation from the mere biological pattern of experience (181–9, 262–70).

Moreover, the law of integration is of fundamental importance for understanding the dramatic subject as well. This crucial law declares that "the initiative of development may be organic, psychic, intellectual, or external, but the development remains fragmentary until the principle of correspondence between different levels is satisfied" (471). Every initiative of development on one level thus "invites complementary adjustments" (472). Accordingly, for the dramatic subject to achieve the integration requisite to becoming an existential work of art, every development within one pattern of experience must continually be met with complementary adjustments in the other patterns.

For the dramatic subject to properly govern this developing interplay of complementary patterns of experience, there is required a spirit of "genuineness" (475). Now there are two kinds of genuineness. There is that spontaneous kind proper to the "simple and honest soul innocent of introspection and depth psychology" (476) and "another genuineness that has to be won back through a self-scrutiny that expels illusion and pretense" (475). Genuineness of either kind requires a commitment to and appropriation of the truth. Lonergan spells out what is involved in such an appropriation in an often overlooked passage:

To appropriate truth is to make it one's own. The essential appropriation of truth is cognitional. However, our reasonableness demands consistency between what we know and what we do; and so there is a volitional appropriation of truth that consists in our willingness to live up to it, and a sensitive appropriation of truth that consists in our adaptation of our sensibility to the requirements of our knowledge and our decisions (558).

The similarities of these three kinds of self-appropriation in *Insight* to the three kinds of conversion, to which Lonergan later refers as intellectual, moral, and psychic, are not coincidental.

First, we need to distinguish the self-appropriation of one's mere cognitional activities from the full intellectual possession of all one's activities as a dramatic subject, that is, cognitional self-appropriation in the fullest sense of the word. The former refers to the self-affirmation of the knower in so far as one appropriates the activities found in the intellectual pattern of experience, while the latter involves taking possession of all the other patterns of experience as well (biological-organic, aesthetic-affective, practical-moral, mystical-religious) plus objectifying the operations of sensitive and volitional self-appropriation. However, these latter self-appropriations, while they can be thematized in cognitional self-appropriation, are not intellectual exercises themselves.

For Lonergan, all the sense imagery in our experience is always accompanied by emotional associations (193). While the aesthetic-artistic pattern of experience can in no way be identified with this realm of affectivity, nevertheless it is primarily through the symbols of artistic creation that the dramatic subject comes to terms with its affectivity (189). Moreover, Lonergan repeatedly argues that only the "retrospective education" of one's affectivity (457) can provide the "psychic liberation" (203n) needed to implement one's intellectual blueprints for the good of society (472). Sensitive self-appropriation is thus not an intellectual affair but the therapeutic negotiation of our feelings that frees them up so as to be capable of ongoing adaptation to the exigencies of our knowledge and decisions.

Moreover, the ongoing process from implicit to explicit volitional self-appropriation is well expressed in Lonergan's description of the "drama of living" as one in which "out of the plasticity and exuberance of childhood, through the discipline and the play of education, there gradually is formed the character of man" (188). Thus to be fully genuine, the dramatic subject must transform the error-plagued "habitual background" of its moral character (476). The subject will thereby learn how to choose genuine values over mere satisfactions.

Lonergan states clearly that "cognitional appropriation of truth is solidary with volitional and sensitive appropriation" (561). Here again we see the fundamental law of integration and the logic inherent in the distorted dialectic. Indeed, Lonergan argues that these three self-appropriations are interdependent: they "condition and are conditioned by adaptations" called forth by the others (561). What seems like a vicious circle to reason, however, is not so in practice (478). Since self-appropriation is always a matter of degree, from being merely latent and implicit to becoming more and more explicit, one can begin with any self-appropriation at whatever level of explicitness in order to help foster the development of the other modes of self-appropriation. These in turn will help foster one's initial act of self-appropriation in an ongoing solidary manner.

According to Lonergan, then, "the concrete being of man . . . is being in process" (625). The logic of solidarity involved in our ongoing development, however, can be seen as a vicious circle, constituting what Lonergan calls the "problem of liberation." This is especially the case when we consider the social dimensions of moral impotence (628–9). Lonergan observes that the problem of liberation "lies in an incapacity for sustained development" (630). As long as tension and development mark human nature, it is always possible for the series of ongoing adaptations to break down, relapse in one self-appropriation leading to relapse in the others. One can arrive at a correct philosophy, but it "will not appear workable to wills with restricted ranges of effective freedom" (631). One can achieve a good will, but "who will tell which proposals" ought to be implemented (629–30)? Indeed, one can even have a transformed psyche, but it will only remain frustrated if the subject fails to have the proper understanding and hopeful good will (472). Lonergan concludes that what is needed is a new "higher integration of human living" (632–33).

Of course these new habits that are needed to achieve ongoing development, for Lonergan, are none other than the faith, hope, and charity that come from our religious relationship with God (723). The mystical pattern of experience, therefore, is unlike all the other patterns, because its differentiation makes possible the self-appropriation that ensures the genuineness of the interaction of all other patterns. But how does one predispose oneself to receiving this gratuitous higher integration of living?

Indeed, "how is one to be persuaded to genuineness and openness, when one is not yet open to persuasion?" (624). It is now that we can discuss Lonergan's brief account of satire and humor in the context of this problem of liberation.

Lonergan refers to Kierkegaard's three spheres of being and attempts the following initial analogy: "The aesthetic and the ethical spheres would seem to stand to the whole man, to the existential subject, as the counter-positions and the positions stand to the cognitional subject" (624). However, he then points out that the problem with this analogy is that the spheres are existential while the positions and counterpositions are intellectual theories (625). Human beings, for Lonergan, simply do not exist in either an ethical or aesthetic sphere, as the "either/or" of Kierkegaard's system seems to suggest. Rather, we live in "some blend or mixture" of the various patterns of experience and reveal "little inclination to a rigidly consistent adherence to the claims either of pure reason or of pure animality" (625). Indeed we can just as well achieve progress in our integrated development as we can show signs of disintegration.

How then can we find the means to go forward if we seem to be involved in a vicious circle? Each self-appropriation requires a solidary advance on the part of the other two. Moreover, without the emergence of the mystical pattern and our reception of God's grace, such solidary self-appropriation cannot sustain itself. However, the logic of solidarity also applies to the mystical pattern and its relation to the three modes of self-appropriation. Lonergan knows full well that perfect faith is not a possibility in this world. And so he invites the reader of *Insight* to attempt to struggle to make one or more of the three self-appropriations first, in hopes that one's faith can be thereby stimulated later in a dialectical manner. The logic of solidarity refuses to give causal priority to either the mystical pattern or the three self-appropriations, resulting in what seems like a vicious circle with no way out.

Lonergan, however, urges that we learn how to reframe this apparent *aporia*. The problem of liberation, that is, the fact that we are always in process, can have a positive spin put upon it. Lonergan contends that the dramatic subject should not be "discouraged by his failures, that rather he is to profit by them both as lessons on his personal weaknesses and as a stimulus to greater efforts" (627). This realization that we need not despair, despite our ongoing failures to maintain genuine development, is achieved, however, "not by argument but by laughter" (626). Lonergan points out that "if men are afraid to think, they may not be afraid to laugh" (626).

He treats Kierkegaardian irony as a form of satire and argues that "satire laughs at, humor laughs with" (626). For Lonergan, these two forms of laughter can help dispel our illusions and prejudices. Satire ridicules our imperfections in hopes of promoting development, while humor keeps our ideals "in contact with human limitations and human infirmity" (626). Indeed, "if satire becomes red with indignation, humor blushes with humility" (626). Moreover, Lonergan argues that we should not judge these forms of laughter in terms of the limited results they might achieve, but in terms of the "transcendent . . . potentialities they reveal" (626). He concludes that "as satire can help man swing out of the self-centeredness of an animal in a habitat to the universal viewpoint of an intelligent and reasonable being, so humor can aid him to the discovery of the complex problem of grasping and holding the nettle of a restricted effective freedom" (626).

Let us now relate Lonergan's account of laughter to our prior interpretations of Kierkegaard, Aristotle, Eco, and Kuschel. Lonergan's notion of satire seems comparable to Aristotle's eutrapelia, Kierkegaard's irony, and those possibilities in Eco and Kuschel that we linked earlier to these Aristotelian and Kierkegaardian concepts. All these forms satirize our vices in order to promote their correction. Lonergan's notion of humor, moreover, bears an uncanny resemblance to the laughter evoked by Aristotle's comic hero and Kierkegaard's religious incognito as well as to those interpretations of Eco and Kuschel that stress their acceptance of human limitations in a manner that does not verge on nihilism.

Like Kierkegaard, Lonergan opts for a process view of the self, open to dialogue with God and others. However, he displays a more complex understanding of what needs to be achieved by Kierkegaard's ethical stage: both cognitional and volitional self-appropriation. Moreover, Lonergan seems more aware than Kierkegaard of the possibility of relapse in the development of the existential subject. And the reason is because Lonergan uses a logic of dialectical solidarity, while Kierkegaard is committed to the progressive integration of lower levels by higher stages. Finally, laughter for Lonergan is not simply the reflective point of view that humor is for Kierkegaard. On the contrary, it is charged with affectivity through and through, as in Aristotelian laughter.

Lonergan avoids the abyss of postmodern relativism by his inclusion of a directed finality in his depiction of the developing existential subject. However, he avoids the charge of advocating a naive foundationalist philosophy by means of his portrait of God, the self, and truth as dynamic processes that never realize total actuality in this temporal world of ours. Moreover, laughter, for him, not only spurs ongoing development of the dramatic subject (satire) but also keeps it in touch with the necessary incompleteness of its being (humor). Finally, this way of reframing the vicious circle of our development also keeps us open to the possibility of being transformed by divine grace.

We are thus back to the fundamental problem of the ambiguity of postmodern laughter. Is it necessarily nihilistic or open to the possibility of dialogue with Christian conceptions of humor promoted by Kuschel, Kierkegaard, and Lonergan? The answer, of course, depends in part upon whether Westphal and Marsh are correct about the postmodern dimensions involved in the thought of Kierkegaard and Lonergan. The fact that I have advocated a reinterpretation of Aristotle's theory of humor is indicative of my own preference for positions that are "both/and" rather than "either/or." And if laughter is a matter of discerning positively the contradictions of our existence, then perhaps humor itself opts for bringing together these curious bedfellows of postmodernism and Christian philosophy.

Notes

1. See Ronald H. McKinney, S.J., "Lonergan's Hermeneutical Theory, *International Philosophical Quarterly* 23 (1983): 277–90; "Beyond Objectivism and Relativism: Lonergan versus Bohm," *Modern Schoolman* 64 (1987): 97–110.

2. See Ronald H. McKinney, S.J., "Deconstructing Lonergan," *International Philosophical Quarterly* 31 (1991): 81–93.

3. Bernard Lonergan, *Insight: A Study of Human Understanding* (London: Longmans, Green, and Co., 1957), 624–6.

4. Umberto Eco, *The Name of the Rose*, trans. William Weaver (New York: Harcourt Brace Jovanovich, 1983).

5. Umberto Eco, "The Frames of Comic Freedom," in *(Carnival!) Approaches to Semiotics* 64, ed. Thomas Sebeok (Berlin: Mouton, 1984), 8.

6. Karl-Josef Kuschel, *Laughter: A Theological Essay* (New York: Continuum, 1994), xi–xii.

7. See Richard Janko, *Aristotle on Comedy: Towards a Reconstruction of "Poetics II"* (Berkeley: University of California Press, 1984); Lane Cooper, *An Aristotelian Theory of Comedy* (New York: Harcout, Brace, 1922).

8. All translations of Aristotle will be taken from Richard McKeon's edition of *The Basic Works of Aristotle* (New York: Random House, 1941) and cited within the text itself.

9. Janko, *Aristotle on Comedy*, 141.

10. Robert Torrance, *The Comic Hero* (Cambridge, MA: Harvard University Press, 1978), 1.

11. Martha Nussbaum, *The Fragility of Goodness: Luck and Ethics in Greek Tragedy and Philosophy* (Cambridge: Cambridge University Press, 1986), 79–81.

12. Nussbaum, "Equity and Mercy," *Philosophy and Public Affairs* 22 (1993): 95.

13. Michael Davis, *Aristotle's Poetics: The Poetry of Philosophy* (Lanham, MD: Rowman and Littlefield, 1992), 72.

14. Janko, *Aristotle on Comedy*, 216–8.

15. Cooper, *Aristotelian Theory of Comedy*, 18–41.

16. Ibid., 19.

17. Ibid., 182.

18. Charles Paul Segal, "The Character of Dionysius and the Unity of the *Frogs*," in *Twentieth Century Interpretations of* The Frogs, ed. David Littlefield (Englewood Ciffs, NJ: Prentice Hall, 1968), 55–6.

19. Kenneth McLeish, *The Theatre of Aristophanes* (New York: Taplinger, 1980), 16.

20. Ibid., 60, 66, 93.

21. See Merold Westphal, *Becoming A Self: A Reading of Kierkegaard's* Concluding Unscientific Postscript (West Lafayette, IN: Purdue University Press, 1996); Sylvia Walsh, *Living Poetically: Kierkegaard's Existential Aesthetics* (University Park, PA: Penn State University Press, 1994); C. Stephen Evans, *Kierkegaard's "Fragments" and "Postscript": The Religious Philosophy of Johannes Climacus* (Atlantic Highlands, NJ: Humanities Press International, 1983).

22. Evans, *Kierkegaard's "Fragments" and "Postscript,"* 12–3, 33, 46.

23. Walsh, *Living Poetically*, 51, 70–7.

24. Ibid., 110–6.

25. Ibid., 136–65.

26. Westphal, *Becoming a Self*, 154, 161.

27. Ibid., 165–9, 194.

28. Ibid., 168.

29. Walsh, *Living Poetically*, 212–21.

30. Ibid., 216.

31. Evans, *Kierkegaard's "Fragments" and "Postscript,"* 186–205.

32. Ibid., 195.

33. Walsh, *Living Poetically*, 9.

34. Ibid., 22, 247–50.

35. Westphal, *Becoming a Self*, viii.

36. Ibid., ix.

37. Ibid., ix.

38. McKinney, "The Role of 'Conversion' in Lonergan's *Insight*," *Irish Theological Quarterly* 52 (1982): 268–70.

39. Lonergan, *Insight*, 422.

40. Ibid., 217–45.

41. James Marsh, "Reply to McKinney on Lonergan: A Deconstruction," *International Philosophical Quarterly* 31 (1991): 97–8.

42. McKinney, "Navigating Scylla and Charybdis: Contemporary Philosophy and GC 34," in *Promise Renewed: Jesuit Higher Education for a New Millennium,* ed. Marty Tripole (Chicago: Loyola Press, 1999), 260–1.

43   Lonergan, *Insight,* 233.

44. Robert Doran, *Psychic Conversion and Theological Foundations: Toward a Reorientation of the Human Sciences* (Chico, CA: Scholars Press, 1981), 33, 83,163.

45. Lonergan, *Insight,* 385.

Works Cited

Abbey, Ruth. *Charles Taylor.* Princeton, NJ: Princeton University Press, 2000.

Anderson, Joel. "The Personal Lives of Strong Evaluators: Identity, Pluralism, and Ontology in Charles Taylor's Value Theory." *Constellations* 3, no. 1 (1996): 17–38.

Aristotle. *The Basic Works of Aristotle.* Translated and Edited by Richard McKeon. New York: Random House, 1941.

Bauman, Zygmunt. *Postmodern Ethics.* Cambridge: Blackwell, 1993.

Beaudrillard, Jean. *The Perfect Crime.* Translated by Chris Turner. London: Verso, 1996.

Benjamin, Walter. "On Language as Such and On the Language of Man." In *Critical Theory Since Plato*, edited by Hazard Adams. Orlando, FL: Harcourt Brace Jovanich, 1992.

Boyne, Roy. *Foucault and Derrida: The Other Side of Reason.* London and New York: Routledge, 1990.

Burrell, David B. "How Complete Can Intelligibility Be? A Commentary on *Insight:* Chapter XIX." *Proceedings of the American Catholic Philosophic Association* 41 (1967): 250–53.

Campbell, John Angus. "Insight and Understanding: The 'Common Sense' Rhetoric of Bernard Lonergan." In *Communication and Lonergan: Common Ground for Forging the New Age*, edited by Thomas J. Farrell and Paul A. Soukup. Kansas City, MO: Sheed & Ward, 1993.

Caputo, John. *Against Ethics: Contributions to a Poetics of Obligation with Constant Reference to Deconstruction.* Bloomington: Indiana University Press, 1993.

———. "For Love of the Things Themselves: Derrida's Hyper-Realism." *Journal for Cultural and Religious Theory* 1, no. 3 (August, 2000). <http://www.jcrt. org/archives/01.3/index.html?page=caputo.shtml>.

———. *The Prayers and Tears of Jacques Derrida: Religion without Religion* Bloomington: Indiana University Press, 1997.

Chanter, Tina. "Reading Hegel as a Mediating Master." In *Levinas and Lacan: The Missed Encounter*, edited by Sarah Harasym. Albany: State University of New York Press, 1998.

Chalier, Catherine. "Ethics and the Feminine." In *Re-Reading Levinas*, edited by Robert Bernasconi and Simon Critchley. Bloomington: Indiana University Press, 1991.

Clark, R. Michael. "Byway of the Cross." *Lonergan Workshop* 12 (1996).

Conn, Walter. "The Desire for Authenticity: Conscience and Moral Conversion." In *The Desires of the Human Heart: An Introduction to the Theology of Bernard Lonergan*, edited by Vernon Gregson. Mahwah, NJ: Paulist Press, 1988.

Cooper, Lane. *An Aristotelian Theory of Comedy*. New York: Harcourt, Brace & Co., 1922.

Copeland, Shawn. "Memory, Emancipation, and Hope: Political Theology in the 'Land of the Free.'" *The Santa Clara Lectures* 4, no. 1 (1997): 1–20.

Critchley, Simon. *The Ethics of Deconstruction: Derrida and Levinas*, 2nd ed.West Lafayette, IN: Purdue University Pres, 1999.

———. *Ethics-Politics-Subjectivity: Essays on Derrida and Levinas and Contemporary French Thought*. London: Verso, 1999.

Danesi, Marcel. Introduction to *Signs: An Introduction to Semiotics*, by Thomas A. Sebeok. Toronto and Buffalo: University of Toronto Press, 1994.

Davis, Michael. *Aristotle's Poetics: The Poetry of Philosophy*. Lanham, MD: Rowman and Littlefield, 1992.

De Beauvoir, Simone. *The Second Sex*. Translated by H. M. Parshley. New York: Bantam Books, 1961.

De Boer, Theodore. *The Rationality of Transcendence: Studies in the Philosophy of Emmanuel Levinas*. Amsterdam: Geiben, 1997.

De Lauretis, Teresa. "The Female Body and Heterosexual Presumption." *Semiotica* 67 (1987): 259–79.

Deleuze, Gilles, and Guattari, Felix. *Anti-Oedipus: Capitalism and Schizophrenia*. Translated by Robert Hurley, Mark Seem, and Helen R. Lane. Minneapolis: University of Minnesota Press, 1983.

Derrida, Jacques. *Deconstruction in a Nutshell: Conversations with Jacques Derrida*. Edited with a commentary by John D. Caputo. New York: Fordham University Press, 1997.

———. "Faith and Knowledge: The Two Sources of 'Religion' at the Limits of Reason Alone." In *Religion*, edited by Jacques Derrida and Gianni Vattimo. Stanford, CA: Stanford University Press, 1998.

———. *Points . . . : Interviews, 1974–1994*. Edited by Elisabeth Weber. Translated by Peggy Kamuf et al. California: Stanford University Press, 1995.

———. *Specters of Marx*. Translated by Peggy Kamuf. New York: Routledge, 1994.

———. *Writing and Difference*. Translated by Alan Bass. Chicago: University of Chicago Press, 1978.

Descartes, René. *Meditations on First Philosophy*. Edited by Stanley Tweyman. London: Routledge, 1993.

Doane, Janice, and Devon Hodges. *From Klein to Kristeva: Psychoanalytic Feminism and the Search for the "Good Enough" Mother*. Ann Arbor: University of Michigan Press, 1992.

Doran, Robert. *Psychic Conversion and Theological Foundations: Toward a Reorientation of the Human Sciences*. Chico, CA: Scholars Press, 1981.

————. *Theology and the Dialectics of History*. Toronto: University of Toronto Press, 1990.

Eco, Umberto. "The Frames of Comic Freedom." In *(Carnival!) Approaches to Semiotics*, edited by Thomas Sebeok. Berlin: Mouton, 1984.

————. *The Name of the Rose*. Translated by William Weaver. New York: Harcourt Brace Jovanovich, 1983.

————. *A Theology of Semiotics*. Bloomington: Indiana University Press. 1976.

Evans, C. Stephen. *Kierkegaard's "Fragments" and "Postcript": The Religious Philosophy of Johannes Climacus*. Atlantic Highlands, NJ: Humanities Press International, 1983.

Farrell, Thomas J., and Paul A. Soukup, editors. *Communication and Lonergan: Common Ground for Forging the New Age*. Kansas City, MO: Sheed and Ward, 1993.

Fiorenza, Francis Schüssler. Introduction to *Spirit in the world*, by Karl Rahner. Translated by William Dych. New York: Continuum, 1994.

Foucault, Michel. *The Foucault Reader*. Edited by Paul Rabinow. New York: Pantheon Books, 1984.

————. *Power*. Edited by James D. Faubion. Translated by Robert Hurley et al. Vol. 3 of *Essential Works of Foucault 1954–1984*, edited by Paul Rabinow. New York: New York Press, 1994.

————. *Religion and culture: Michel Foucault*. Edited by Jeremy R. Carrette. New York: Routledge, 1999.

Fraser, Nancy. "The Uses and Abuses of French Discourse Theories for Feminist Politics." In *Revaluing French Feminism: Critical Essages on Difference, Agency, and Culture*, edited by Nancy Fraser and Sandra Lee Bartky. Bloomington: Indiana University Press, 1992.

Furman, Frida Kerner. *Facing the Mirror: Older Women and Beauty Shop Culture*. New York: Routledge, 1997.

Gadamer, Hans-Georg. "Dialogues in Capri." In *Religion*, edited by Jacques Derrida and Gianni Vattimo. Stanford, CA: Stanford University Press, 1998.

————. *Truth and Method*. Translated by Garrett Barden and John Cumming. New York: Seabury, 1975.

Grosz, Elizabeth. "The Body of Signification." In *Abjection, Melancholia and Love*, edited by John Fletcher and Andrew Benjamin. London: Routledge, 1990.

Hart, Kevin. "Jacques Derrida (b. 1930): Introduction." In *The Postmodern God: A Theological Reader*, edited by Graham Ward. Oxford: Blackwell Publishers, 1997.

Heft, James. *A Catholic Modernity? Charles Taylor's Marianist Award Lecture*. Oxford: Oxford University Press, 1999.

Heidegger, Martin. *Being and Time*. Translated by John Macquarrie and Edward Robinson. New York: Harper and Row, 1962.

Irigaray, Luce. "Questions to Emmanuel Levinas: On the Divinity of Love." In *Re-Reading Levinas*, edited by Robert Bernasconi and Simon Critchley. Bloomington: Indiana University Press, 1991.

Janko, Richard. *Aristotle on Comedy: Towards a Reconstruction of "Poetics II."* Berkeley: University of California Press, 1984.

Jardine, Alice. "Opaque Texts and Transparent Contexts: The Political Difference of Julia Kristeva." In *The Poetics of Gender*, edited by Nancy K. Miller. New York: Columbia University Press, 1986.

Jardine, Murray. "Sight, Sound, and Epistemology: The Experiential Sources of Ethical Concepts." *Journal of the American Academy of Religion* 44, no. 1 (1996): 1–25.

Kanaris, Jim. *Bernard Lonergan's Philosophy of Religion: From Philosophy of God to Philosophy of Religious Studies*. Albany: State University of New York Press, 2002.

———. "Calculating Subjects: Lonergan, Derrida, and Foucault." *Method: Journal of Lonergan Studies* 15, no. 2 (1997): 135–50.

———. "Engaged Agency and the Notion of the Subject." *Method: Journal of Lonergan Studies* 14, no. 2 (1996): 183–200.

———. "Lonergan and Contemporary Philosophy of Religion." In *Explorations in Contemporary Continental Philosophy of Religion*, edited by Deane-Peter Baker and Patrick Maxwell. New York: Rodopi Press, 2003.

Kaufmann, Walter. *Nietzsche: Philosopher, Psychologist, Antichrist*. 4th ed. Princeton, NJ: Princeton University Press, 1974.

Kristeva, Julia. *Desire in Language: A Semiotic Approach to Literature and Art*. Edited by Leon S. Roudiez. Translated by Thomas Gora, Alice Jardine, and Leon Roudiez. New York: Columbia University Press, 1980.

———. "Interview: *The Old Man and the Wolves*." In *Julia Kristeva Interviews*, edited by Ross Mitchell Guberman. New York: Columbia University Press, 1996.

———. *In the Beginning Was Love: Psychoanalysis and Faith*. Translated by Arthur Goldhammer. New York: Columbia University Press, 1987.

———. "Modern Theatre Does Not Take (A) Place." Translated by Alice Jardine and Thomas Gora. *SubStance* 18–19 (Winter-Spring 1977): 131–34.

———. *The Old Man and the Wolves*. Translated by Barbara Bray. New York: Columbia University, 1994. Originally published as *Le vieil homme et les loups* (Paris: Librairie Arthème Fayard, 1991).

———. *Powers of Horror: An Essay on Abjection*. Translated by Leon Roudiez. New York: Columbia University Press, 1982. Originally published as *Pouvoirs de l'horreur* (Paris: Seuil, 1980).

———. "The Semiotic *Chora* Ordering the Drives." In *Revolution in Poetic Language*, translated by Margaret Waller. New York: Columbia University Press, 1984.

———. *Strangers to Ourselves*. Translated by Leon Roudiez. New York: Columbia University Press, 1991. Originally published as *Etrangers à nous-même* (Paris: Fayard, 1989).

Kuschel, Karl-Josef. *Laughter: A Theological Essay*. New York: Continuum, 1994.

Lamb, Matthew. "The Notion of the Transcultural in Bernard Lonergan's Theology." *Method: Journal of Lonergan Studies* 8, no. 1 (1990): 48–73.

———. *Solidarity with Victims: Toward a Theology of Social Transformation*. New York: Crossroad, 1982.

Lawrence, Fred. "The Fragility of Consciousness: Lonergan and the Postmodern Concern for the Other." In *Communication and Lonergan: Common Ground for Forging the New Age,* edited by Thomas J. Farrell and Paul A. Soukup. Kansas City, MO: Sheed & Ward, 1993.

———. "The Fragility of Consciousness: Lonergan and the Postmodern Concern for the Other." *Theological Studies* 54 (1993): 55–94.

———. "Lonergan, The Integral Postmodern?" *Method: Journal of Lonergan Studies* 18 (2000): 95–122.

———. "The Subject as Other: Lonergan and Postmodern Concerns." *Catholic Theological Society of America Proceedings* 53 (1998): 163–65.

Lechte, John. *Julia Kristeva.* London: Routledge, 1990.

Levinas, Immanuel. *Difficult Freedom: Essays on Judaism.* Translated by Seán Hand. London: The Althone Press, 1990.

———. "Enigma and Phenomenon." In *Basic Philosophical Writings,* edited by Adriaan T. Peperzak, Simon Critchley, and Robert Bernasconi. Indianapolis: Indiana University Press, 1996.

———. "God and Philosophy." In *Of God Who Comes To Mind,* translated by Bettina Bergo. Stanford, CA: Stanford University Press, 1998.

———. "The Idea of the Infinite in Us." In *Entre Nous: On Thinking-of-the-Other,* translated by Michael B. Smith and Barbara Harshav. New York: Columbia University Press, 1998.

———. *The Levinas Reader.* Edited by Seán Hand. Oxford: Basil Blackwell, Ltd., 1989.

———. "Love and Filiation." In *Ethics and Infinity, Conversations with Philippe Nemo.* Translated by Richard A. Cohen. Pittsburgh, PA: Duquesne University Press, 1985.

———. *Otherwise Than Being or Beyond Essence.* Translated by Alphonos Lingis. Boston: Kluwer Academic Publishers, 1991.

———. "The Rights of Man and Good Will." In *Entre Nous: On Thinking-of-the-Other,* translated by Michael B. Smith and Barbara Harshav. New York: Columbia University Press, 1998.

———. *Totality and Infinity: An Essay on Exteriority.* Translated by Alphonso Lingis. Pittsburgh, PA: Duquesne University Press, 1969.

———. "Transcendence and Height." In *Basic Philosophical Writings,* edited by Adriaan T. Peperzak, Simon Critchley, and Robert Bernasconi. Indianapolis: Indiana University Press, 1996.

Lonergan, Bernard J. F. "Bernard Lonergan Responds." In *Language, Truth, and Meaning: Papers from the International Lonergan Congress 1970,* edited by Philip McShane. Notre Dame: University of Notre Dame Press, 1972.

———. *Collection.* Vol. 4 of *Collected Works of Bernard Lonergan,* edited by Frederick E. Crowe and Robert M. Doran. Toronto: University of Toronto Press, 1988.

———. *Insight: A Study of Human Understanding.* London: Longmans, Green, and Co., 1958. Reprint, San Francisco: Harper & Row, 1978.

———. *Insight: A Study of Human Understanding.* Vol. 3 of *Collected Works of Bernard Lonergan,* edited by Frederick E. Crowe and Robert M. Doran. Toronto: University of Toronto Press, 1992.

———. "Lectures on Existentialism." Typewritten transcript, Nicholas Graham. Boston College, 1957. Photocopy.

———. *The Lonergan Reader.* Edited by Elizabeth Morelli and Mark Morelli. Toronto: University of Toronto Press, 1997.

———. *Method in Theology.* Toronto: University of Toronto Press, 1972.

———. "Natural Right and Historical Mindedness." In *A Third Collection: Papers by J. F. Lonergan, S.J.,* edited by Frederick E. Crowe, S.J. Mahwah, NJ: Paulist Press, 1985.

———. "Notes on Existentialism." Author's notes for lectures given at Boston College. Montreal: Thomas More Institute, 1957. Photocopy.

———. *Philosophical and Theological Papers 1958–1964.* Vol. 6 of *Collected Works of Bernard Lonergan,* edited by Robert C. Croken, Frederick E. Crowe, and Robert M. Doran. Toronto: University of Toronto Press, 1996.

———. *Philosophy of God, and Theology: The Relationship Between Philosophy of God and the Functional Specialty, Systematics.* London: Longman & Todd, 1973.

———. "Response to Father Burrell." *Proceedings of the American Catholic Philosophical Association* 41 (1967): 258–9.

———. *A Second Collection.* Edited by William F.J. Ryan and Bernard J. Tyrrell. Toronto: University of Toronto Press, 1974.

———. *The Subject.* Milwaukee: Marquette University Press, 1995.

———. *Topics in Education.* Vol. 10 in *Collected Works of Bernard Lonergan,* edited by Frederick E. Crowe and Robert M. Doran. Toronto: University of Toronto Press, 1993.

———. *Understanding and Being: The Halifax Lectures on "Insight."* Edited by Elizabeth A. Morelli and Mark D. Morelli. Revised and augmented by Frederick E. Crowe with the collaboration of Elizabeth A. Morelli, Mark D. Morelli, Robert M. Doran, and Thomas V. Daly. Vol. 5 of *Collected Works of Bernard Lonergan,* edited by Frederick E. Crowe and Robert M. Doran. Toronto: University of Toronto Press, 1990.

MacCannell, Juliet Flower. "Kristeva's Horror." *Semiotica* 62 (1986): 345–51.

Marsh, James. *Critique, Action and Liberation.* Albany: State University of New York Press, 1995.

———. *Post-Cartesian Meditations.* New York: Fordham University Press, 1988.

———. "Post-Modernism: A Lonerganian Retrieval and Critique." *International Philosophical Quarterly* 35 (1995): 159–73.

———. *Process, Praxis and Transcendence.* Albany: State University of New York Press, 1999.

———. "Reply to McKinney on Lonergan: A Deconstruction." *International Philosophical Quarterly* 31 (1991): 97–8.

McCance, Dawne. *Posts: Re-Addressing the Ethical.* Albany: State University of New York Press, 1996.

McKinney, Ronald. "Beyond Objectivism and Relativism: Lonergan versus Bohm." *Modern Schoolman* 64 (1987): 97–110.

———. "Deconstructing Lonergan." *International Philosophical Quarterly* 31 (1991): 81–93.

———. "Lonergan's Hermeneutical Theory." *International Philosophical Quarterly* 23 (1982): 277–90.

———. "Navigating Scylla and Charybdis: Contemporary Philosophy and GC 34." In *Promise Renewed: Jesuit Higher Education for a New Millenium*, edited by Marty Tripole. Chicago: Loyola Press, 1999.

———. "The Role of 'Conversion' in Lonergan's *Insight*." *Irish Theological Quarterly* 52 (1982): 268–70.

McLeish, Kenneth. *The Theatre of Aristophanes*. New York: Taplinger, 1980.

Miller, Jerome. "All Love is Self-Surrender: Reflections on Lonergan After Post-Modernism." *Method: Journal of Lonergan Studies* 15 (1995): 53–81.

———. *In the Throe of Wonder: Intimations of the Sacred in a Post-Modern World*. Albany: State University of New York Press, 1992.

Morelli, Elizabeth. "Oversight of Insight and the Critique of a Metaphysics of Presence." *Method: A Journal of Lonergan Studies* 18 (2000): 1–15.

Nussbaum, Martha. "Equity and Mercy." *Philosophy and Public Affairs* 22 (1993): 83–125.

———. *The Fragility of Goodness: Luck and Ethics in Greek Tragedy and Philosophy*. Cambridge: Cambridge University Press, 1986.

Nye, Andrea. "Woman Clothed with the Sun: Julia Kristeva and the Escape from/to Language." *Signs: Journal of Women in Culture and Society* 12 (1987): 664–86.

Ong, Walter J. *Orality and Literacy: The Technologizing of the Word*. London: Methuen, 1982.

Parsons, Susan Frank. *Feminism and Christian Ethics*. Cambridge: Cambridge University Press, 1996.

Payne, Michael. *Reading Theory: An Introduction to Lacan, Derrida, and Kristeva*. Cambridge: Blackwell Publishers, 1993.

Peperzak, Adriaan. *Before Ethics*. Atlantic Highlands: Humanities Press, 1997.

Plants, Nicholas. "From the Disengaged Subject to the Subject as Subject in Taylor and Lonergan." Ph.D. diss., Saint Louis University, 2000.

———. "Loneran and Taylor: A Critical Integration." *Method: Journal of Lonergan Studies* 19 (2001): 143–72.

———. "The Surpassing Subject." Paper presented at the annual meeting of the Fallon Memorial Lonergan Symposium, Los Angeles, March 2001.

Purcell, Michael. *Mystery and Method: The Other in Rahner and Levinas*. Milwaukee, WI: Marquette University Press, 1998.

Ricoeur, Paul. "The Task of Hermeneutics." In *Paul Ricoeur: Hermeneutics and the Human Sciences: Essays on Language, Action and Interpretation*, edited by John B. Thompson. Cambridge: Cambridge University Press, 1981.

Robbins, Jill. *Altered Reading: Levinas and Literature*. Chicago: University of Chicago Press, 1999.

Ross, Susan A. *Extravagant Affections: A Feminist Sacramental Theology*. New York: Continuum, 1998.

Scott, Joan W. "The Evidence of Experience." In *Questions of Evidence: Proof, Practice, and Persuasion Across the Disciplines*, edited by James Chandler, Arnold I. Davison, and Harry Harootunian. Chicago: University of Chicago Press, 1994.

Sebeok, Thomas A. *Signs: An Introduction to Semiotics.* Toronto and Buffalo: University of Toronto Press, 1994.

Segal, Charles Paul. "The Character of Dionysius and the Unity of the *Frogs.* In *Twentieth Century Interpretations of* The Frogs, edited by David Littlefield. Englewood Cliffs, NJ: Prentice Hall, 1968.

Soper, Kate. "Postmodernism, Subjectivity and the Question of Value." In *Principled Positions: Postmodernism and the Rediscovery of Value*, edited by Judith Squires. London: Lawrence & Wishard, 1993.

Stanton, Domna. "Difference on Trial: A Critique of the Maternal Metaphor in Cixous, Irigaray, and Kristeva." In *The Poetics of Gender*, edited by Nancy K. Miller. New York: Columbia University Press, 1986.

———. "Language and Revolution: The Franco-American Dis-Connection." In *The Future of Difference*, edited by Marilyn Eisenstein and Alice Jardine. Boston: G. K. Hall, 1980.

Tallon, Andrew. *Head and Heart: Affection, Cognition, Volition as Triune Consciousness* New York: Fordham University Press, 1997.

Taylor, Charles. "Consciousness." In *Explaining Human Behavior*, edited by Paul Secord. London: Sage Publications, 1982.

———. *The Ethics of Authenticity.* Cambridge, MA: Harvard University Press, 1991.

———. *Human Agency and Language.* Vol. 1 of *Philosophical Papers.* Cambridge: Cambridge University Press, 1985.

———. "Inwardness and the Culture of Modernity." In *Philosophical Interventions in the Unfinished Project of the Enlightenment*, edited by Axel Honneth, Thomas McCarthy, Claus Offe, and Albrecht Wellmer. Cambridge, MA: MIT Press, 1992.

———. "Overcoming Epistemology." In *Philosophical Arguments.* Cambridge, MA: Harvard University Press, 1995.

———. "Rorty in the Epistemological Tradition." In *Reading Rorty*, edited by Alan Malachowski. Cambridge: Basil Blackwell, 1990.

———. *Sources of the Self: The Making of Modern Identity.* Cambridge, MA: Harvard University Press, 1989.

Taylor, Mark C. *Erring: A Postmodern A/theology.* Chicago: University of Chicago Press, 1984.

Torrance, Robert. *The Comic Hero.* Cambridge, MA: Harvard University Press, 1978.

Walsh, Sylvia. *Living Poetically: Kierkegaard's Existential Aesthetics.* University Park, PA: Penn State University Press, 1994.

Westphal, Merold. *Becoming a Self: A Reading of Kierkegaard's* Concluding Unscientific Postscript. West Lafayette, IN: Purdue University Press, 1996.

———. *Suspicion and Faith: The Religious Uses of Modern Atheism.* Grand Rapids, MI: Wm. B. Eerdmans, 1993.

White, Allon. *Carnival, Hysteria, and Writing*. Oxford: Clarendon Press, 1993.

Wiles, Maurice. Review of *The predicament of postmodern theology: Radical orthodoxy or Nihilist Textualism?*, by Gavin Hyman. *Theology Today* 60, no. 1 (2003): 116.

Williams, Robert. "Sin and Evil." In *Christian Theology: An Introduction to Its Traditions and Tasks*, edited by Peter C. Hodgson and Robert H. King. Philadelphia: Fortress Press, 1985.

Winquist, Charles E. *Desiring Theology*. Chicago: University of Chicago Press, 1995.

———. *The Surface of the Deep*. Aurora, CO: Davies Group, 2003.

Contributors

JOHN D. CAPUTO is the Thomas J. Watson Professor of Religion and Humanities at Syracuse University. His most recent books are *On Religion* (Routledge, 2001), *More Radical Hermeneutics: On Not Knowing Who We Are* (Indiana University Press, 2000). He is also the editor of *Blackwell Readings in Continental Philosophy: The Religious* (2001). He has also co-edited *Questioning God* (Indiana University Press, 2001) and *God,the Gift and Postmodernism* (Indiana University Press, 1999), which are collections of studies based on a series of conferences he has co-directed at Villanova University featuring Jacques Derrida in dialogue with major postmodern religious thinkers. He is also chairman of the editorial board of *The Journal for Cultural and Religious Theory*.

MARK J. DOORLEY is Assistant Director of the Ethics Program and Visiting Assistant Professor at Villanova University. He is the author of *The Place of the Heart in Lonergan's Ethics: The Role of Feelings in the Ethical Intentionality Analysis of Bernard Lonergan*, (University Press of America, 1996). His interests include the possibility of ethical foundations in a postmodern world as well as the notion of authenticity in ethical analysis. He is also interested in the pedagogical value of community service in the teaching of ethics.

CHRISTINE E. JAMIESON is Assistant Professor and Graduate Program Director in the Department of Theological Studies at Concordia University in Montreal. Her specialization is social ethics. Her dissertation involved exploring Julia Kristeva's contribution to moral theology. She has given several presentations bringing the work of Bernard Lonergan and Julia Kristeva into dialogue. In addition, another paper, "To Begin Anew: Reflections on Freedom, Destiny and Ethics in the Thought of Julia Kristeva and Bernard Lonergan," is forthcoming in *The Lonergan Workshop Journal*, edited by Fred Lawrence, Vol. 18 (Atlanta: Scholar's Press).

JIM KANARIS is Faculty Lecturer in Philosophy of Religion at McGill University's Faculty of Religious Studies. His interests include philosophical-theological hermeneutics, religion and the sciences, and the thought of Bernard Lonergan,

Jacques Derrida, and Michel Foucault. He is the author of *Bernard Lonergan's Philosophy of Religion: From Philosophy of God to Philosophy of Religious Studies* (State University of New York Press, 2002).

FREDERICK LAWRENCE is Associate Professor of Theology at Boston College. He wrote his dissertation on Lonergan and Hans-Georg Gadamer, under the direction of Gadamer. Professor Lawrence has published extensively on the thought of Lonergan and is also known for his English translations of the works of German philosopher Jürgen Habermas. He is also the founder and director of the Lonergan Workshop at the Lonergan Institute, Boston College; he edits the Lonergan Workshop series published annually.

JAMES L. MARSH is Professor of Philosophy at Fordham University. He teaches and writes in the areas of phenomenology, hermeneutics, Lonergan, Marx, critical theory, Hegel, and postmodernism. Marsh has published over sixty articles and seven books in the above areas, the last two of which are *Unjust Legality: A Critique of Habermas' Philosophy of Law* and *Ricoeur as Another* co-edited with Richard Cohen (State University of New York Press, 2002).

RONALD H. MCKINNEY, S.J., is a professor of philosophy and Director of the Special Jesuit Liberal Arts Program at the University of Scranton. He has published numerous articles on Lonergan's thought as well as on postmodern literature and moral theory in *Philosophy Today, International Philosophical Quarterly New Literary History*, and other journals. He is currently trying to mount a production of his musical drama about the Holocaust, entitled *Terezin*!

A recent lecturer in philosophy at Mount Saint Mary's College in Emmitsburg, Maryland, NICHOLAS PLANTS has published two other articles pertaining to Lonergan, both of which can be found in *Method: Journal of Lonergan Studies*. In addition to exploring the integration of Lonergan and Charles Taylor, both in his dissertation and in *Method*, he has published an article concerning Richard Rorty's hermeneutics that earned him the American Catholic Philosophical Association's Young Scholar of the Year Award in 1998.

MICHELE SARACINO is Assistant Professor of Religious Studies at Manhattan College in Riverdale, New York, where she specializes in the area of Catholicism and Culture. This essay is part of her larger interest in the constructive intersection between Catholic thought and contemporary continental theory, in which she has a book entitled, *On Being Human: A Conversation with Lonergan and Levinas* (Marquette University Press, 2003). Currently, she is researching the theological implications of cultures of entitlement.

Index